HOME HINTS & TIPS

The new guide to natural,
safe and healthy living

ROSAMOND RICHARDSON

PHOTOGRAPHY BY RUSSELL SADUR

DK Publishing

DK

LONDON, NEW YORK, MUNICH, MELBOURNE, and DELHI

To Kay, with thanks and appreciation

Project Editor Bella Pringle **Art Editor** Jane Forster
US Editor Margaret Parrish
Senior Editor Jennifer Jones **Managing Editor** Gillian Roberts
Senior Art Editor Karen Sawyer **Art Director** Tracy Killick
Category Publisher Mary-Clare Jerram
DTP Designer Sonia Charbonnier **Production Controller** Joanna Bull

IMPORTANT NOTICE

First American edition, 2003
03 04 05 10 9 8 7 6 5 4 3 2 1

First published in the United States by
DK Publishing, Inc.
375 Hudson Street
New York, New York 10014

Library of Congress Cataloging-in-Publication Data
Richardson, Rosamond, 1945-
  Home hints and tips / Rosamond Richardson
    p. cm.
  Includes index.
  ISBN 0-7894-9299-7 (alk.paper)
  1. Home economics. I. Title.

TX158 .R58 2003
640--dc21   2002025996

Color reproduced in Singapore by Colourscan
Printed and bound in Singapore by Star Standard

See our complete product line at
www.dk.com

CONTENTS

INTRODUCTION

This book is a practical guide to creating a healthy, safe, and natural home. It shows how, instead of using synthetic and often toxic chemicals, we can easily change to using natural substances that are equally effective but have no side effects.

The book is packed with detailed information designed to raise awareness of the effects of our everyday housekeeping on our health and safety, and to show how easy it is to change even long-term habits. It offers straightforward practical advice in the form of hints and tips. Many of these are time-honored ideas based on readily available materials, while a comprehensive Resources section lists where to find more unusual products. Animal rights, fair trade, and environmental impact are all issues involved in the decisions we make, and these are addressed, too.

The book also offers useful tips on reusing and recycling, which play their part in dealing with the issue of what happens to items once we have used them. Everything has to go somewhere and the planet is fast running out of dumping places. Plastic, for example, does not biodegrade but sits in landfill sites, leaking toxic gases and polluting the water supply. Depositing at sea is no solution, nor is incineration, since it releases toxic fumes.

We leave our "ecological footprints" behind us in the way in which we live our lives as consumers or users. We have choices to make. Buying less, and more thoughtfully, reusing and recycling, using less gas by cutting down on unnecessary travel or going by bicycle instead, reducing our use of plastic, choosing organic foods and making choices that encourage biodiversity, cutting back on processed foods whose manufacture impacts on the environment, switching to nontoxic cleaning products, and using natural rather than synthetic materials in the home—all these are areas of our lives over which we have control, and even small changes can add up to something significant if we all make them.

This is the new housekeeping.

Rosamund Richardson

HOME BASICS

Many of us have heard of "sick building syndrome" in air-conditioned offices where toxic emissions from the synthetic building fabric affect the air within the structure, but few of us have realized that our homes can also be affected—until now, that is. Increasingly, we are becoming aware that health and environmental concerns need to be taken into account at home, too. In response to this new awareness, specialized "biological architects" and some environmentally conscious builders are designing houses that are not detrimental to health or to the local ecology. They build on carefully selected sites, and use sustainable construction materials from nearby sources that do not need to be transported long distances, a process that avoids consuming large amounts of fuel.

CREATING A HEALTHIER HOME

Not all of us can build new houses for ourselves. Often we must make the best of the homes we have, built with more conventional construction methods. With a few simple measures—choosing nontoxic finishes and natural furnishings to improve air quality, for example, or changing the way we use energy to conserve natural resources—we can do much to make our homes healthier and more environmentally sound.

Buy secondhand tools with wooden handles. They will do the job just as well as their plastic-handled equivalents, and will also save you money.

Building materials p11

Wood flooring p12

Conserving water p14

Improving air quality p17

THE NATURAL HOME

It is perfectly possible to use construction materials derived from natural resources when building or repairing a house, instead of synthetic materials that are based on chemicals and have a heavy impact on the environment. Using wood (from sustainable sources), cellulose, ceramics, metal, or stone is a sound way of ensuring a healthy home.

HOME HEALTH CHECK

An absolutely safe and healthy home is the ideal, but this is difficult to achieve in the real world. If you are moving, you should avoid those properties with a low "health score." If not, there are still ways to make your present home safer.

● If possible, avoid living in a building close to power lines or cell phone towers. These emit electromagnetic radiation at various frequencies and intensities that may be harmful (*see Resources page 163*). The health implications of EMFs are not proven, but they may be associated with fatigue and short-term memory loss.

● Avoid properties close to busy roads and industrial sites, since these cause air pollution.

● Choose a home built on well-drained land to decrease the risk of a wet basement, a precaution against damp.

● If buying an older property, have a search done for lead-based paint and lead pipes—lead contaminates the water supply—and asbestos, which is hazardous when disturbed during house repairs.

● Test the gas supply for leaks, and have faulty or old wiring replaced to prevent fire.

● Have your home tested for radon and take the necessary steps to keep it out of the building (*see Resources page 163*). Radon, which occurs as a colorless, odorless gas, is a type of natural radiation, and is known to cause lung cancer.

● If your garage is attached to the house, create an airlock between it and the living space, or install a well-sealed door,to prevent toxic fumes from entering the living quarters.

● Insulate your home for both energy saving and good air exchange.

When renovating an old house, have separate boxes for sorting wood, metal, and electrical wires for recycling.

RESTORING & RENOVATING

In old houses, most of the materials used in the original construction will have stopped releasing toxins, but take care when removing old insulation, since it can be hazardous.

● Wear a mask if you intend to remove old insulation or particle board. Foam insulation and fiberglass, lead in paint, and wood treated with pesticides are all dangerous and may cause respiratory and other health problems. Asbestos is hazardous when disturbed, since it contains microscopic fibers that can be inhaled, causing permanent damage to lungs.

● If an area containing asbestos needs to be repaired or removed, get an expert in to deal with it safely (*see Resources*

page 163). Never handle asbestos yourself, even if it is present in only small quantities.
● Salvage materials to reuse at a later date in the house, or sell them to a wrecker yard: bricks, stones, wood flooring, window frames and beams, tiles and slates are expensive to buy new or secondhand, so remove them carefully and store until they are required. Metals, glass, and thermo-plastics can be reused, and so can lumber that is still in good condition. Wood that is rotten can be chipped and added to the compost heap (see pages 82–83), along with paper products used in natural insulation.
● Use recycled materials for your renovations: find a wrecking yard that stocks old doors, shelving, and masonry that match the style and period of your house.

(see pages 82–83)

PRESSED-WOOD PRODUCTS

Avoid using these, since they are made with toxic resins and are treated with hazardous chemicals. They include:

• Laminated boards (plywood and blockboard)
• Particle boards (wood chipboard)
• Hardboard and softboard
• MDF (medium-density fiberboard)

NEW MATERIALS CHECKLIST

Whether you are building, renovating, or doing a small repair job, check that your choice of new materials meets the following criteria before you buy.

● Nontoxic: many processed construction materials are toxic. Pressed-wood products (see box) are great offenders: opt for solid woods instead.
● Ecologically sound: check that the material has a certificate to verify that it comes from a sustainable source. This will ensure that the manufacturer is not contributing to the pollution of the environment.
● Local: by buying local materials you avoid the pollution caused by transporting them.
● Biodegradable: new paper-based insulation products break down and do not add to landfill sites (see Resources pages 163).

NATURAL BUILDING PRODUCTS

● Clay or lime plaster for walls
● Lime mortar for brickwork
● Rush and lath plaster—especially good for ceiling work
● Gypsum drywall for interior walls and ceilings
● Clear silicone for caulking
● Stone, marble, slate, and granite for floors and other surfaces—excellent for kitchens and bathrooms
● Ceramic tiles, brick, concrete, and natural linoleum for flooring
● Copper pipes for plumbing with lead-free soldering and joints
● Solid wood from sustainable sources for carpentry and flooring (see page 12)
● Cellulose-based insulation materials (see page 24)

Linseed oil putty is made from flax seed. Not only does it smell natural, but it is also a filler that allows wood to breathe.

SUSTAINABLE WOODS

Most people are aware that softwoods come from fast-growing trees, which make well-managed woodland easy to sustain. Buy hardwoods from responsible suppliers, but avoid tropical hardwoods if possible.

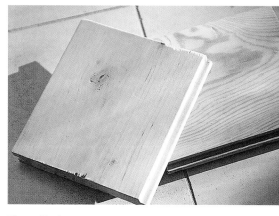

ACCEPTABLE SOFTWOODS

The common softwoods used to make low-cost furniture include pine and birch. Check the origin of the wood before purchase and look out for items made of willow—very fast-growing–bamboo, cane, and coconut, all of which are renewable resources.

Pine and larch are pale-colored softwoods with a light grain. Responsible suppliers will tell you their origin, and whether they have been treated with pesticides and preservatives.

ACCEPTABLE HARDWOODS

● Sustainable hardwoods include alder, apple, sycamore, aspen, beech, elm, hickory, lime, oak, pear, plane, European and black walnut, ash, box, cherry, maple, myrtle, and olive.
● Try to buy native hardwoods from a local supplier, to avoid unnecessary shipping.
● Avoid tropical hardwoods

such as mahogany, teak, iroko, African walnut, agba, bubinga, ebony, Honduras cedar, Indian laurel, obeche, sapele, tulip wood, wenge, and zebrano. Felling them depletes the rain forests, and they also need to be transported across vast distances, which is an energy-intensive process.

● Check that hardwood timber is free from toxic pesticides or preservatives.
● Buy recycled lumber from wrecking yards.

Maple, walnut, elm, white oak, cherry merbau, and sustainable Rhodesian teak are all hardwoods with a rich color and distinctive grain, and are available from reputable suppliers.

WOOD TREATMENTS

Many softwood trees, including yew, poplar, pine, larch, hemlock, and spruce, are treated with chemicals to produce high-yielding crops

and, once the wood is milled, it is often treated with a chemical finish. Familiarize yourself with the following toxins used in timber production and, if possible, avoid them. Timber treated with less toxic substances is also available.

• Lindane, an organochloride insecticide, is a suspected carcinogen; it has also had a devastating effect on the world bat population.
• The insecticide dieldrin and the preservatives pentachlorophenol (PCP) and tributyltin oxide (TBTO) are toxic and are now banned for home wood treatments in many countries.
• PVC (polyvinyl chloride) is used in flooring products and replacement window frames. Some vinyl products may give off chemical fumes.
• Formaldehyde, used as an adhesive in pressed-wood

products, is a volatile organic compound (VOC) and gives off vapors at normal room temperature. It can cause irritation to the eyes, nose, and throat, breathing difficulties, and allergic reactions.
• Melamine, a thermoplastic used to coat kitchen units and worktops to make them easy to wipe clean, may also contain formaldehyde resins.
• Insecticides made from synthetic pyrethroid (the active ingredients to look out for on the label is permethrin) are far less toxic, and are more bat-friendly than lindane (*see left*).
• Timber preservatives based on inorganic borates have low toxicity and low environmental impact. Inorganic borates are also highly effective as preventative and remedial treatments for wet and dry rot. Borax is a fire retardant and suppresses mold growth.

VARNISHING WITH SHELLAC

Unlike most other wood varnishes, which are made from petrochemicals, shellac is a 100 percent natural gum derived from "lac," a scale-insect secretion. Use it to varnish wood shelves and other wooden fixtures to create a clear, hardwearing surface. Shellac is also very good for sealing any treated wood surface that you have inherited from a previous homeowner, since it will prevent the wood from emitting toxic vapors. Shellac is available from most home improvement stores, is quick and easy to apply, smells good, and dries to a matte finish in 2–3 hours.

1 Using fine grade sandpaper or steel wool, gently rub down the painted or plain wood surface.

2 Paint on the shellac in smooth strokes. Leave it to dry for 2–3 hours, then apply a second coat.

CONSERVING WATER

The average homeowner uses 32–53 gallons (120–200 liters) of water per day but, by being a little more careful, we can reduce this to 21 gallons (80 liters). Furthermore, sources of water worldwide are becoming increasingly polluted with fertilizers, pesticides, and slurry from agriculture, while sewage, detergents, and toxic chemical residues are poured into the water system. By taking responsibility for our water use and for the ways in which we dispose of liquid toxic waste, we can make a positive contribution to water quality.

To save water, refrigerate filtered water rather than running the faucet until the water is cold enough to drink.

USING LESS WATER

Water is an increasingly scarce commodity, so reducing water use can make a real difference, especially when you consider that home use accounts for 65 percent of all consumption. Here are some ideas for saving water in the home and yard.

Spray faucets use far less water than steady-flow faucets, and they also wash the dirt off fruits and vegetables effectively.

AROUND THE HOME

● Install a water meter to measure your water use. Figures show that people who use meters consume 10–20 percent less water on average.
● Check for leaks: one drip per second wastes 1 gallon (4 liters) of water per day.
● Install a combination boiler or instant water heater. These heat only as much hot water as needed, and so cut down on water use (and save energy).

IN THE KITCHEN

● Wash dishes by hand in a basin, not under constant running water.
● Run the dishwasher only when you have a full load, to save water and energy.
● Run your washing machine on full loads only; a full load uses less water than two half loads, since each cycle uses up to 22 gallons (100 liters).
● When you buy a new washing machine, make sure you get a water-efficient one: this could reduce your water consumption by 5 percent.
● Always try to use the economy cycle when machine-washing any item.

USING THE TOILET

- Put a water-saving device in your cistern. Water authorities supply these, or you could improvise your own. Fill a bottle with water, replace the cap, and float it in the cistern. This displaces some of the water and reduces the quantity used in each flush. Alternatively, cut a plastic bottle in half, half-fill with pebbles or marbles to weigh it down, and place in the cistern.
- If you have an old-fashioned toilet with a high, suspended tank, do not replace it: these use less water than most modern flush cisterns.
- Install a dual-flush system that uses only a small amount of water for liquid waste and a larger volume for solid waste (*see Resources page 163*).
- If practical, install a low-flush toilet (*see Resources page 163*) that reduces the average flush from 2.5 gallons (9 liters) to 1 gallon (4 liters).

IN THE BATHROOM

- Turn off the faucet when brushing your teeth: running water for 1 minute uses up 3–4 gallons (10–14 liters).
- Take showers rather than baths, since they use less water.
- Install a water-saving showerhead (*see Resources page 163*) that fills each droplet with air, giving three times the efficiency of a normal showerhead but saving water at the same time, while also reducing lime buildup.

WATER TREATMENT PLANTS

Water for domestic use is pumped from rivers, aquifers, and reservoirs to treatment plants where it is filtered, and sterilized with chemicals such as chlorine before it reaches the faucets in our homes. Some companies use ultraviolet radiation instead of chlorine to disinfect water supplies, which is more environmentally friendly, since it is chemical-free and the radiation doses are far too low to be a health risk. We can ensure that our drinking water is clean—or as clean as possible—by always filtering tap water (*see page 99*) before we drink it.

IN THE YARD

- Be conscientious about reducing the amount of water you use in the yard, especially during the hot summer months: in 30 minutes a garden sprinkler uses as much water as a family of four in a day, or 264 gallons (1,000 liters) per hour or 1 pint (500 ml) every two seconds.
- Mulch your flowerbeds with compost or bark chippings to avoid moisture loss by evaporation (a mulch will also suppress weeds).
- Consider reducing the area of lawn and having a low-maintenance gravel area instead.
- Install a "graywater bypass" system for channeling used water (from bathtubs, showers, sinks, dishwashers, and washing machines) by rerouting your pipes into a discharge tank (*see Resources page 163*). This can be used for watering the yard.
- Install a compost toilet (*see Resources page 163*), which uses no water at all. You can use the resulting compost in the yard.

Collect rainwater in a large rain barrel so that you can water plants without using the hose.

AIR QUALITY

Indoor pollution is a major health concern, especially since many of us now spend more time indoors than out. According to research carried out by the Environmental Protection Agency, the concentration of toxic compounds can accumulate inside buildings, making them 200–500 times higher than outdoors. If you are concerned, buy a home kit to test levels of pollutants, or call in a professional tester. But above all, keep the house well ventilated: even colds and the flu will occur less often than in tightly sealed buildings.

AIR POLLUTANTS

The Environmental Protection Agency has compiled a list of the products that it considers are the worst air pollutants in the home. These are outlined below. They are easily avoided, since effective natural or "soft chemistry" alternatives are available.

AIR FRESHENERS
These synthetic fragrances disguise bad smells by releasing a chemical that coats the nasal passages with a film of oil, or deadens the olfactory nerves.

AEROSOL SPRAYS
Used for hairsprays and insecticides, these emit a fine mist that is easily inhaled, and contain CFCs, which damage the ozone layer. Use pump sprays as an alternative.

CLEANING PRODUCTS
Formaldehyde, PVC, acrylics, polyethylene, fluorocarbons, polystyrene, polyester, and polyurethane are present in the contents and packaging of many everyday products.

IMPROVING AIR QUALITY

There are many inexpensive ways of instantly improving the air quality in your home. Here are a few ideas to help you achieve germ- and pollutant-free air.

- Decorate and furnish your home with as many natural materials as possible (*see pages 32–43*).
- Make your household a no-smoking zone.
- Open doors and windows to encourage air circulation.
- Avoid overheating your home: the higher the ambient temperature, the greater the "outgassing" of toxic vapors.
- Air dry-cleaned garments outside before hanging in the closet: perchloroethylene used in the process is a suspected human carcinogen.
- Use safe household plastics made from cellulose fibers.
- Replace smaller plastic items, such as wastebaskets, with natural fibers such as wicker.
- Limit your use of chemical household products.

Heat up a few drops of essential oil such as citronella, and its vapor will scent and freshen the air naturally.

Scented geranium leaves or herbs in bowls of humidifying water close to radiators act as an air freshener.

ELECTRIC HEATING
Homes heated by radiant electric systems have lower levels of pollution than those heated by other methods. But hot air can dry out the atmosphere, causing sore throats as well as damaging wood furniture and plants. To improve air humidity, place bowls of water close to radiators. This will keep humidity levels at 30–50 percent—a level that is best for controlling biological contaminants. Buy a simple hygrometer to check humidity levels in your home (*see Resources page 163*). If possible, keep heating on a constant low temperature. This is cheaper and less energy-intensive than a sudden blast of heat.

GAS HEATING
Gas heaters emit carbon monoxide, nitrogen dioxide, and other combustion pollutants, so make sure that they are well vented. Service gas heaters regularly and make sure that you place a CO_2/combustion-products detector nearby.

FIREPLACES
An open fire can emit benzopyrene, so make sure that it is well vented. Have the chimney cleaned regularly by a professional contractor.

MINIMIZING THE MOLD
Mold spores and airborne bacteria are common in poorly ventilated homes. Counteract them by installing extractor fans in kitchens and bathrooms. Cover pans while cooking, and open windows to let steam escape.

AIR IONIZERS
Ionizers increase the amount of beneficial negative ions (electrically charged atoms) in the air, counterbalancing the positive ion charge from heating systems and other domestic equipment which can cause lethargy, tiredness, and susceptibility to illness.

HELPFUL HOUSEPLANTS
Certain houseplants are good at filtering the surrounding air—spider plants can even remove formaldehyde fumes. Plants also increase oxygen levels, act as humidifiers, and may also be fragrant. The following plants can significantly improve the air quality of your home by reducing the vapors released by synthetic chemicals.

Aloe vera (*Aloe vera*)
Bamboo palm
  (*Chamaedorea seifrizii*)
Boston fern
  (*Nephrolepis exaltata*)
Chinese evergreen
  (*Aglaonema crispum*)
Chrysanthemum
  (*Chrysanthemum morifolium*)
Corn plant (*Dracaena fragrans*)
Dracaena (*Dracaena deremensis*)
Dwarf banana (*Musa cavendishii*)

Pygmy date palm
  (*Phoenix roebelenii*)
English ivy (*Hedera helix*)
Gerbera (*Gerbera jamesonii*)
Lady palm (*Rhapis excelsa*)
Peace lily (*Spathiphyllum*)
Philodendron (*Philodendron*)
Rubber plant (*Ficus robusta*)
Schefflera (*Brassaia actinophylla*)
Spider plant (*Chlorophytum comosum*)
Weeping fig (*Ficus benjamina*)

The peace lily mops up ammonia, acetone, ethyl acetate, benzene, and formaldehyde from the atmosphere.

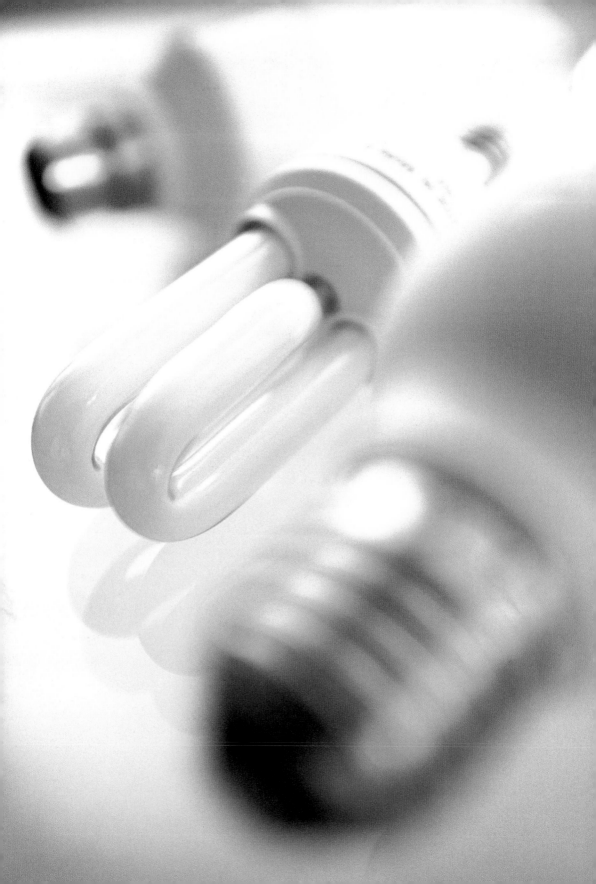

SAVING ENERGY

Most of us take our supply of energy for granted and are wasteful without realizing how much we can save just by being careful or by changing old habits. Small gestures, like carpooling rather than traveling to work in separate cars, soon add up to significant energy savings.

Maximizing daylight p20

LIMITED RESOURCES

Fossil fuels provide us with most of our heating, lighting, and transportation needs. In doing so, they release carbon dioxide, which causes health problems and global warming. The good news is that our homes can now be connected to electricity based on renewable, clean resources such as wind, wave, and solar power—in fact, it is possible to meet nearly half of an industrial country's electricity needs from pollution-free sources. Houses and apartments can also be insulated to prevent heat loss, but need to be well ventilated too, since overinsulation can trap unwanted smells and toxic gases in the home.

Insulating hot water pipes p25

REDUCING ENERGY CONSUMPTION

This chapter shows you how you can cut down on the amount of energy expended to light and heat the home and run household appliances. It also suggests energy-saving adaptations, and puts forward ways to save energy when taking a short trip or using the car. Most of these tips require little extra effort and have the positive benefit of reducing household bills.

Low-energy appliances p26

Low-energy bulbs are widely available and fit into regular sockets. They are long-lasting and help to reduce bills.

Energy-saving transportation p28

LIGHTING

Maximizing natural light in the house has many advantages, not least the beneficial effect on your own sense of well-being. Ultraviolet rays are "germicidal," which means that they are able to kill off dust mites in carpets and other soft furnishings. This is one of the reasons why it is a good idea to air household items outdoors in the sun. However, too much exposure to sunlight may cause damage to household goods: fabric colors can fade, natural wood surfaces may bleach, and paper lampshades can turn yellow if regularly exposed to direct sun.

NATURAL LIGHT

Just by making the most of the available natural daylight that the exposure of your house has to offer, you can heat and light your home without having to draw on gas or electricity supplies.

- Place key work surfaces—in the kitchen and the home office—near windows.
- Install skylights in upper-story rooms to provide a source of natural light all day long.
- If you have a yard, consider installing French doors to open out onto the area.
- Install roller blinds or add tiebacks on your curtains to allow maximum daylight in.
- Keep window panes and skylights clean.

Diffused natural daylight is provided by a wall of glass bricks that lets light in, saves on electrical lighting bills, and offers privacy from neighboring homes.

CHOOSING LIGHTBULBS

Something as simple as your choice of lightbulb can affect the demands you place on household energy supplies. Decide whether you need task or ambient lighting, or perhaps both, depending on the room's function, and then use this information to help you choose the right lightbulb.

INCANDESCENT BULBS
- These offer a steady white light that does not cause eye strain, and give good color rendition.
- They have a relatively short life expectancy and are expensive in comparison to other bulbs.
- Their large heat output wastes energy, so always turn them off when they are not in use.

If switching to energy-saving bulbs, start by replacing the lightbulbs in the rooms that you use most often, since this will save the most energy and money. Energy-saving bulbs give out the same amount of light as incandescent bulbs without losing energy in heat. They are considerably more expensive than regular bulbs, but you recoup your initial outlay quickly with the money you save on electricity bills.

HALOGEN BULBS

● These last longer than incandescent bulbs.
● They emit a brilliant white light ideal for task lighting.
● They give off a lot of heat but use less energy than incandescents.

"FULL-SPECTRUM" BULBS

● These are designed to imitate daylight, not always effectively.

● They are usually fluorescent, but choose those without enhanced UV rays; they are more eco-friendly.

FLUORESCENT BULBS

● These are the least energy-intensive of bulbs, using one-fifth of the energy of incandescent bulbs and lasting up to eight times longer.
● They use argon gas and mercury—a highly toxic metal.
● They flicker rapidly from 100–30,000 times per second, which is stressful, affects the eyes, and causes headaches.
● They require special fixtures.

COMPACT FLUORESCENT BULBS

● These are the standard energy-saving bulbs. During its lifetime, each bulb saves 400 lb (180 kg) of coal and keeps 286 lb (130 kg) of carbon out of the atmosphere.
● They last 10 times longer than incandescent bulbs.
● They are excellent for task lighting.

● Compact fluorescent bulbs can be fitted into regular incandescent light sockets.
● The bulbs last longer if left on for a period rather than being switched on and off.

Dormer windows allow natural light to flood in. An adjustable desk lamp offers good directional light.

DIMMER SWITCHES

Lighting is important in creating the right atmosphere in a room, and dimmers are the ideal solution if you want to be able to change the light levels and save energy.

Operating dimmer switches reduces the flow of electric current to the light sources and therefore uses less energy. Installing dimmer switches so that you can adjust light levels to just what you need, rather than having brighter lighting than you require, and can save fossil fuels as well as reducing your electricity bill.

Standard light switches can quickly and easily be replaced with a dimmer mechanism by a professional electrician without having to change the wiring.

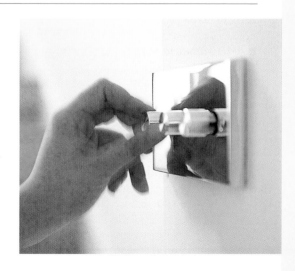

HEAT & INSULATION

Over 50 percent of our energy bills goes on hot water and heating. There are ways of regulating and saving heat to reduce this expensive energy load, and simple ways of making the most of solar energy. The following advice includes hints and tips for conserving heat and covers the obvious benefits of turning to solar energy.

CONSERVING HEAT

There are numerous practical ways, all very simple, of saving on your heating bill. You will also be doing your part in reducing carbon emissions that pollute the environment: even small changes can have a big impact if everyone makes them!

● Insulate your hot water tank: this can reduce the heat loss by 75 percent.
● To make the most of rising heat, have your living room upstairs.

● Warm air rises, so if you have high ceilings, design a platform area that will be warm and comfortable, and that will you give you more living space.

WINDOW REPAIRS
● Up to 23 percent of heat loss occurs through the gaps in poorly installed windows.
● If installing new windows, especially if you are enlarging an opening, you may need to get a building permit from your town or city hall.

ATTIC INSULATION
● Make sure that your attic is properly insulated. About 3 in (8 cm) of insulation material will save around 20 percent of your heating costs—natural insulation materials, which include recycled paper and vermiculite (*see page 24*), are now more widely available (*see Resources pages 165*).
● Insulating your attic makes the space colder, so if your water heater is in the attic, make sure that you insulate the hot water tank and water pipes to avoid freezing in winter (but not underneath, so that they receive rising heat from below).
● Weatherstrip and insulate the attic door.

A light and airy sunroom kitchen has energy-efficient windows that create a comfortable, well-insulated room.

CENTRAL HEATING
● Set your thermostat to 69°F (20°C) when the house is occupied. If you go out for more than two hours, turn the thermostat down to 60°F (15°C).
● A timer switch that turns the heating system on and off automatically will avoid wasting heat on an empty house. Install an up-to-date electronic timer so that you can change the program easily whenever your daily routine or the weather changes.
● Radiator heating systems are cheaper, provide better water pressure, and give you more space because they don't need a large water storage tank.
● Make sure that your registers produce the right output for the room size and are not overheating it.
● Put shelves over registers or radiators to help direct warm air into the room as it rises.
● Close registers in unused rooms, and keep doors closed.
● Underfloor heating radiates

heat and is less wasteful than conventional systems.
● Consider other methods of heating such as electric storage heaters or a wood burner.

AIR–CONDITIONING
● Air-conditioning systems are very energy-intensive. Consult the manufacturer about energy-saving options, such as thermostatic controls for when you are out at work, or zoning systems to cool only the rooms you are using at any one time.
● Set the system a few degrees higher, to save energy.
● About one-third of unwanted heat comes in through the roof. Prevent heat buildup by applying a reflective coating to your roof, or staple reflective foil to the roof rafters (*see Resources page 165*). Installing louver windows or roof vents can reduce the temperature in the attic by up to 30 degrees.
● Install ceiling fans or floor-standing fans instead.
● Hang a dampened sheet or

Install thermostatic radiator valves to vary room temperatures as required, and save energy.

curtain over a window to catch the breeze and cool the air.
● Keep curtains closed in direct sunlight.
● Plant deciduous trees on the sunny side of your home to shade it. A vine on a trellis serves the same purpose.

HOT WATER SUPPLY
● Attach a thermostat to your hot water cylinder and set it at around 130° F (55° C).
● Insulate the hot water pipes between the boiler and tank.
● Old water heaters are far less energy-efficient than modern ones. Replacing a 15-year-old heater can cut your energy use by up to 20 percent.
● Instantaneous water heaters provide instant hot water. There is no storage tank to hold hot water, so no energy is wasted in heat loss as water travels along pipework.

SOLAR HEATING
It makes sense to use solar heat: fuel reserves are expendable and fuel pollution causes problems to human health and to the environment. Solar energy is secure, clean, and inexhaustible. Here's how to make the best use of natural sunlight.
• Buy a south-facing house to benefit from natural light.
• Install large windows on the sunny side of the house.
• Heat-absorbent building materials—brick, concrete, stone—will store up heat during the day and release it gradually in cool temperatures.
• Invest in a solar wall: this is a transparent insulation panel attached to a masonry wall that collects solar energy. It heats up the solid wall, which then transmits this heat to the internal wall.
• Install a solar-powered hot water system (*see Resources page 165*).
• Install solar panels on the roof of your house to capture heat from the sun, which is then stored and used to heat your house or water supply. If well-positioned, you can supply at least 40–50 percent of your heating from a roof-sized solar collector.

WHY INSULATE?

Heat loss from walls, roofs, windows, and heat lost through drafts can be greatly reduced by insulation. However, over-insulation can cause indoor air pollution (*see pages 16–17*). So the secret is to reduce heat loss while keeping the house well ventilated. Insulating an existing home may seem expensive, but your property could be eligible for an energy-saving grant. This is worth discussing with your state or local government. Even if you have to pay for the insulation yourself, the noticeable reduction in household energy bills will soon cover the cost of your initial outlay.

NATURAL INSULATION MATERIALS

Not all insulation products are beneficial to the environment, even though they save energy. Try to avoid insulation products that cause pollution and are difficult to reclaim when manufactured, such as polystyrene (a by-product of petroleum), expanded polystyrene (bead board), polyurethane foam, and urea formaldehyde foam (or polyiscyanurate foam). The following natural materials are microporous and "breathe," so reducing the risk of condensation and problems caused by mold.

A wide range of 100 percent natural insulation materials are readily available from hardware outlets.

CELLULOSE FIBER
Made from recycled newspaper, or recycled jute sacking, cellulose is treated with borax to make it fire-resistant. It is available in shredded paper or fiber-pellet form for loose-fill insulation, or as fiberboards for insulating floors, walls, ceilings, and roofs.

WOOD FIBERBOARD
This is recycled wood, bonded together with its natural resins. It is used for exterior insulation in timber-frame construction, and as boards for floor and wall insulation, and soundproofing.

SHEEP'S WOOL FELT
This acoustic and thermal wool felting is treated with borax to make it fireproof and insect-resistant. It is used to insulate walls, ceilings, and roofs.

HEMP FIBER
A fast-growing crop, hemp is used to make loose-fill cavity insulation, while a hemp and lime mix is used for insulation fiberboards.

COCONUT FIBER
This is made into thermal and acoustic insulation board.

MINERAL FIBERS
These include:
● Perlite (from vitreous rock, which comes in the form of enamel-like globules)
● Vermiculite (a natural scale-like mineral based on silicates of aluminum and magnesium)
● Foamed glass (glass in cellular form)

FLAX
This fast-growing crop is made into wadding that is used to insulate ceiling joists and rafters, and also for thermal and acoustic wall and floor insulation.

CORK
Cork tiles provide excellent, warm floor insulation, but make sure they are not treated with a polyurethane finish.

SYNTHETIC INSULATION MATERIALS

These insulation materials are used in modern house construction, so they may already be present in your home. However, if you are doing your own insulating and have a choice in what you use, try to avoid products that contain any of the following.

- PVC (polyvinyl chloride) plastic found in some window frames is produced using toxic chemicals. This process creates polluting waste, including dioxins. If PVC is burned, it also emits dioxins, and the ash may contain heavy metals. If disposed of in landfill sites, other chemicals found in PVC products may leach into the soil.
- Manufactured mineral fibers (MMFs) are known generically as "rockwool" and are used as thermal and acoustic insulators in walls, attics, and for pipe lagging. Slag wool, stone wool, mineral wool, and fiberglass all come into this category. Their particles may become airborne during handling and may be highly irritant to the respiratory system. They may cause eye and skin damage, and are suspected carcinogens.

MAKING THE RIGHT CHOICE

The natural insulation material you choose will depend on the area of your home you want to insulate. The following suggestions list the best fibers for each location.

WALLS
- Use cellulose fiber, wood fiber, loose-fill hemp, sheep's wool felt, or vermiculite.

DRAFT–PROOFING

• Cover old-fashioned letter slots or keyholes.
• Use stuffed draft-excluders made from remnants of fabric along the bottom of doors.
• Use commercial draft strips for doors (brass "atomic" strip works best).
• Hang thick, lined and interlined curtains over drafty windows and doors.
• Install spring hinges to allow doors to swing shut.
• Install compression seals in strip form for windows, or wiper seals for sash windows.
• Close the chimney damper when not in use.

- Polystyrene beads, although manufacturing-intensive, are far better than MMFs.
- Effective insulation on external walls includes lime plaster render, coats of natural resin, wood cladding, tiles, or slates.
- Line internal walls with thermal boards made from natural materials.

FLOORS
- Wall-to-wall carpeting using natural materials (*see pages 42–43*) prevents heat loss.
- Use recycled rubber or cork for an insulating underlay.
- Layers of old newspapers under carpet or natural resin linoleum make good natural floor insulators.

ATTICS
- Use vermiculite under the floorboards and in the eaves.
- Cellulose fiber is also very effective in attic spaces.

Lag indoor pipes with an eco-friendly thermoplastic product instead of expanded foam pipe sections.

- Insulate the cold water tank with sheep's wool felt (*see opposite*).

HOT WATER TANKS
- Cover with a fitted thermal jacket to reduce heat loss by 75 percent.
- Insulate hot water pipes with a CFC- and HCFC-free thermoplastic product.

HOUSEHOLD APPLIANCES

When buying or replacing household appliances, check their energy-efficiency ratings. Appliances in a dealer's showroom are required by law to have a yellow-and-black EnergyGuide label attached to them. Some appliances may also carry the EnergyStar logo, which indicates that they are substantially more energy-efficient than comparable models. Just by upgrading your refrigerator or freezer, for example, harmful carbon dioxide emissions can be greatly reduced.

BUYING APPLIANCES

By making informed choices when we buy various household appliances, we can reduce or minimize the impact these products have on the environment.

- Buy good-quality appliances that will last—and buy only what you really need.
- Choose energy-efficient equipment: hand- or battery-operated gadgets are often just as effective as their electric equivalents. Solar-powered flashlights, radios, and battery chargers are also available.
- Consider renting rather than buying a TV and VCR to reduce the demand for manufacture.
- Buy metal rather than plastic items: plastics release fumes when hot and break more easily.
- Take old appliances to a recycling center for disposal.

TOP TIP

Fill your teakettle with only as much water as you need, and you can dramatically reduce your daily energy consumption. But make sure the kettle is free of lime deposits or power will go to waste.

WASHING MACHINES

- Front-loading machines use less water and energy than top-loaders.
- If possible, sign up for a time-of-use plan with the electric company, and run your machine during the lower rate hours.
- Always read the manual to get the best out of your washing machine.
- Excessive vibration can damage working parts, so make sure that your machine stands level on the floor.
- Use a water softener in hard water areas to prevent mineral deposits, or add washing soda to your powder.
- Use the correct settings for the size of load and type of fabrics (see page 64).
- Always wait until you have a full load before using the machine, or else use the half-load or economy functions.
- Use the lowest possible temperature setting.
- Presoaking garments (see page 64) and treating stains (see pages 66–69) reduces the amount of detergent required, and makes a cooler wash cycle possible.

A hand-operated carpet sweeper is great for a quick cleanup and only requires your energy to power it.

FRIDGES & FREEZERS

● A cool pantry can save on refrigerator space and a smaller refrigerator reduces the quantities of damaging CFCs released into the atmosphere.

Dust the coils at the back of the refrigerator—dust can increase energy consumption by up to 30 percent.

● Avoid buying a refrigerator that is bigger than you need, and check its energy rating.
● Buy a hydrocarbon-cooled model rather than one using CFCs.
● Insulate the sides of the refrigerator to save energy.
● Keep the refrigerator temperature at 38–48°F (3–9°C), and the freezer at 32–23°F (0 -°5C).
● Avoid leaving the refrigerator door open for longer than necessary, since this allows cold air to escape.
● Let food cool before putting it into the refrigerator, and keep it covered.
● Although refrigerators are now very well insulated, try to avoid placing this appliance next to your stove or oven: it may have to work harder.
● Connect your refrigerator

Defrost the freezer when ice builds up so that it works to maximum efficiency. Full freezers need defrosting less often.

to an energy-saving plug, which works by matching energy to the load required.
● Find out if your municipality offers a recycling service for old appliances.

DISHWASHERS

● Buy the most energy-efficient in terms of amounts of water used and units of electricity used.
● Try not to buy a bigger dishwasher than you really need: the compact models hold very practical amounts of crockery and cutlery.

● Use the economy cycle for every wash.
● Running a dishwasher on an economy cycle with full loads can use less water than washing by hand.
● Turn off the machine when it reaches the drying cycle to save energy: just open the door.

TV, VCR, & STEREO

● Keep stereo units (CD player, amplifier, tuner, tape player) as close as possible to each other so that they can operate from the same power supply. Separate power supplies will increase your electricity bill.
● Never leave machines on standby: it wastes a large amount of energy and is a cause of electrical fires.

● Use battery-powered cordless headphones. Not only do they save energy, but they also protect neighbors from unwanted noise.
● Buy a windup radio, the ultimate eco-friendly gadget. A mere 25 seconds of winding will give you 30 minutes of playing time, at no cost to yourself or the environment.

AVOIDING EMFs

Electrical equipment gives off EMFs, or electromagnetic frequencies, a type of radiation that may cause health problems. The following tips will reduce your exposure to them:
● Unplug appliances when not in use (they still produce EMFs when switched off).
● Try to do without microwave ovens and electric blankets.
● Sit as far away as possible from televisions, stereo systems, and computers.
● Keep beds at least 4 ft (1.2 m) away from electrical items, such as electric heaters, or clock radios with LCD number displays.
● Use your cellular phone as little as possible or buy a hands-free earpiece.

TRAVEL

Traveling to work or for pleasure is both energy-intensive and polluting. In terms of toxic fuel emissions, air travel is the most polluting form of transportation because aviation fuel is more polluting than gasoline. Although many of us still prefer the convenience of the car, traveling by train or bus is a better option because both use far less fuel per passenger. If you must go by car, here are some ways to make your journeys more energy-saving.

REDUCING CAR TRAVEL

Traveling by car is often a matter of habit. Try other ways of getting around, and make the most of the car journeys you do take.

- Walk or cycle for short trips—these activities are good for your health as well as for the environment. Studies suggest that a 10 percent increase in the number of cyclists on the road would lead to a 4 percent reduction in heart disease. Wearing a pollution mask helps filter out toxic gases.
- Use the train or bus where possible.
- If you shop by car, do all your shopping in one trip per week, and tie it in with as many other errands as possible.
- Carpool.
- Use the HOV (High-Occupancy Vehicle) lane where available, when car-pooling.
- Use park-and-ride programs.

Try to cycle or walk rather than always taking the car. It will improve your well-being, both physically and mentally.

BUYING A CAR

The car is here to stay, but by driving well and making informed choices about fuel we can all reduce the impact it makes. The internal combustion engine may soon give way to propane gas, fuel cell, and other technologies, but meanwhile, follow these tips.

- Buy secondhand—it has far less environmental impact than buying new, and it is much cheaper.
- Buy small: usually, small means less polluting, while four-wheel drive increases fuel consumption by 5 percent.
- Buy a stick-shift: automatics use more gas.

- Choose a car with low pollution features like good fuel efficiency, a catalytic converter, and electronic ignition.
- Avoid diesel cars. Diesel is far more polluting, containing more than 40 recognized toxic pollutants that cause major health problems, including

cancer, and pollute the environment. If you do have a diesel engine, use biodiesel, which is based on waste food oil—but check first that your car will run on this. Otherwise, try a low-sulfur diesel (see Resources page 165), which is a cleaner version of regular diesel.

ENERGY-SAVING DRIVING

The way we drive makes a quantifiable difference to fuel consumption, as well as to wear and tear on the vehicle. Slamming on the brakes, using gear changes to slow down, and revving the engine can increase your bills by 20 percent.

- Drive more slowly. Speeding along at 70 mph (113 km/h) can gobble up 30 percent more gas than 55 mph (88 km/h).
- Accelerating gently uses less gas: drive smoothly.
- Have your car serviced regularly and keep it in good repair.
- Keep tires correctly inflated: low tire pressure increases fuel consumption by 1 percent.
- Remove a roof rack when it is not in use—wind resistance increases fuel consumption.
- Use air-conditioning only when necessary—it uses fuel.
- Don't idle the engine when standing: turn it off.
- Drive in the highest gear possible: 37 mph (60 km/h) in third gear uses 25 percent more fuel than fifth gear.
- Convert your car to propane: conversion is expensive, but the fuel is cheap and less polluting than gasoline.
- Use reformulated gasoline, a low-emission unleaded gas that requires no vehicle modification.

CLEANING THE CAR

It is not strictly necessary to use chemical cleaners on your car: there are some natural alternatives that work just as well. For example, you could use the window cleaner on page 50 to clean all the glass. Here are some other suggestions.

- Baking soda mixed with a little water is excellent for removing insects from headlights, windshields, and paintwork, and cleans up grease spills.
- Save water: rather than using the hose to wash the car, fill a bucket with warm water and add "soft chemistry" liquid detergent, and clean with a cellulose sponge.
- To clean the windshield, put soda water into a spray bottle, squirt over the glass, and wipe dry.
- To clean battery terminals, sprinkle baking soda around them, spray with water, and leave for an hour. Sponge off with water and leave to dry.

CAR-CLEANING POLISH

Use this natural homemade preparation to remove surface dirt and give your car a long-lasting shine.

YOU WILL NEED
4 oz (100 g) soapflakes
 or grated hand soap,
water, to cover
6 drops of jojoba oil
½ oz (15 g) beeswax

Before mixing the ingredients, dissolve the soapflakes in water overnight. To apply, dab on with a soft cloth, and buff to a shine with a chamois cloth.

1 Melt the beeswax and jojoba oil in a bowl over simmering water. Pour the melted wax into the dissolved soap flakes. Beat until the mixture is creamy.

2 Place in a lidded jar ready for use.

DECORATING
& FURNISHING

Decorating a home is an opportunity to create a sanctuary where we can live comfortably in surroundings which give us pleasure. Our choice of materials is key, and natural ones almost always look, feel, and smell better than synthetic products. There is growing concern, too, over the cocktail of chemicals used in the manufacture of paints and textiles. Often there is no list of ingredients on these products, which adds to the difficulty of making an informed choice.

NONTOXIC PAINTS FOR HOME DECORATING

You can now buy paints that are made without the hazardous substances that harm the air quality in your home. Natural paints offer a smooth, matte finish and are available in a wide range of colors.

NATURAL TEXTILES & FABRICS

Bedlinen, upholstery, curtains, and towels in pure linen or cotton, silk and wool are ideal for the natural home. As well as feeling luxurious, they are also practical, resilient fabrics. An "organic" or "untreated" label means that they are derived from fiber crops grown and processed without toxic pesticides, fertilizers, and chemical finishes. Unlike mass-produced fabrics, they are free of vinyl, formaldehyde, and other toxic substances that may cause allergies and sickness. This chapter aims to show you why it makes sense to choose natural paints and fabrics. It describes how and where to apply them, and how to clean and care for them so that they last.

Natural paints are now available in an extensive range of soft colors, and do not "outgas" during or after application. Pure cottons and linens make durable covers for furniture.

Making milk paint p33

Natural brush cleaner p34

Applying limewash p33

Choosing flooring p42

PAINTING & DECORATING

Although some mainstream manufacturers are now reducing the quantity of chemicals used in housepaints, most commercial paints on the market contain large amounts of hazardous substances. The high levels of toxicity present in paint soon become evident when you begin examining the warnings paint manufacturers are legally obliged to display on cans. Oil paints are the worst offenders. They contain toxic volatile organic compounds (VOCs), resins, pigments, and additives such as defoamers (chemicals that break down the foam caused by chemical reactions), deodorizers, stabilizers, and preservatives. Water-based latex paints contain vinyl resins, which have been linked to various health problems. And although commercial water-based paints may contain low levels of VOCs, their chemical content is still three times higher than that of natural paints.

Organic water-based paints that are free of artificial pigments and chemicals are now available by mail order, so they are easily obtainable nationwide.

AVOIDING TOXIC INGREDIENTS

In 1999, a Johns Hopkins University study showed that over 450 toxic chemicals may be present in house paint. By familiarizing yourself with the dangers associated with chemicals in paints you can make an informed decision about whether to use them in moderation or to opt for a natural alternative.

VOLATILE ORGANIC COMPOUNDS (VOCS)

Most oil-based house-paints contain 40–60 percent VOCs, a large family of chemical compounds that evaporate easily. These organic solvents are mainly used to help particles in paint to disperse and bind together. Water-based paints contain lower amounts of VOCs (about 10 percent). VOCs found in paint may include toluene, xylene, and formaldehyde, all hazardous chemicals. VOCs "outgas" at room temperature, and are responsible for the typical new paint odor. The fumes may trigger asthma, allergies, disorders of the nervous system, and flulike symptoms. VOCs also contribute to the formation of ozone at ground level in summer, commonly known as smog.

PAINTING TIPS

If you are using paints that contain VOCs, here are some hints to reduce their impact.
• Ventilate the room during and after applying paint.
• Wear protective clothing, gloves, and even goggles to protect your skin and eyes.
• Avoid moving into a newly painted room right away. Leave it to "outgas" first for about a week.
• Paint at cooler times of the year to reduce vapor levels.
• Reduce the temperature of your home and keep humidity below 35 percent to limit the release of toxic chemicals.

NATURAL PAINTS

Paints made from natural raw materials (*see Resources page 166*) have been used successfully for centuries. The principal ingredients are linseed oil, lime from limestone, casein from milk, and natural solvents such as turpentine and/or oils derived from citrus fruits. Chalk and natural pigments make up the remainder. There are now also water-based gloss and satin paints for interior and exterior wood, metal, plaster, and masonry. They may be more expensive, but the benefit is that they contain no fungicides or preservatives. Because they are preservative-free, natural paints do have a limited shelf life: about nine months if unopened. Use the same technique for applying natural paints as you would for any other house paint; however, some require more drying time because they lack chemical drying agents.

Limewash paint has no smell and is nontoxic. It dries quickly, so apply it with a large, natural bristle brush in broad strokes for a smooth finish.

ADVANTAGES OF NATURAL PAINTS

● Natural paints are micro-porous, so they allow the walls to "breathe." This means blistering and peeling do not occur (as may happen with synthetic paints), nor does moisture accumulate, since it can evaporate naturally.
● The process used to make natural paints produces far less toxic waste than synthetic paint manufacture.
● Natural paints are safe for the environment and are not tested on animals.
● They are less likely to trigger sensitivities and allergies than paints high in chemicals.

● Brushes and rollers can be cleaned with soapy water.
● The packaging is recyclable.
● Although drying time is longer (with the exception of limewash), the paint settles into a smooth, enamel-like coating, free from brushmarks and hairline cracks.

MAKING MILK PAINT

Casein powder, a by-product of milk, can be mixed with water and a small amount of natural pigment to make a wonderfully smooth, matte paint for interior walls.

1 Mix ½ lb (250 g) casein powder with 1½ cups (340 ml) water. Whisk to make a thick batter and stand for 30 minutes.

2 Add a further ½ cup (125 ml) water and whisk to a creamy consistency. Let stand for 15 minutes.

3 Mix 2 oz (50 g) of pigment powder with a little water to make a thin paste. Add to the casein mix, stir, and use.

WORKING WITH PAINT

Paints made from natural ingredients have different properties from ordinary commercial brands. Use these application guidelines to achieve successful results.

● Natural paint is more fluid than other types of paint. When applying it to a ceiling, cut a slit in a sponge and thread it onto the handle of the brush to prevent drips from running down your arm.

● To achieve the smooth, enamel finish characteristic of natural paint, you need to use high-quality bristle brushes with fine ("combed") tips.

● Rolling produces a different finish from brushing, so avoid mixing these two methods of application.

● Spraying with a paint spray gun produces a smooth finish.

● Allow 24 hours for natural paints to dry.

● Although most natural paints are odorless or have a citrus-fruit aroma, you can remove unwanted smells by placing a few slices of onion in a dish of water.

BRUSH-CLEANING PRODUCTS

The most common brush cleaners for oil paints are mineral and methylated spirits, but since these are based on petrochemicals they are best avoided. Instead, clean your brushes with solvent-free, water-based products. These have no toxic effects and minimal VOC content (*see Resources page 166*).

DISPOSING OF PAINT

● Contact your local recycling center for guidelines for the disposal of paint, strippers, and finishes, which are defined as hazardous waste products. Paint waste contains many toxins and heavy metals, and should not be dumped in a landfill.

● Keep any leftover paint for retouching paintwork.

● Donate unused paint to local community groups or charities.

GARDEN USES

● Organic paints are not harmful to plants and contain natural oils and minerals, so any dried-up remains can safely be added to compost.

● Leftover limewash paint can be brushed onto the trunks of fruit trees to deter pests.

NATURAL BRUSH CLEANER

Turpentine, derived from the natural resin of coniferous trees, is an excellent brush cleaner for oil paints. It can be rinsed down the sink, since it does not harm the environment. All you need is a glass jar, dishwashing liquid, and clean water for rinsing.

1 Pour enough turpentine into the jar to cover the bristles. Leave the brush to soak for 20–30 minutes.

2 Clean off any excess paint with lukewarm water and a small amount of "soft chemistry" dishwashing liquid.

3 Rinse out the soapy water and paint under the faucet. Shake the brush, then dry it flat to keep the bristles straight.

WORKING WITH WALLPAPER

Wallpaper manufacturers often give a vinyl or plastic finish to decorative papers to make them easier to wipe clean. Wallpaper pastes also contain chemical solvents. Some wallpaper manufacturers, however, now produce a range of papers from recycled cotton or paper pulp, as well as clay-coated papers. Water-based wallpaper pastes are also available, and these offer a preferable alternative to chemical solvent-based glues.

TOP TIP

Instead of using chemical products to remove wallpaper, try a steam stripper. To save energy, fill the stripper with hot water to reduce the time needed to bring the water to a boil.

AVOIDING CHEMICAL SOLVENTS

Chemical wallpaper strippers are based on sodium hydroxide, which can burn the skin, while products to remove wallpaper glue may contain methylene chloride, which is known to be carcinogenic. Consider the following natural alternatives:

● "Soft chemistry" solvent strippers are available, but may need to be left on overnight to allow time for them to work. Apply a second coat of stripper before peeling off the wallpaper.

● Some wallpapers may peel off dry. If not, follow the technique described below.

NATURAL WALLPAPER STRIPPER

The following step-by-step sequence shows how you can remove wallpaper without the use of chemical solvents. A simple solution of hot water and white vinegar is applied to the paper and left to soak in. This reacts with the wallpaper paste and loosens it, making it much easier to peel off with a scraper. If you wish to paint the walls afterward, you may need to remove any traces of wallpaper solvent by rubbing gently with sandpaper to create a smooth surface, then wipe down the wall with a damp cloth and leave to dry before redecorating.

1 Using a utility knife, score the wallpaper to be removed.

2 Pour ½ pint (300 ml) white vinegar into a bucket of hot water. Brush onto the paper with a wallpaper brush, and leave the solution to penetrate the paper.

3 The vinegar solution reacts with the wallpaper paste and helps to loosen it. This will allow you to gently ease the paper away from the wall surface with a metal scraper.

SOFT FURNISHINGS

Synthetic fibers may now dominate the textile market, but natural fabrics—especially those derived from organic sources and colored with natural dyes—are better for our health and sense of well-being, and far gentler on the environment. Although more expensive than synthetic fibers, good-quality natural fabrics are perhaps a better investment in the long term, since we are more inclined to take care of them and repair them before throwing them out. To maintain soft furnishings in pristine condition, always read the care instructions before cleaning, and follow the advice given below.

LINEN

Linen is made from the fibers of the flax plant, and is often sold in its natural, unbleached ivory color. The plant has few insect predators but, unless organically grown, it may still be treated with some pesticides. In its natural state linen is crisp, cool, and dries quickly. Since it may shrink slightly when washed, it is often preshrunk. It is vulnerable to mildew but not to moths. Linen and cotton blends are common and often have a chemical antiwrinkle treatment that may wash out, leaving the fabric limp.

Organic linen is an attractive fabric with a pleasing natural color and texture.

Iron linen tablecloths on the reverse side of the fabric with a cool iron to prevent shine.

CARING FOR LINEN

● Detergents (*see page 70*) can alter the color or produce dappling on linen: use "soft chemistry" options on a gentle washing cycle for delicate articles; a hot cycle for bedlinen.
● Never tumble-dry: this wrinkles linen fibers badly, and also uses up energy.
● Use the natural bleaching powers of the sun to dry white bedlinen and tablecloths, but keep dyed linen out of sunlight or it may fade.
● To prevent shine, do not use too hot an iron on linen, and iron it on the wrong side. Work around seam lines carefully so that they do not mark the right side of the fabric.
● Fold articles such as tablecloths and sheets in a different way each time they are ironed, to avoid weakening the fibers along the fold line.
● Prolong the life of bedlinen by putting freshly laundered items at the bottom of the pile so that they are all used in turn, with equal frequency.

COTTON

Cotton is a cellulose fiber, and its quality is determined by the length of that fiber. Cotton plants are susceptible to attack from pests and diseases so are treated with fungicides, herbicides, and pesticides. Cotton manufacture reduces the residue in the yarn itself, but try to buy organically grown cotton that is free of chemicals, and processed without dyes, bleaches, or formaldehyde finishes. Untreated cotton fiber comes in various natural colors, from ivory to light browns. Sheets and towels made from unbleached cream-colored cotton are increasingly available.

CARING FOR COTTON

- Most cotton furnishing items are machine-washable. Wash knitted cotton throws and cushion covers on a gentle cycle, and dry flat to maintain their shape.
- Bleach white cotton sheets and pillow cases using a "soft chemistry" bleach and dry in the sunshine, to maintain the whiteness of the fabric.
- Try to avoid exposing colored cotton tablecloths, curtains, and bedspreads to direct sunlight, since the dyes may fade unevenly.
- Iron cotton furnishings with a hot iron, unless they have been treated with crease-resistant chemicals, in which case reduce the temperature setting and iron the cotton fabric on the wrong side to prevent shine.

WOOL

Woolen fabric is woven from the shorn fleece of sheep and is one of nature's most comfortable materials, whether in the form of carpets and rugs, cushion covers, throws, or bedcovers. The natural oils in wool keep you dry as well as warm, yet wool is also porous, letting your skin breathe. The fibers can be spun and woven into durable fabrics, making wool practical for upholstery and floor coverings.

CARING FOR WOOLENS

- Wash according to the care label. Wool shrinks in hot water, but is less likely to do so if mixed with synthetic fibers.
- Washing can cause wool fibers to "pill" (gather into small matted knots): wash cushion covers inside out to protect the outer surface.
- Wool is fairly stain-resistant: liquids penetrate the fibers slowly because of their natural oil (lanolin) content, allowing time to blot up the stain with absorbent paper towel.
- Woolen blankets and bedcovers are often treated with toxic chemicals to make them mothproof. Choose untreated blankets and store with herbal mothbags (*see page 60*).

Accidental spills on wool can be blotted up quickly with absorbent paper towel. The oily lanolin in the fibers acts as a repellent so that liquid does not immediately soak in.

Silk furnishings can safely be handwashed using warm water and soapflakes. Smaller items, such as cushion covers, can be washed in a bowl, and larger ones in the bathtub.

SILK

Silk fiber comes from the cocoon of the silkworm. A fine, soft, lightweight material, pure silk defies copying by even the most skillful synthetic methods. The fiber is used to make a variety of fabrics, from the finest organza and crêpe de chine to heavier silk velvet or rough-textured raw silk. It can be dyed in a range of colors, but also stains easily. Silks make luxurious curtains, cushion covers, and bedspreads.

CARING FOR SILK

Dry cleaning is often recommended, but since this is a chemical process, a better alternative is to wash silk furnishings by hand. Keep them separate from other items because the dye may run, and do not soak them for more than a few minutes to avoid weakening the fibers. Dry in the shade to prevent fading. Iron on the reverse while still damp, using a cool iron.

HEMP, JUTE, & RAMIE

Fibers from the inner bark of plants are absorbent and durable, and are becoming increasingly available (*see Resources page 166*). Hemp is quick-growing and produces a fiber that is stronger than cotton. It is used for canvas, furnishings, and rope.

Jute is an inelastic fiber useful for bags and burlap. Ramie, also called China grass, is taken from a stingless nettle. It is blended with cotton for clothes, knitwear, and upholstery to increase durability. Care for these fibers is as for linen (*see page 36*).

BEDDING FIBERS

The absorbency and feel of natural fibers make them ideal for bedding. Synthetic fibers do not "breathe" and so are often uncomfortably hot to sleep in. Polyester sheets may be covered with a formaldehyde finish to make them crease-resistant. Mattresses made from polyurethane foam are often sprayed with fire retardant. Acrylic blankets, polyester-filled pillows, and synthetic pillowcases further add to the chemical content of bedding, which you will be in close contact with during sleep.

HEALTHY SLEEP

Choose a cotton mattress, or an organic cotton, linen, or wool futon. Wool is particularly suitable for bedding because it both insulates and absorbs humidity well—the body produces considerable amounts of moisture during sleep. To protect the mattress from perspiration and soiling, cover it with a natural mattress pad. Also try organic wool- or kapok-filled pillows.

NATURAL BEDCLOTHES

Because they keep you warm while at the same time allowing your skin to breathe, bedclothes made from natural materials help to regulate your body temperature while you sleep so that you do not become too hot. Natural fabrics also feel particularly pleasant to the touch.

● Buy organic unbleached cotton, cotton-flannel, muslin, or linen sheets and pillowcases. These soften with repeated washes.
● Try pure silk sheets and pillowcases. Although expensive, these will keep you cool in summer and warm in winter.
● Choose a natural cotton comforter filled with feathers and/or down. These may, however, be plucked from living birds and you may prefer a wool-filled comforter instead. Both types work by trapping warm air in the filling.
● For warm yet lightweight coverings, choose open-weave pure wool blankets, which trap warm air in the weave, or cashmere blankets.
● Organic cotton throws and organic cotton decorative quilts are also available.

Hanging your comforter out to air on a cold morning will kill off dust-mite eggs and guarantee allergy-free bedding.

Vacuum your mattress when you change your bedlinen to remove dust. If you have asthma, protect the mattress with an allergy-free cover that will deter dust mites.

CARING FOR BEDDING

Since we spend at least seven hours every night in bed sleeping, this environment should be as healthy as possible. This is particularly important if you or your children are asthma or allergy sufferers, since dust mites can penetrate the mattress and mattress cover. Keep the bedroom well ventilated by opening the windows and airing the room daily. The suggestions below should help you maintain a healthy bedroom.
● Change and launder sheets, pillowcases, and blankets once a week.
● Wash pillows regularly. You can handwash pillows in the bathtub, using soapflakes, and rinse several times. Dry in the sunshine. Air them outside at least once a month.
● Mattress covers or pads are often overlooked. Wash them once a week.
● Turn the mattress regularly to ensure even wear. Air it outside on a sunny day twice a year.
● Clean comforters once or twice a year, preferably using a gentle machine wash rather than dry-cleaning. Give them a good airing outside in cold weather to kill off dust mites.

SYNTHETIC FABRICS

With their easy-care qualities, synthetic fibers are undeniably useful for people with busy lifestyles. They are also generally cheaper to buy than most natural fabrics. However, synthetic fabrics and finishes do have one major drawback: they are made from plastics, which are derived from petrochemicals, and they may "outgas" these chemicals throughout their lifetime. They also release fibers that can cause respiratory problems.

COMMON SYNTHETICS

Synthetic materials, including nylon, polyester, acrylic, acetate, and PVC (polyvinyl chloride), are found in many household furnishings. Viscose rayon is another common synthetic. Although pure rayon is composed of natural ingredients, such as cellulose and wood pulp, viscose rayon—which accounts for about 95 percent of rayon on the market—is far from natural. Most soft furnishing fabrics also contain PVC and formaldehyde to make them flameproof and resistant to shrinking and creasing.

Before buying new soft furnishings, find out the proportion of synthetic to natural fibers so you can make an informed choice.

A fake fur throw is one of the few examples where synthetic is preferable to natural—not only is fake fur cruelty-free, but it is also washable, instead of needing chemical dry-cleaning. Wash it in a mild detergent solution and dry it flat outdoors.

DISADVANTAGES OF SYNTHETIC BEDLINEN

- Synethic sheets, pillow covers, and other bedlinen give off vapors when they warm up against the skin, which may cause sensitive skin to itch.
- They absorb little moisture but also inhibit evaporation, so make the body feel hot and sweaty, especially in summer.
- They retain grease, which only strong detergents have the power to remove.
- They have static cling, unless treated with strong chemical antistatic agents.

CHECKING FOR FORMALDEHYDE FINISHES

Formaldehyde-resin finishes on furnishing fabrics have a tendency to break down with wear, washing, and ironing. This chemical breakdown has been linked to both minor and severe health problems. The following tips will alert you to their presence in fabrics:
- Unless otherwise stated, all cotton–polyester blend fabrics have formaldehyde finishes, especially bedlinen because it requires frequent laundering.
- Formaldehyde is used on nylon to render it flameproof.
- Some "pure cotton" fabrics are given a formaldehyde finish for easy care. If labeled "shrink-resistant" or "noniron," they will have this finish.

FLAME RETARDANTS

Some synthetic fibers, such as polyester, are designed to be flame-resistant. Other fibers have flame-retardant chemicals, such as TRIS and formaldehyde, added during manufacture. In many countries, the use of flame-retardant chemicals on fabrics is a legal requirement.

FABRIC DYES

Dyes used to color fabrics are unstable chemicals. They can be released from damp fabrics and absorbed if in contact with the skin. Some fabric dyes such as dichlorobenzidene (used to color cottons) are carcinogenic and may be present in imported fabrics.

AVOIDING TOXINS

• Wash synthetics before use to remove excess chemicals.
• Choose good-quality soft furnishings that will last longer, or buy secondhand.
• Extend the life of your fabrics by cleaning them carefully.
• Avoid dry cleaning to reduce chemical emissions in the home (*see page 73*).
• Choose unlined curtains and covers that you can wash by hand rather than dry-clean.
• Read fabric labels to check for the dyes used.

CARING FOR SYNTHETICS

The guidelines below explain how to maintain synthetic soft furnishings. Extending the lifespan of an item with good care reduces the amount of synthetic waste going into the environment, as does recycling worn-out items.

● Read the care label. Failure to launder according to instructions may result in a ruined fabric. Too hot a cycle may shrink or even melt a synthetic fabric.
● Synthetic fibers seem to retain stains and odors more than natural fibers, so wash items regularly.

● Wash delicate articles by hand (*see page 71*).
● Most synthetics do not absorb water well and retain oils, so they are difficult to get really clean without the use of strong detergents. Try presoaking items in water before washing.
● Use a "soft chemistry"

fabric softener to reduce static cling in synthetic fibers.
● Lay knitted acrylic throws flat to dry, so that they retain their shape.
● Most synthetics do not require much ironing. If you have to iron them, however, use a low setting; otherwise the fabric may melt.

▲ **Turn synthetic cushion covers** inside out before washing to protect the fabric and reduce the chance of pilling.

▶ **To check for color run,** steam synthetic fabric between two pieces of white cloth to see if the color comes out.

CARPETS & NATURAL FLOORING

The majority of modern carpets are made from synthetic fibers—typically about 80 percent nylon and 20 percent plastic. As many as 120 chemicals may be used in their production, including volatile organic compounds (VOCs) such as toluene and xylene, and the known carcinogen benzene. If there is wool in the carpet, the pesticide permethrin is often added to protect the fibers from moths, and styrene is used to make the synthetic latex backing. The problem with the chemical constituents of carpet is that they may "outgas" for long periods, polluting the air in the home, while the solvents used to fix natural floorings to a hardboard base are also hazardous. Children and pets are the most likely to suffer the health effects of regular chemical exposure because they are in closer contact with the floor.

New natural flooring materials include coir, sisal, and jute, which offer attractive and hardwearing floor coverings for heavy-traffic areas of the home.

CARPET FACTS

Unfortunately, all carpet fibers attract and accumulate the dust and pollutants brought into the home on shoes and on the paws of pets. Close scientific analysis of carpet pile has shown that it harbors residues of many compounds, including toxic substances from household cleaning products, hair, cigarette smoke particles, and dust mites, all of which are an inevitable part of modern living.

The industrial processes used in carpet manufacture also cause considerable damage to the environment: carpet factories use huge quantities of water, approximately 20 gallons per square yard (75 liters per square meter), consume petrochemicals, and pollute air and water supplies with waste products.

LAYING CARPET

● If you decide on wall-to-wall carpeting, use carpet tacks to fasten it to the floor. This will avoid the need to affix the carpet in place with a strong chemical adhesive.
● After installation, try to steam-clean a new carpet with water to remove chemical residues present on the surface.
● Leave windows and doors open after laying a new carpet, until the fumes have subsided.

CHOOSING CARPETS & RUGS

Natural flooring materials are not only a healthy choice because they limit toxic emissions—they are an aesthetic one, too, since they look and feel wonderful. Check carefully, though, before choosing. Although a 100 percent pure wool carpet may seem like a "natural" option, many wool carpets have a latex backing made with styrene, which may "outgas" for a long time. Bare floors with loose woven wool or cotton rugs, or coir (made from coconut fibers), hemp, jute, sisal, seagrass or even paper matting are perhaps a better, nontoxic solution, particularly if you wish to create an allergy-free home environment. Many beautiful handcrafted floor rugs can also be bought through fair-trade organizations (*see Resources page 166*).

Fasten a wool rug to a natural wood floor with a nonslip felt mat with an adhesive base, to prevent accidents.

HARD FLOOR CHOICES

Wooden floors are a classic choice, and linoleum is making a comeback. Both have a place in the healthy home.

● Hard- or softwood flooring may be made of pine, beech, oak, or maple. New floors should preferably be made from recycled planks or renewable sources of wood. An existing wooden floor can be sanded, but wear a suitable mask to prevent inhalation of the dust from old varnish. Unsealed wood floors can be treated with oil or carnauba wax (*see page 51*), solvent-free varnish, natural stains or paint.

● Linoleum is made in an environmentally responsible way, from linseed oil (a product of flax crops), ground cork, wood, flour, and resins. These are baked slowly at high temperatures and fixed under pressure to a natural jute or burlap backing material. Linoleum is also static-free, and kills off harmful bacteria found on the floor. (It should not be confused with vinyl,

or PVC, flooring, which is a synthetic plastic product. This contains phthalates, chemicals used as softeners in PVC, which are released from vinyl flooring into the air; see also page 141. Since small children often like to play on the floor, they are more likely to be exposed to phthalates. Pets are similarly vulnerable.)

Linoleum is soft and warm underfoot and will insulate your home. This 100 percent natural product is a good solution for those who like the warmth and color of carpet combined with an easy-to-clean, hard floor surface.

TREATING STAINS
(*See pages 66–69*)

CLEANING THE HOME

A clean, chemical-free home is a delight to be in—it looks and feels good and smells wonderful, too. To achieve it, it is important to establish well-defined cleaning routines. These in turn will prevent flooring, furniture, and fixtures from becoming so dirty that you have to resort to heavy-duty chemical cleaners. (Most modern households in the developed world contain 4–12 gallons/15–45 liters of chemically based cleaning materials.) A file divided into sections for different chores acts as a useful reminder for when each of these tasks are due to take place. In your file, you can also include a note of the useful recipes for natural cleaners to be found in this chapter.

KEEPING DIRT OUT

Follow common sense measures to prevent dirt from entering your home in the first place, such as keeping a doormat in front of each exit, and if possible a second mat on the other side. Getting into the habit of removing shoes when you come in from outdoors cuts down on dirt, too.

WATER POWER

The best cleaner in the world is water: soaking is one of the most effective ways of removing dirt, whether it be burned food in pans, smears on glassware, or obstinate marks on stoves or floors. We rely too much on heavy-duty cleaners when milder solutions are perfectly efficient— they are cheaper and less harmful to our health and the environment too.

Chemical-free aids to store in your natural cleaning cupboard include soapflakes, glycerine, and steel wool.

Natural air freshener p49

Multisurface cleaner p53

Cleaning grouting p51

Beeswax furniture polish p56

NATURAL CLEANERS

Cleanliness is vital for a healthy home, but generally we use too many chemical cleaning products and in too great a quantity, and are oblivious to their side effects. There are time-honored natural alternatives that are just as effective, do not have such a harmful impact on our health or the environment, and will leave your home smelling delightfully fresh and fragrant—so get rid of all your old household cleaners and start anew with the natural alternatives.

SOFT CHEMISTRY

Some manufacturers have devised alternatives to chemical cleaning products based on sustainable vegetable sources. These are known as "soft chemistry" products. They are not tested on animals, are packaged in recyclable materials and, unlike most commercial brands, contain no additives or detergents. In addition, some drugstores now sell low-allergy cleaning products. These contain no additives or irritants and fewer pollutants (*see Resources page 168*).

CHEMICAL CLEAROUT

All these chemical cleaning products can be replaced with safer "soft chemistry" or natural alternatives:

Degreasing cleaners for sinks
  and bathtubs
Multisurface cleaners
Dishwashing liquid
Dishwasher detergents
Toilet bowl cleaners
Floor cleaners
Polishes
Window cleaners
Disinfectants and bleaches
Metal cleaners and scourers
Air fresheners

HOMEMADE CLEANERS

In addition to the "soft chemistry" options that you can buy, you can easily make your own natural household cleaners. These have several advantages: the ingredients are easy to obtain, inexpensive, and have no damaging effect on the environment; they contain no additives, so are unlikely to cause allergic reactions; they are not tested on animals; and they come in recyclable packaging. A list of ingredients and their uses appears opposite.

Fresh lemon, blocks of beeswax, white vinegar, liquid soap, washing soda, baking soda, table salt, and essential oils are some of the key ingredients for a completely natural cleaning kit.

PURE SOAP
Hot water and plain soapflakes with a little washing soda will perform most cleaning jobs. It sounds simple—and it works.

BAKING SODA
Baking soda (bicarbonate of soda) is a naturally occurring mineral and a versatile cleaner. It has an infinite number of other household uses. Buy in bulk from the grocery store.

TABLE SALT
Salt is a mild disinfectant and makes a gently abrasive scouring powder.

WHITE VINEGAR
The acetic acid in white vinegar cuts through dirt efficiently. You can use it to clean glass and tiles and to remove stains from coffee mugs, coffee pots, and teapots. Mixed with salt or baking soda, it will polish brass and copper.

LEMON JUICE
Citric acid is one of nature's great cleaners. Versatile, safe, and fragrant, it cleans fantastically well.

WASHING SODA
Washing soda (sodium carbonate) is a natural water softener and cuts through grease, making it an effective heavy-duty cleaner for painted walls, hard floors, and kitchen surfaces. It is an entirely natural product, and has no negative impact on health or the environment.

BORAX
Also known as sodium tetraborate decahydrate, this is a naturally occurring mineral and may be used in small quantities for treating stains and mildew, and removing odors. However, it contains the element boron, which cannot biodegrade, and consequently should only be used sparingly.

ESSENTIAL OILS
Tea tree, citrus, thyme, sage, and eucalyptus oils all have disinfectant properties and can be added to any of the natural cleaners above to introduce fragrance. Be sure to buy high-quality, unadulterated oils, and store them in a cool, dark place. Grapefruit seed extract also acts as a disinfectant.

THE NATURAL CLEANING CUPBOARD
Your natural cleaning cupboard should contain the following key ingredients:

Pure soapflakes
Liquid soap (no additives)
Baking soda
Table salt
White vinegar
Washing soda
Borax
Beeswax polish (*see page 57 for recipe*)
Steel wool
Bristle brush
Cellulose sponges
Lemon juice

Bristle scrubbing brushes, steel wool, and linen scree cloths make useful and long-lasting cleaning tools, in preference to synthetic sponges and plastic brushes with nylon bristles.

CLEANING TOOLS
Use old garments and sheets to make rags for your household cleaning, rather than buying synthetic ones. When choosing sponges, it is better to purchase the cellulose type (the kind used for cleaning the car) rather than plastic. To get maximum use from each sponge, you can cut it into smaller pieces. Instead of buying treated steel-wool pads, buy varying grades of steel wool and make your own scourer. Use a wooden bristle brush for dishwashing rather than a plastic brush with nylon bristles.

AVOIDING HOUSEHOLD CHEMICALS

Cleaning the "easy" way with heavy-duty chemicals may not bring the harmony and sweetness to your life that manufacturers would have you believe. Fewer than one-quarter of the 70,000 chemicals used in cleaning products and toiletries have been fully tested for safety, and substances classified as hazardous waste are found in many common cleaning fluids.

DETERGENTS

Pure soap—our oldest natural and biodegradable washing agent—is only effective in soft water. So industrial chemists have devised detergents that can cut through dirt, but when they leach into the water supply, harm living organisms. Most common brands of dishwashing liquid and dishwasher products contain detergents derived from crude oil, a limited resource, making these detergents not only a harmful but also an unsustainable option.

CHLORINE

Most dishwasher detergents contain chlorine, a disinfectant, in its dry form. This releases toxic fumes into the kitchen, which can cause headaches, burning eyes, and breathing difficulties. Residues can adhere to the dishes and can leach into the food.

PHOSPHATES

Phosphates (salt of phosphoric acid) act as a water softener and have been added to cleaning products since the 1940s. They may be found in wool-washing agents, multipurpose cleaners, dishwasher detergents, and scouring cleaners. Phosphates are responsible for excessive growth of algae in water systems.

BLEACHES

Most household bleaches are based on sodium hypochlorite, which has a known effect on hormone levels. Bleached toilet paper, kitchen towels, and facial tissues may contain residues of toxic dioxins and brighteners.

DISINFECTANTS

These synthetic germ-killers, used in toilet cleaners, contain volatile chemicals, and the fumes they give off can be dangerous to inhale. They can damage the kidneys, liver, lungs, pancreas, and spleen, and interfere with the central nervous system.

READ THE LABEL

Most cleaning and washing products list their ingredients. They may include surfactants, enzymes, phosphates, bleach, solvents (with a warning about solvent abuse), and perfumes. Many contain warnings: that they may release dangerous gases (chlorine); that they are irritants to skin and eyes; and that, if swallowed, immediate medical advice is required. If a cleaning product contains these substances, try to avoid it. Use the natural alternatives on pages 46–47 or buy "soft-chemistry" options instead.

PRODUCT FACTS

● The colorings that are added to most cleaning materials are synthetic, and contain heavy metals that damage the environment.

● Sulfates are used in cleaning materials. These are salts that make freshwater rivers brackish and cause corrosion in waste-water treatment plants.

● Synthetic fragrances are based on petrochemicals and can cause allergic reactions.

● Products may be preserved with formaldehyde, known for its allergenic properties.

SAFETY FIRST

All cleaning materials, natural and otherwise, must be kept out of the reach of children.

THE FRAGRANT HOME

Keeping your home fresh and sweet-smelling not only makes it a pleasant environment to live in, but can also be beneficial psychologically, calming or uplifting the spirits.

NATURE'S SCENTS

• Buy scented houseplants, such as jasmine or hyacinths, or fragrant cut flowers, such as freesias or lilies.
• Hang aromatic rosemary or bay in your kitchen, and crush the leaves to release the scent.

ELIMINATING ODORS

● Air your home daily by opening the windows.
● Install extractor fans in the kitchen and/or bathroom to remove moisture.

● Keep your house comfortably warm and dry.
● Empty trash cans frequently, and sprinkle baking soda into the garbage bag.

HOMEMADE AIR FRESHENER

To eliminate bad odors, create this simple natural air freshener with water and essential oils—lemon and cedarwood are both excellent. Not only can this air freshener be custom-made with your own favorite fragrance, but it will not have a harmful impact on the environment.

YOU WILL NEED:
½ cup (125 ml) water
10 drops of essential oil (neroli is a favorite of mine)

HOMEMADE POTPOURRI

To make your own potpourri, use the leaves from dried herbs or flower petals. Choose from peppermint, sage, pine, thyme, lemon verbena, bay leaves, rosemary, bergamot, rose geranium, lemon-scented geranium, scented roses, and lavender. Mix with ground cinnamon or cloves and a sprinkling of ground orris root (a natural preservative), and put in a bowl. Gently toss the potpourri from time to time to release the fragrance. As it loses its scent, revive it by sprinkling with a few drops of essential oil.

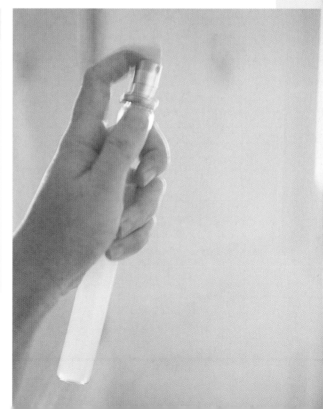

1 Fill a spray bottle with water and then add the drops of essential oil. Replace the top and shake.

2 A few squirts aimed upward into the air will make your room fragrant and eliminate pungent odors.

WINDOWS, WALLS, & FLOORS

Products designed to clean windows, walls, and floors often contain synthetic perfumes that are made up of numerous—and often untested—chemicals. Some carpet cleaners may contain the solvent perchloroethylene, a suspected carcinogen, and naphthalene, a toxic insect repellent. You can look after your health—and your money, too—by opting for the following natural cleaning alternatives in your home.

CLEANING WINDOWS

There is no need to rely on chemical sprays to keep windows clean. Instead, use the following tried-and-tested natural methods.

● An effective window cleaner can be made from 1 part white vinegar to 1 part water, with the addition of a few drops of liquid soap.
● To make it easier to see streaks when cleaning glass, use up-and-down strokes on one side and side-to-side strokes on the other.
● Remove the waxy deposit left by commercial window cleaners with a little washing soda solution (2 tablespoons to 1 pint/500 ml water).
● If you have a plastic window, do not use a cleaner containing ammonia—it will leave the surface permanently cloudy. Use a handful of pure soapflakes mixed with 1 tablespoon of washing soda and 1 pint (500 ml) warm water.
● To clean venetian blinds, take crusts of fresh bread and hold the crusts around each slat as you run them along its length.

For sparkling windows, rub the glass with a sheet of crumpled newspaper and a spray solution of equal parts white vinegar and water, with a few drops of liquid soap added to it.

CLEANING WALLS

Vacuuming will keep painted or papered walls generally free of dirt. For more thorough cleaning, try the following remedies. Unlike chemical products that are designed for spot-cleaning walls only, these can be applied to the entire surface.

● Spot-clean matte latex paint with a paste of baking soda (*see page 52*). This will remove furniture scuffs, crayon or ink marks, grease spots, and other stains. Leave on for 10 minutes, then wipe off with a damp cloth.
● Clean satin finishes and gloss with a solution of ½ cup (125 ml) white vinegar and 1 oz (25 g) washing soda mixed with 1 pint (500 ml) water.
● For grease marks on wallpaper, cover the spot with blotting paper or paper towels and apply a warm iron so that the paper absorbs the grease.

CLEANING HARD FLOORS

Natural hard flooring, such as wood or tile, is a beautiful surface and one that is easy to keep fairly clean simply with regular sweeping. Untreated wood needs care, including nourishing with wax. Here are some of my tips for natural floor care.

WOOD
● For unsealed floors, apply raw linseed oil on a soft cloth, allow it to sink in, then mop with a little more oil until a shine develops.
● Hard carnauba wax is nourishing for untreated wood floors and brings up a good sheen on the surface.
● Sealed wooden floors need regular sweeping and occasional wiping with a damp cloth or sponge. Wax occasionally to improve the shine.

LINOLEUM
● Mop with a weak solution of a "soft chemistry" cleaner, or my all-purpose surface cleaner (see page 53).
● Polish linoleum floor tiles with carnauba wax when they start to lose their luster.
● Rub off scuff marks with neat turpentine and fine steel wool. Wipe clean with a damp cloth.

TILES
● Cleaning unglazed and terra-cotta floor tiles with soap makes them turn cloudy. Use a 50:50 solution of water and white vinegar.

Clean grouting between floor tiles with baking soda and water on an old toothbrush. Work the baking soda paste into the grout, then rinse off.

● Wipe down glazed wall and floor tiles with baking soda on a damp sponge.
● Remove hard water spots with white vinegar.
● After cleaning, polish tiles with a soft towel.

STONE
● Never use soap on stone floors. It cannot be absorbed and makes them slippery. Clean instead with a solution of 2 pints (1 liter) water to 2 tablespoons of washing soda powder.

MARBLE
● Clean with my all-purpose surface cleaner (see page 53). Never use detergent.

CARPET CARE

With a handful of simple ingredients, you can keep your carpets clean without resorting to chemicals. Baking soda is particularly effective, removing grease, dirt, smells, and even pet stains from both natural and synthetic carpets.

● To remove general stains, mix 1 part "soft chemistry" dishwashing liquid with 4 parts boiling water. When cool, whip to a foam. Sponge on, then wipe off with a damp cloth.
● For pet or urine stains, apply baking soda or a solution of 3 tablespoons vinegar and 1 tablespoon liquid soap. Leave to work for 15 minutes, then vacuum or rinse.
● Heavy grease or oil stains that resist the baking soda treatment can be cleaned in the same way with cornstarch.
● Steam-clean your carpets using just plain water.

To remove spot marks, sprinkle the area with baking soda. Leave to absorb the stain and then vacuum up.

THE NATURAL KITCHEN

Fresh lemon juice, baking soda, white vinegar, and salt can all be used as natural cleaners, since they have cleansing, scouring, and antiseptic properties. They are just as effective as products that use strong chemicals, and are a lot cheaper. For washing dishes, use a "soft chemistry" dishwashing liquid (*see Resources page 168*).

GENERAL CLEANING & CARE

Here are my favored, environmentally sound methods for cleaning kitchen surfaces and equipment, and maintaining them in good condition. Some of them use the two natural cleaning agents that I have given recipes for: a baking soda paste and an all-purpose surface cleaner.

WATER SOFTENERS

• If you have hard water, add a small handful of baking soda to your dishwashing water as a natural softener.
• Instead of using store-bought detergent in your dishwasher, make up your own using 2 teaspoons of borax and 2 teaspoons baking soda.
• Add 2 tablespoons of baking soda to the dishwasher salt compartment to eliminate hard water streaks.

KITCHEN FLOORS
● To remove grease from cork, ceramic, wood, or stone tiles, use the all-purpose surface cleaner (*see page 53*).
● Sprinkle heavier grease marks with baking soda, leave for 30 minutes, then rub clean.

KITCHEN SURFACES
● Scrub dirty or odorous wooden surfaces, such as cutting boards, with the juice of half a lemon mixed with 1 tablespoon of table salt. Alternatively, use the baking-soda-paste recipe below.

SINKS
● Clean out the sink with a solution of 1 oz (25 g) table salt to 1 cup (250 ml) water. Salt is a disinfectant and an abrasive.
● A cut lemon removes tea and coffee stains—just rub the cut surface over the stained area.

POTS & PANS
● Rub in baking soda paste (*below*) with a damp cloth or an abrasive pad, then rinse off.
● For burned pans, sprinkle a thin layer of baking soda into the pan and add boiling water to cover it. Leave overnight, then scour with steel wool.

BAKING SODA PASTE

Baking soda is one of the most useful natural products to keep in your kitchen. It can be put to many different uses, from deodorizing refrigerators and garbage cans to removing stains. As an all-purpose surface cleaner, baking soda paste is unbeatable. It is non-abrasive, so it can be used to clean chrome and aluminum surfaces, pots and pans, and fridge interiors. Rub on the paste with a soft cloth and buff to a brilliant sheen.

1 Dissolve 4 tablespoons of baking soda in 4 tablespoons of water.

2 Using a soft cloth, rub the paste onto the surface to be cleaned. Wipe off with a clean cloth and buff to a shine.

ALL-PURPOSE SURFACE CLEANER

This cleaner removes grease and dirt, smells beautifully fresh, is cheap and nontoxic, and will keep indefinitely. Use it on stainless-steel sinks and draining boards, tiled and wooden surfaces, and plastic finishes (such as telephones).

YOU WILL NEED:
1 pint (500 ml) white vinegar
1 cup (250 ml) water
20–30 drops eucalyptus oil

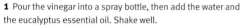

1 Pour the vinegar into a spray bottle, then add the water and the eucalyptus essential oil. Shake well.

2 Pour a little of the mixture onto a soft, damp cloth and rub over the surface to be cleaned. There is no need to rinse.

KEEPING APPLIANCES CLEAN

It is important to use the correct non-abrasive cleaner on kitchen appliances, since their surfaces are often easily scratched and damaged. Here are my tips for maintaining naturally clean and hygienic kitchen appliances.

REFRIGERATORS
● Clean the inside of the fridge with baking soda paste (*see opposite*). The paste will also work to eliminate any stale refrigerator odors.
● Charcoal absorbs smells inside fridges; so does cat litter. Fill a dish and leave in the fridge for a day.
● Wipe the door clean with a damp cloth. Use baking soda paste for obstinate marks.

WASHING MACHINES
● Keep your machine clean by running it empty on a hot wash with ¼ cup (60 ml) vinegar in the detergent drawer. Do this every 20 washes.
● Clean out the detergent compartment regularly: remove it carefully, soak it, then scrub clean any residues that may cause blocking.

COFFEEMAKER
● To clean your coffeemaker, empty it and pour in white vinegar. Leave for 1 hour. Rinse with cold water. Pour fresh water into the coffeemaker. Run it through, then throw this water away.

OVENS
● To clean the interior of the oven, rub with wet steel wool, then sprinkle baking soda over the dirty surfaces and rub clean with a damp cloth.

MICROWAVES
● To clean and deodorize your microwave, mix ½ cup (125 ml) water with 2 teaspoons of baking soda in a microwave-safe bowl. Place the mixture in the microwave, set on maximum power, and run for 2 minutes. Remove the bowl and wipe the oven clean.

THE NATURAL BATHROOM

The bathroom is one room in the home where it may seem necessary and even justifiable to use heavy-duty chemicals. It is reassuring to know, then, that natural cleaners are equally effective. They are also less abrasive, so they will not scratch enamel surfaces and are kinder to hands.

Rub lemon juice around drainage hole to remove grease and limescale.

TUBS, SINKS, & SHOWERS

Most of the cleaners here are natural homemade products, although there are "soft chemistry" options that you can buy. The tools you use are also important. For example, instead of an abrasive scourer to clean a very dirty bathtub, why not use a bristle brush? For hard-to-reach areas behind faucets, an old toothbrush comes in handy.

BATHROOM SURFACES

● Use a baking soda paste (*see page 52*) to clean sinks, tubs, toilet surfaces, and faucets. Rub persistent dirty marks with a cut lemon.

● Rub stubborn stains on sinks and tubs with turpentine oil. Rinse with hot water mixed with a little "soft chemistry" dishwashing liquid.

● To loosen dirt on enamel, pour "soft chemistry" dishwashing liquid into the bath as it is running out, then rinse and brush clean.

DRAINS AND FAUCETS

● Clean drains by rubbing with a cut lemon.
● For brown stains caused by dripping faucets, rub with a mixture of 1 oz (25 g) salt to ⅔ cup (150 ml) white vinegar.
● Brown staining also responds well to a paste of cream of tartar, made in the same way as baking soda paste (*see page 52*).
● Remove hard water deposits

from chrome with a salt and vinegar mix (*see left*).
● Remove lime from faucets with a soft cloth dipped in white vinegar.
● Scrub away rust and grime around faucets with an old toothbrush coated with a mixture of 1 teaspoon salt to 1 tablespoon lemon juice.
● A little toothpaste on a damp cloth cleans up chrome.

SHOWERHEADS & CURTAINS

● Sponge shower curtains with water and baking soda.
● For showerheads clogged with limescale, soak the showerhead overnight in straight white vinegar.

● Wipe hard water deposits on glass or plastic shower doors with straight white vinegar. Leave for 10 minutes before rinsing off and buffing to a shine with a soft cloth.

Use a darning needle to unblock the holes in a showerhead, then rinse out the head with white vinegar.

TOILET TREATMENTS

When it comes to toilet cleaning, most people feel tempted to make liberal use of strong chemicals, such as bleach, in order to disinfect the area thoroughly. But, as elsewhere in the bathroom, there are "soft chemistry" and natural alternatives that do the same job but without the same potential for environmental harm.

● To clean the bowl, pour ⅔ cup (150 ml) straight white vinegar into it and brush before flushing.
● Disinfect the bowl with a solution of 10 drops of tea tree oil in ½ cup (125 ml) of water. Leave it in the bowl until the next flush.
● Wipe the toilet seat with all-purpose surface cleaner (*see page 53*).

● For hard water deposits, apply a mixture of 2 oz (50 g) borax powder and 1 cup (250 ml) white vinegar and leave for 2–3 hours before flushing.

TOP TIP

Lighting a match in the toilet after use eliminates bad smells —simple but miraculous!

CLEARING DRAINS

Prevention is the best strategy here—try to limit the waste matter going into your drains in the first place. Chrome drain-strainers placed over drains work well.

● To keep drains clear, you can use a handful of baking or washing soda mixed with ½ cup (125 ml) white vinegar (this is a stronger solution than using salt) and simply pour it down the drain and leave to work.
● If your drains become clogged, avoid using a strong drain-cleaner, such as caustic soda. Instead, unblock them with a hand-plunger (available from hardware stores).
● "Soft chemistry" options are also available.

MOLD & MILDEW

Bathrooms are humid environments and are particularly prone to mold and mildew. If these are persistent problems, ensure that air circulates near the source of the trouble, and that the area is kept warm and dry.

● Borax prevents mold and mildew from developing. Make a solution of 2 oz (50 g) borax to 1 cup (250 ml) white vinegar and apply with a cloth, or put into a spray bottle to apply to damp walls. Leave for 30 minutes or more before wiping off.
● Spray problem areas with white vinegar, leave for 30 minutes, then wipe off.
● Dry portable items in the sun after treating.

Flush boiling water and a handful of salt down blocked or foul-smelling drains instead of resorting to bleach.

CARING FOR MARBLE

To protect marble bathroom surfaces, blot stains with paper towels, then flush with cold water until the stain disappears. Slight surface scratches may be rubbed off with very fine steel wool.

FURNITURE & ORNAMENTS

Most furniture can be cleaned simply and naturally and does not need heavy-duty cleaners or polishes. Although they are effective at masking wear-and-tear and scratch marks, synthetic chemical wood polishes give off toxic fumes, and are not particularly good for furniture. They produce a milky finish that some find attractive, but I would always opt for the original beauty of the wood, which is better maintained using natural cleaning products. Brass and copperware, silver and pewter, glass and china, and other delicates need especially careful cleaning—the better they are cared for, the longer they will last.

Using a soft cloth, polish wooden furniture with natural beeswax polish (*see recipe opposite*).

WOOD & BAMBOO

Wood is an absorbent material that benefits greatly from careful treatment, as do more fragile fibers such as wicker and bamboo.

CANE, RATTAN, & BAMBOO

These materials are porous, so furniture made from them sometimes has a protective coating. It should be dusted regularly or cleaned with a damp cloth. You can wash it occasionally with soapy warm water, but never soak cane, rattan, or bamboo, since this weakens the pliant fibers.

If possible, air-dry the furniture in the sun and a light breeze, but don't leave it too long once dry—it can become brittle in the heat.

SURPLUS POLISH

Mix 2 tablespoons white vinegar and 2 tablespoons water and use to remove a buildup of polish. Rub off at once. You can also use it to remove stubborn fingermarks.

CARING FOR WOODEN FURNITURE

- Use a beeswax polish to nourish wooden furniture and maintain its shine.
- Use coasters on polished surfaces to protect them from heat marks and scratching.
- Mop up spills on wood immediately.
- If the surface becomes watermarked, polish with a slightly darker-colored wax, or touch up with artist's oil paints. Then polish frequently until the mark fades.
- Treat scratches in the same way as watermarks.
- If you are using liquid polish, use a pumpsprayer. Never use aerosol sprays, since they contain CFCs (chlorofluorocarbons), which damage the ozone layer.

BEESWAX POLISH

Here is my own recipe for an effective and nontoxic polish. The polish will keep indefinitely.

YOU WILL NEED:
3 oz (75 g) pure beeswax
½ cup (125 ml) turpentine oil
10 drops of lavender oil

1 Grate the beeswax into a bowl and place over a pan of warm water.

2 Stir until the wax melts. Add the turpentine oil, and stir thoroughly.

3 Pour into a tin with a lid. Stir in oil, leave to cool, and replace the lid.

METAL FURNITURE & FITTINGS

Metal items must be cleaned regularly or they will tarnish. A tarnished surface is much harder to clean than a dirty one, but there are ways of restoring natural shine.

BRASS & COPPER

● For a homemade polish that will bring a shine to brass and copper, mix 3 tablespoons lemon juice or white vinegar with 1 tablespoon baking soda. Rub on, and buff to a sheen.

● Immerse deeply tarnished articles in hot vinegar mixed with 1–2 tablespoons salt. As soon as a shine appears, rinse very thoroughly. Don't leave items too long in this solution, or new staining may occur.

● Intricate brass and copper objects can be rubbed with the cut side of a lemon, which can penetrate the metal detail without leaving the powdery traces caused by some proprietary chemical cleaners. When clean and shiny, rub dry with a soft chamois cloth.

● When polishing brass fixtures on wooden furniture, you need to be careful not to let your cleaning product mark the surrounding wood. Make a paper "mask" by cutting a hole the exact size and shape of the metal to protect the wood as you polish the fittings.

PEWTER

● Pewter tarnishes easily when it comes into contact with strong chemicals: wash it in warm, soapy (detergent-free) water and polish dry to its lovely dull sheen.

● Never drink fruit drinks or wine from pewter mugs because the acid in these fluids will penetrate the metal and the drinks will take on a metallic taste.

CHROME

● Clean chrome with a solution of 1 tablespoon ammonia to 1 pint (500 ml) of water. (This is especially good for greasy car chrome.)

STEEL

● To clean steel knives, dip in diluted lemon juice and vigorously rub off stains with a steel wool pad.

IRON

● Wipe rusted ironwork with a damp cloth, scrub with steel wool, and dry, then oil lightly with machine oil to prevent further rusting.

● Wash cast-iron articles by hand, and dry. Rub with a thin coating of vegetable oil to prevent the iron from rusting.

SILVER

The beautiful sheen of silver requires thoughtful cleaning. Never put silver in the dishwasher: it is a soft metal that scratches and damages easily and can become tarnished by other metals. Always wash silver items by hand with a mild soap (no detergent) and water.

When cleaning silver plate, do not rub too vigorously because the coating of silver is thin and will wear through. Black stains left by egg yolk can be rubbed with the cut side of a lemon, rinsed, and polished dry.

If you are using a store-bought cleaner on intricate silverware, use a soft-bristle toothbrush to remove the residue from the nooks and crannies. Store silver by wrapping it in soft cloths to prevent it from tarnishing while not in use. Keep it dry.

CLEANING SILVER THE NATURAL WAY

The following method of cleaning silverware is simplicity itself, and involves none of the petrochemicals found in commercial cleaners.

It can be used to clean any silver objects, as long as they do not have cemented-on parts and are small enough to be submerged in a pan of water.

1 Dip the article into simmering water containing a piece of aluminum foil and 2 teaspoons of washing soda.

2 The aluminum attracts the dirt, and the silver comes up bright. Dry thoroughly, and buff to a shine with a soft cloth.

JEWELRY

The setting and stones of most jewelry need to be cleaned regularly, especially if the piece is worn every day, because small particles of dirt can get inside intricate settings and dislodge the stones. Stones also become dull over time, and settings may tarnish with daily wear.

● Always clean jewelry in a bowl rather than a sink because the stones may work loose and accidentally fall down the drain.

● Most jewelry can be cleaned in warm, soapy water. Soak the piece in water for a while to loosen the dirt, then brush gently with a soft toothbrush—be careful not to brush too

hard, though, because you may loosen the stones from their settings.

● Use the point of a wooden toothpick to loosen dirt from crevices. I sometimes use toothpaste to clean my rings quickly.

● Cotton swabs soaked in a little baking soda solution can also dislodge stubborn dirt.

If you clean special finishes with the wrong cleaners you can ruin them. The following old-fashioned methods help to increase the lifespan of beautiful objects.

GILT
Gold leaf is extremely fragile but does not tarnish easily. Simply wipe carefully with a silk cloth.

LACQUER
Antique lacquer is extremely fragile, easily scratched, and distorted by water. The best way to clean it is to rub it gently with a silk cloth. Modern lacquer can be cleaned with a damp cloth.

MOTHER-OF-PEARL
Clean mother-of-pearl by rubbing with a soft cloth. If it is really dirty, wash it in mild soapy water, but avoid chemical detergents, which may damage the surface.

CHINA & METALWORK

Delicately glazed or hand-painted china, or metalwork such as gilt should always be washed by hand. Washing in the dishwasher will fade, chip, or damage it.

- Rinse china plates immediately after use if they have had acidic food such as tomatoes on them.
- Don't leave delicate china soaking for long because the water may seep under the glaze and damage it.
- Use warm soapy water to clean delicate china. Always wipe clean with a dishcloth rather than a bristle brush.
- Wash china ornaments as above, and use a soft toothbrush to loosen dirt. Wash items one at a time to keep them from knocking against each other and breaking.
- Remove hard water deposits with vinegar on a damp cloth.

GLASSWARE

Hot, soapy water containing a little vinegar is one of the best glass cleaners. Here are some other tips.

- To clean drinking glasses, squeeze the juice of half a lemon into the dishwater, and add a little washing soda as a water softener. Wash the glasses, then dry them immediately to avoid streaking. Polish to a shine with a soft cloth.
- Never apply ammonia to glass because it turns it cloudy.
- Clean glass flower vases each time they are used so that staining does not build up. Soak in pure vinegar or salty water (2 tablespoons salt to 1 pint/500 ml water), and rinse thoroughly afterward.

CRYSTAL

Crystal is more delicate than it looks, and is easily damaged. Follow these tips to help preserve your crystal items.

- Never put crystal into the dishwasher or the microwave: it scratches easily, and goes irreversibly cloudy. Instead, carefully handwash items one at a time in mild soap with a soft brush. Dry immediately.
- To remove wax from a crystal candlestick, allow it to harden first, pull it off, then rub off any residue with ethanol alcohol.

Newly washed crystal should be dried immediately and polished to a sheen with a soft cloth to prevent streaking.

HOUSEHOLD PESTS

Insects and vermin are facts of life and have to be dealt with—but the safe way. Many insecticides are poisonous and should be avoided. Children who are exposed to insecticides are known to have a significantly increased risk of developing a cancer known as non-Hodgkin's lymphoma. There are tried-and-tested natural ways of dealing with household pests that are harmless to humans and leave no damaging traces in the environment. To reduce the incidence of pests, keep your foodstuffs in tightly sealed containers and your storage cupboards clean, don't leave crumbs around, and empty trash cans frequently.

Place muslin sachets of herbs such as dried lavender among clothes and bedlinen in drawers to deter moths.

MOTHS

Mothballs contain naphthalene, a highly toxic substance derived from petrochemicals, or the insecticide paradichlorobenzene. Mothball vapors irritate the lungs and can cause kidney and liver damage, headaches, nausea, and depression after prolonged exposure. If you use naphthalene mothballs, reserve them for well-ventilated areas only, separate from your living quarters—or, better still, replace them with natural alternatives.

● Create your own natural moth repellents by filling muslin sachets with dried lavender, a mixture of rosemary and mint, dried tobacco, peppercorns, or cedarwood chips. Place in your drawers among items that are not used frequently.
● To protect fabric items that are to be stored for a long period, make sure they are completely clean, wrap them in paper, and place in drawers or boxes, with herb sachets.
● If you suspect an infestation, put the items in the freezer for at least 48 hours. Place them in a plastic bag first, squeeze out excess air, then seal tightly. Afterward, shake them and hang them in the sun. Moth eggs cannot survive extremes of hot and cold.

MICE & RATS

Chemical vermin killers can contain arsenic, strychnine, or phosphorus. Natural alternatives include:
• Keeping a cat to keep mice down, or a terrier for rats.
• Using mousetraps. Keep the bait fresh daily, and place all around the house.

ANTS & COCKROACHES

ANTS
● Sprinkle their trail with baking soda, cayenne pepper, paprika, or borax.
● Plant mint just outside your house: ants detest and avoid it.

COCKROACHES
● Make a killer cockroach cocktail. Mix equal parts powdered sugar and baking soda or borax. Leave the mixture out near their trail and they won't come back.
● Make a trap by putting chocolate, banana, or raisins in the bottom of a tall glass jar. Smear inside the neck thickly with grease. Cockroaches can climb in but cannot get out.

FLIES

There are several nontoxic ways to repel flies. They dislike citrus scents, so burning lemon or grapefruit oils in a vaporizer will deter them, as will eucalyptus oil. Hang muslin bags filled with cloves around the room, and bunches of eucalyptus, bay, or mint leaves by doors and windows—or spot a few drops of lavender oil inside a lampshade to release its scent when warmed by the heat of the light.

HOMEMADE FLYPAPER

Here is a natural and traditional method of catching flies that gives off no toxic fumes or bad odors. All you need is sugar, corn syrup, and strips of brown packaging tape.

1 Mix together equal parts by volume of sugar, corn syrup, and water. Boil the mixture until thick, stirring occasionally.

2 Cool, then dip strips of tape in the sticky mixture. Leave to dry outside for about 30 minutes.

3 Hang up with string. The flies will be attracted to—and trapped on—the sticky coating.

MOSQUITOES

Commercial mosquito repellents contain diethyltoluamide, an irritant that can damage plastic and painted surfaces. Long exposure may, in rare cases, cause tremors and brain disorders, and accidental ingestion has proved fatal to children. Try these natural repellents instead to keep mosquitoes at bay.

● Vinegar repels most insects, including mosquitoes. To use, soak a cotton ball in pure vinegar and rub it into your skin daily. This does dry out the skin, however—and may impart a vinegary smell—so you may prefer to combine this remedy with the following scented oil repellent.

● Essential oils of citronella and peppermint both act as powerful deterrents to insects,

including mosquitoes. Dilute about 3–4 drops of essential oil in 1 fl oz (29 ml) base oil, such as sunflower, almond, or wheatgerm. Dab onto your skin in the same way as perfume, once or twice a day.

● Dab pure oils along the hems of your clothes.

● Burn citronella candles, or add a few drops of the essential oil to a vaporizer.

● Mosquitoes are not fast movers, so when they are resting on the wall you can vacuum them up, or use a handheld bug vacuum, which sucks the insects up into a disposable cartridge.

● Sleep under a mosquito net.

FLEAS & HOUSEMITES
(See PEST CONTROL pages 146–147)

WASHING & LAUNDRY

Washing requires four simple components: time, motion, water at the right temperature, and chemical action. While the synthetic detergents developed by industrial chemists in the second half of the 20th century are extremely efficient at cleaning clothes, the "soft chemistry" options have improved with each decade. These vegetable-based cleaning products are derived from natural and renewable sources such as coconut, sugar cane, lemon, spices, chalk, sand, and lime. They do not have harmful side effects, nor do they pollute the environment—and they are often produced in recyclable packaging. Natural soapflakes can also be bought at the supermarket or drugstore for gentle handwashing.

A GENTLER WAY

Apart from using these vegetable-based cleaners, you can minimize your impact on the local and wider ecology by arranging for your power supply to be based on renewable resources, reducing your energy consumption by making sure that your machine uses hot water from the water heater, and choosing products that are not tested on animals.

This section is full of energy-saving tips and suggestions for washing clothes and fabrics the natural way, making it safe and healthy for both you and your family—and for the environment, as well.

Hanging just-laundered bedlinen out to dry naturally on a windy day will save energy spent on tumble-drying. It will also give it a delicious fresh-air smell impossible to achieve any other way.

Removing candle wax p68

Keeping colors bright p64

Handwashing delicates p71

Decalcifying a steam iron p73

LAUNDRY KNOW-HOW

Before you wash a new garment or fabric, always make sure that you have read the care label, and organize your laundry into separate categories. Restock your utility cupboard with "soft chemistry" washing products and try to eliminate the use of harsh detergents when using a washing machine. Avoid half-loads, since these waste energy, using up a great deal of water and electricity for only a small amount of laundry. Fill the drum but do not overload it—leave a "hand-breadth" of space at the top.

Before washing, soak bright-colored items in a bowl of cold salty water to "fix" the color so that it will not fade.

ORGANIZING LAUNDRY

To get the best results, separate laundry into different piles according to fabric type—synthetic or natural—and the washing method each type needs—machine-hot, non-colorfast or gentle cycle, or handwashing. This kind of attention will ensure that laundered items last longer.

THE RIGHT CYCLE

- Wash acetates and acrylics, cotton and linen, and wool on different wash cycles.
- Always wash darks separately from lights, and nonfast dyes separately from colorfast items.
- Don't trust delicate items to the machine: wash by hand.

PRESOAKING LAUNDRY

- For heavily soiled fabrics, give them a long soak in water before washing. Forget heavy-duty cleaners—water and time are your best allies.
- Treat stains separately (see pages 66–69) before washing.
- To prevent denim from fading, presoak items in a solution of vinegar and water (¼ cup/60 ml to 10 pints/ 5 liters water) for 30 minutes.

CUTTING DOWN ON LAUNDRY

- Wear a T-shirt or slip to reduce the need to wash outer garments so often.
- Wear an apron or smock when you are cooking, cleaning, or gardening.
- Avoid lying on the bed in clothes worn outdoors.
- Wash your hands and face before going to bed—a bath or shower is even better—to prevent soiling bedlinen.

READ THE LABEL

Reading the care label on washable fabrics is the key to success. Natural fibers shrink in too hot or too long a wash, and synthetics can lose their suppleness and crease-resistant qualities. Check that dyes are colorfast (see page 41) before you add fabrics to a machine wash, or the other items will take on the color of the dye and be ruined. To prolong the life of an item and save energy, wash at the lowest recommended temperature—even whites turn yellow if washed in water that is too hot. Symbols on garment labels indicate whether an item can be machine-washed and at what temperature. Handwash and dry-clean-only articles are also indicated.

HOMEMADE PREWASH CLEANER

Follow this recipe to make your own general prewash cleaner. It costs next to nothing, and can be made from natural household ingredients. It works well on garments that only need a quick spot-clean before washing, or that are dry-clean-only. Keep it for occasional use. It will keep indefinitely if stored in a cool, dry place.

YOU WILL NEED:

½ cup (125 ml) white vinegar
2 tablespoons ammonia
4 tablespoons baking soda
2 tablespoons liquid soap

1 Place all the ingredients together in a glass bowl and stir until thoroughly mixed. Pour into a lidded jar.

2 Shake the mixture vigorously before use. Dab it on with a clean cloth, and rinse off after 1 minute.

SOFT & SWEET

Fabric conditioners help sustain the suppleness of fibers and reduce static. Try one of the "soft chemistry" products based on natural fatty acids from vegetable sources, such as lecithin or coconut oil (*see Resources page 168*)—or make your own.

● If you live in a hard-water area, try adding 1 tablespoon of white vinegar to the fabric conditioner compartment of the washing machine. In my experience, this has just the same effect as a manufactured chemical conditioner.

● Many synthetic fragrances added to laundry products contain allergenic chemicals. To make your laundry smell good, mix the vinegar conditioner (*right*) with 4–5 drops of essential oil—lemon or lavender are favorites.

HOMEMADE FABRIC CONDITIONER

Mix together 1 cup each of washing soda, white vinegar, and water. Stir in a few drops of essential oil (lavender, lemon, cedarwood, or geranium). Store in a capped bottle, and use as you would a commercial conditioner.

TIPS FOR MACHINE-WASHING

However gentle the setting, the mechanical action of the washing cycle as items of clothing are turned in the drum is fairly vigorous. To keep clothing in good condition over a lifetime of machine-washing, follow these guidelines.

● Make sure pockets are empty.
● Turn corduroy inside out, or else the pile will pick up fluff and fibers from other fabrics.
● Turn denim jeans inside out to prevent them from fading.
● Machine-washable knitwear

may "pill," and benefits from being turned inside out.
● Rub a moistened bar of mild soap over dirt lines on shirt collars and cuffs, then brush with an old toothbrush to loosen dirt before washing.

● Place delicate fabrics inside a pillowcase to protect them inside the machine drum.
● Soak soiled handkerchiefs overnight in salty water (1 tablespoon to 1 pint/500 ml) before machine washing.

NATURAL STAIN REMOVERS

There are several "soft chemistry" stain removers to turn to in an emergency. These contain solvents based on ethanol (the same alcohol that is present in wine and beer), which breaks down rapidly in the environment and has no known side effects. Glycerine, a by-product of soap manufacture, is an effective cleaning agent that is available from most drugstores. Washing soda is one of the oldest products used for cleaning. It is also a natural water softener and helps remove grease as well as dirt. Turpentine is a mild, natural solvent for oily stains. As well as being effective on fabric, it can be used to clean brushes used with oil paints, and its method of production encourages sustainable forestry practices.

PRODUCTS TO AVOID

The following substances are all strong chemical stain removers: they emit vapor, cause damage to eyes and skin on contact, and may be based on unsustainable resources. Chemical solvents may also leave marks at the edge of treated stains, which are then difficult to remove.

COMMERCIAL STAIN OR SPOT REMOVERS
Some of these may contain, amongst other ingredients, dry-cleaning solvents such as perchloroethylene (see page 73) and trichloroethylene, petroleum-based compounds. Sodium hypochlorite, an essential component of bleach (see below), may also be an ingredient in some removers.

ACETONE
The main ingredient in nail polish removers, with a distinctive sweet odor, acetone may remove certain stains but it is so powerful that it melts synthetic cellulose fibers and removes dye color from other synthetic fibers. It is irritating to the eyes, nose, and throat.

CHLORINE BLEACH
Bleach damages natural fibers —your beautiful wools and silks and velvets will be ruined. It is irritating to skin, eyes, and the respiratory tract.

METHYLATED SPIRITS AND MINERAL SPIRITS
Both are derived from petrochemicals and are neither sustainable nor ecologically sound. Avoid them completely.

METHANOL
A type of alcohol, this is a wood derivative, also known as wood alcohol, wood spirits, or methyl alcohol. It was once used by hat makers to dilute their colors and mold their forms. The fumes not only caused blindness but caused

dementia—hence the saying "as mad as a hatter." Sometimes present in paint removers, it is a severe skin and eye irritant.

ISOPROPYL ALCOHOL
Used to treat a range of stains. This is a petrochemical derivative, and is to be avoided.

THE WATER TREATMENT

Nature's greatest solvent is water, and this, coupled with speedy action on your part, is the key to successful stain removal. When an accident occurs, do the following:

● Mop up any excess at once with absorbent paper towel.
● Soak the stained area with lukewarm water (not hot—this may "cook" the stain and set it). Soda water and sparkling water are both excellent solvents, especially for treating red wine spills (see also page 67) and removing pet stains.
● Never rub hard—just dab, so as not to damage fibers.
● Work the stain from the inside outward.

REMOVING PROTEIN STAINS

To remove stains such as blood and egg (but not butter which is a grease stain), try the following. Do not use hot water (this "fixes" the stain), but soak in lukewarm water and apply a soap-based or salt solution before washing.

● Egg stains on clothes and soft furnishings respond well to a solution of borax (see below), or to soaking in salt water. Scrape off as much egg as you can first with a dull blade before treating the fabric.
● The albumen protein in bloodstains is broken down by salt, so soak in cold salty water while the stain is fresh.
● Chocolate stains can be easily removed with lukewarm soapy water or borax solution (see below), or try using glycerine. Soak the stained fabric in a bowl of glycerine for 30 minutes, then rinse out.
● For a dried-on protein stain, dab with a little ammonia diluted with cold water.

STAIN REMOVER CHECKLIST

Washing soda (sodium carbonate)
White vinegar
Fresh lemon
Salt (sodium chloride)
Baking soda (sodium bicarbonate)
Turpentine
Glycerine
Fuller's earth (for grease stains)

For occasional use in small amounts only:
Ethanol (pure alcohol)
Borax
Ammonia

HOMEMADE BORAX STAIN REMOVER

This stain remover works well on protein stains. Have a supply ready-mixed for emergency stain removal.

YOU WILL NEED:
1 oz (25 g) borax
1 pint (500 ml) cold water

1 Fill a bottle with the correct quantity of water, and add the borax.

2 Replace the bottle cap and shake the solution well, to mix.

3 Dab the solution onto the stain with a clean cloth. Leave to dry, then launder.

67

REMOVING COLORED STAINS

The following tips suggest ways to remove colored food and drink stains. Berry fruits, coffee, tea, and red wine are among the most tiresome but, if you act quickly, they can be removed without recourse to chemicals.

- Apply a dab of fresh lemon juice or white vinegar to the stain, or soak the stain in a "soft chemistry" bleach before laundering.
- For wine stains on clothes, pour salt onto the affected area to absorb the moisture before soaking the garment in a "soft chemistry" bleach. Or splash with soda water, then launder.
- For old red wine stains, try using the glycerine method given for chocolate stains (see page 67). This stain-removal technique also works for beet, red cabbage, and dark fruit stains.
- When red wine is spilled on carpet, mop up the excess liquid and then pour white wine over the patch to saturate it. Let the wine soak into the carpet fibers for 10 minutes, then rinse with lukewarm water.
- To remove tea or coffee stains, work glycerine into the area. Leave the glycerine to soak into the fabric, and then rinse out with warm water.
- For tea-stained upholstery, use homemade borax stain remover (see page 67). Treat coffee stains in the same way.
- Soak grass stains in glycerine before laundering. This works well on baseball and football uniforms, which are prone to grass staining. Soak in a solution of washing soda (4 oz/110 g to 1.5 gallons/ 5 liters water), then rinse.

Dabbing a soft fruit juice stain with freshly squeezed lemon juice will bleach out the color naturally.

REMOVING GREASE STAINS

The following tips work on greasy makeup stains, candle wax spills, butter, margarine, mayonnaise, cooking oil, and engine oil.

- Pretreat the fabric with baking soda paste (see page 52), then soak in warm water with a "soft chemistry" washing powder. For the machine-wash, add 2 tablespoons of baking soda to your laundry detergent.
- Dab pure ethanol alcohol on obstinate stains.
- Draw out ordinary grease stains by covering with a generous sprinkling of fuller's earth powder. Leave it on for several hours or overnight, then brush off with a stiff bristle brush. This also works well on cooking fat.
- Dab lipstick stains with eucalyptus oil. Leave

To remove wax, place brown paper over the wax stain and melt it with a warm iron. It will lift off onto the paper.

the oil to soak in before laundering the garment. Lipstick and cosmetic stains can also be treated as for grass stains (*see opposite*).

● White handkerchiefs and table napkins stained with lipstick can be boiled clean in hot water.

● Treat oil, tar, and grass stains with a few drops of eucalyptus oil. Rub the essential oil into the stain, then launder the fabric as usual.

● Rub lard into tar stains, then wash the article, adding 2 tablespoons of washing soda to your laundry detergent.

HOUSE PAINT SPILLS

Always act on paint spills while the paint is still wet. Oil paints can be removed with turpentine (*see page 34*), although once the paint is dry this natural solvent will not have an effect. Sometimes a hot vinegar solution will remove oil paint that has just dried. Latex paint spills should be soaked in cold water first, and then gently rubbed off with a sponge and straight turpentine.

COMMON HOUSEHOLD STAINS

Most sticky household stains and colored marks can be removed using natural ingredients and the bleaching effect of sunlight. You should rarely need to use chemical bleach or any of the proprietary stain removers on the market.

● For sticky substances such as glue or chewing gum, first scratch off as much of the substance as possible, then use a citrus cleaner (*see Resources page 168*).

● Chewing gum on clothes may also be treated by holding the affected item over a steaming saucepan until the gum is soft enough to pull off, taking particular care not to damage fabric that has a pile. Alternatively, place the garment in the freezer compartment. When the chewing gum is frozen, it can be lifted.

● Remove laundry detergent residues (left on fabric when washed in an over-full machine) by giving the item a second rinse.

● Scrape off shoe polish, then dab the affected area with neat ethanol alcohol.

● Soak rust stains for 20–30 minutes in a solution made from the juice of 1 lemon mixed with 1 heaped tablespoon of table salt. Rub well, then wash and dry outside in the sun to bleach. Repeat the process until the stain has disappeared.

● Soak sweat stains in water to which 1–2 tablespoons of white vinegar or lemon juice, or a handful of baking soda, has been added. Wash the article according to the care instructions on the label.

SCORCH MARKS

Remove scorch marks with the simplest of remedies—lemon juice and sunlight.

When ironing fabrics on too hot a setting, you may scorch the material. If the scorching is light, and the affected item is 100 percent cotton, such as a napkin, the lemon juice method works well. First soak the scorched area in pure, freshly squeezed lemon juice. Rinse out in warm water and then leave outside to dry in sunlight and benefit from the bleaching action of the sun. Alternatively, use a "soft chemistry" bleach.

Apply lemon juice to the scorched area and place in the sun. Then machine-wash with a "soft chemistry" detergent.

WASHING THE NATURAL WAY

Doing your laundry the natural way has a number of benefits. "Soft chemistry" or homemade powders and liquids are less harsh on the fibers of the fabric, and also limit the quantity of chemicals entering rivers and lakes. They are kinder on the skin, and seem to cause fewer allergic reactions. In contrast, commercial laundry products are based on petrochemicals and contain phosphates, enzymes, and bleaches that are highly toxic. When chemical detergents (described as "surfactants" on labels) enter the environment, they can damage fish, animal, and plant life. Before buying any product, check to see what it really contains.

HOMEMADE POWDER

To make your own allergy-free washing powder, mix together 2 oz (50 g) of soapflakes with 1 oz (25 g) washing soda. Add a bit more washing soda to the mix if you live in a hard water area.

CHOOSING PRODUCTS

"Soft chemistry" products, based on soaps made from coconut, palm, and canola oils, are the best option for laundry (see Resources page 168). Of the more conventional alternatives, powder detergent, ideally in concentrated form, is preferable to liquid products, which contain three to four times more petrochemical-based detergent. Try using half the recommended amount: your wash should come out just as clean, while reducing the tendency for a buildup of soap residues in fibers.

● Check the ingredients listed to make sure that the product is based on vegetable and mineral sources. Check that it is biodegradable, and has not been tested on animals.

● Some laundry detergents contain enzymes that are added to products to help remove protein stains. The enzymes are active only at low temperatures, thus reducing energy costs. However, enzymes can affect other protein molecules too, including human ones, and are thought to increase the incidence of allergic reactions.

Make sure your detergent is enzyme-free, and use natural stain removers (see pages 66–69).

● Optical brighteners, designed to make your washing come out "whiter than white," are derived from petrochemicals, and do not biodegrade easily. They also cause skin allergies and hinder wound healing.

LAUNDRY BALLS

Laundry balls are eco-friendly, using only the cleansing power of water.

This new "green" product claims to replace the need for powder or liquid laundry detergents. It works by producing ionized oxygen that activates water molecules, making them penetrate deeply into fibers to dislodge dirt.

● The balls are hypoallergenic and suitable for sensitive skin.
● They save water—a second rinse is unnecessary.
● They can be reused up to 750 times, making them excellent value (see Resources page 168).

CHEMICAL & NATURAL BLEACHES

Use natural or "soft chemistry" alternatives to chlorine bleach wherever possible.

● Chlorine bleach can be hazardous (*see page 66*), and it pollutes the water supply. Chlorine products should not be mixed with ammonia or acid-based cleaners (including vinegar): the compound produced gives off chloramine, which causes lung problems.

● Powdered bleaches containing borax are active over 140°F (60°C). Boron, a constituent of borax, is a harmful chemical.

● Bleach made from percarbonate is the most environmentally sound chemical bleach. Percarbonate contains soda and oxygenated water, so it is entirely natural (*see Resources page 167*).

● To revive whites, boil them in water with a little soap powder and fresh lemon. Simmer for 10 minutes. The lemon acts as a bleaching agent. (Never boil synthetics.)

USING YOUR MACHINE

If you live in a hard water area, calcium deposits will build up in parts of your washing machine. These threaten its efficiency and shorten its working life. Here's what to do:

● Add 1-2 tablespoons of washing soda to the detergent compartment of your washing machine to reduce calcium deposits. This also reduces the amount of detergent you need by up to 30 percent.

Add washing soda to reduce the amount of detergent you have to use.

● Use powders or liquids that contain ecological water-softening agents such as zeolite or citrate. EDTA and NTA, which are widely used in commercial detergents, are made from petrochemicals, do not biodegrade readily, and are a particular hazard to drinking water.

HANDWASHING

If the label states that a fabric should be handwashed, do not risk machine-washing. Handwash the item in natural soapflakes, or a "soft chemistry" liquid wool wash based on coconut oil (*see Resources page 168*).

● Presoak the fabric in water with mild soapflakes to loosen dirt and grime.
● Rinse out soapflakes in lukewarm water until the fabric no longer feels slippery to the touch.
● For extra body and softness, add 1 tablespoon of baking soda to the last rinse.
● If washing silk, add a dash of vinegar to the final rinse to improve the shine.
● Dry flat on a clean towel in a warm place.

After rinsing, wrap delicate handwashed garments in a towel and press out any excess moisture.

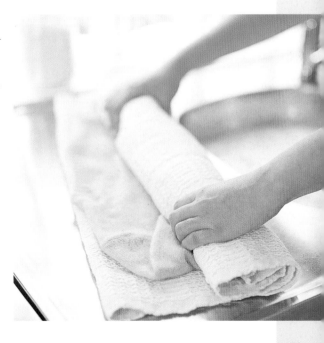

DRYING & PRESSING

Reshape delicate articles and lay them out flat to dry on an absorbent towel.

If you have access to space outdoors, dry your laundry in the fresh air rather than wasting energy tumble-drying. The following points explain how dry cleaning can be kept to a minimum to save money and the environment, and offer ironing tips to enable you to produce well-pressed items without having to resort to the dry-cleaning process.

DRYING THE NATURAL WAY

When hanging clean laundry outside, run a damp cloth along the line to remove any dirt first, and use clothespins. Hang the items evenly, keeping the seams and creases of garments in the right places to retain their shape. This will ensure your laundry dries quickly and efficiently, and reduce ironing to a minimum.

DRYING OUTSIDE

- Choose a windy day, since wind speeds up the process, while sunlight has a bleaching effect.
- Don't hang filled articles such as sleeping bags over the line because the filling will drop to the bottom: dry flat, or on a rack.

DRYING INDOORS

- Dry wool sweaters flat on towels.
- Hang an old-fashioned drying rack from the ceiling in a utility room near a furnace or boiler.
- String an improvised clothes line between chairs placed back-to-back.

BEDLINEN & BLANKETS

The size and weight of larger items of bedding, such as linen double bed sheets, quilt covers, and blankets, mean that they need more space to dry, and also take substantially longer to do so than smaller articles. This is especially true of pure wool blankets whose natural fibers absorb large quantities of water.

- If you have outdoor space, dry sheets in the fresh air.
- You can dry natural cotton or linen sheets over radiators, but beware of doing so with synthetic fibers, since the heat may damage them.
- Fold and smooth noniron sheets when dry, and store in a dry place. Ironing cotton or linen sheets is hard work but worthwhile.

- Avoid buying blankets that require dry cleaning (*see opposite*).
- Line-dry blankets rather than tumble-dry them. Even at low temperatures, frequent tumble-drying may affect the quality of the wool blanket, and it is energy-intensive. Spreading a blanket over two parallel clotheslines will help speed up the process.

TOP TIP

Use your cotton and linen sheets in rotation, putting the newly laundered ones at the bottom of the pile. This will prevent white sheets from yellowing due to lack of use, or discoloring through overuse and repeated washing.

REDUCING DRY CLEANING

Dry cleaning uses a liquid chemical solvent called perchloroethylene (PERC). Studies indicate that the solvent fumes may be carcinogenic and cause organ damage, and they are known to provoke symptoms such as headaches, nausea, dizziness, and nose and throat irritation.

- Don't always take the label at face value: manufacturers often recommend dry cleaning to cover themselves in case garments are ruined by incorrect washing. Very often, careful handwashing of delicate cotton, silk, and wool, and synthetics works perfectly well (*see pages 36–41*).
- Spot-clean clothes (*see pages 67–69*) to save having to send items to the cleaners. Many stains can be treated as for washable fabrics.
- Brush clothes with a soft bristle brush to remove loose surface dirt and dust.
- Hang clothes outside on a sunny day to freshen them up.
- If you do dry clean an item, air it outdoors or in a room with the window open for a few days.

To freshen up dry-clean only items, hang them up in a steamy bathroom.

IRONING TIPS

Follow these guidelines to increase the life of your clothes and prevent damage due to misuse of the iron.

- Always use the correct temperature for the fabric to avoid ruining it: read the label.
- Put a sheet of foil underneath your ironing board cover to reflect heat and save energy.
- To avoid shine, iron on the wrong side of the fabric, and use a damp pressing cloth.
- Steam out wrinkles as you iron: obviously a steam iron is best, but if you do not have one, use a fine plant sprayer filled with clean water.
- Don't iron over buttons: this marks the fabric, and may melt the buttons. Work around them with the tip of the iron.
- Never iron velvet: hold it over a steaming saucepan, stretching it where creased.
- Iron woolens on the wrong side, using a steam iron or a damp pressing cloth (an old, clean dish towel does this job perfectly).

To decalcify a steam iron, mix a little white vinegar with the water that you use for the appliance. Pour the vinegar and water solution the steam cavity, then turn on to hot and allow to steam for 5 minutes. After use, allow to cool, and pour the solution away. Wipe the plate clean with a damp cloth.

TO CLEAN YOUR IRON
When the iron is cold, wipe off any marks with baking soda paste (*see page 52*) to prevent transferring them onto clothes.

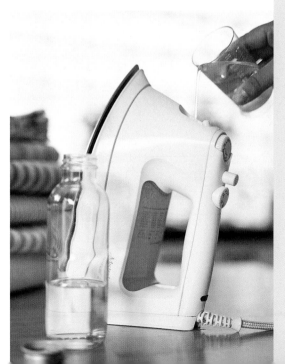

RECYCLING WASTE

It may come as a surprise but more than two-thirds of the materials we throw away as garbage can be recycled. By changing our habits, the three key practices—reduce, reuse, and recycle—will become second nature. The secret is to make it easy for yourself and to organize good recycling facilities in your home so that the process becomes routine.

THE BENEFITS OF RECYCLING

Recycling is really just a matter of reusing items instead of throwing them away. It increases awareness of the amount of waste we produce and gives us a greater sense of collective responsibility as consumers. Old glass bottles go to manufacture new bottles and other glassware, paper is recycled into stationery and newsprint, and plastic is melted down to make containers, patio furniture, and even clothes. Aluminum and steel are recycled into new cans, and organic waste creates rich nutrients when composted for your garden.

RECYCLING FACILITIES

Find out about local recycling facilities. Some municipalities have recycling centers where a range of waste materials can be taken for processing—some even offer curbside collection. If you do not have home collection, take your paper, glass, and metal with you on your weekly shopping trip and drop it off at a recycling center. Allow reusing and recycling to become part of your thinking and part of your life.

Many household items can be recycled. All you need is a little organization and practical storage facilities.

Storing recyclable items p79

Reusing wooden boxes p81

Collecting organic waste p82

Recycling waste paper p86

REDUCING WASTE

When you consider the amount of garbage we generate annually, you will soon grasp why recycling is so vital. Households in the developed world produce millions of tons of garbage each year. Although some of this waste, such as plastic containers, is not biodegradable, about 70 percent of what we consign to the dump could be recycled but isn't. Some countries, notably Denmark, Norway, Sweden, Germany, Austria, and the Netherlands, have had efficient public recycling programs for decades. However, in the United States, only one-quarter of the 220 million tons of trash produced—about 4 lb (2 kg) per person per day—is recycled.

CUT DOWN ON GARBAGE

Waste prevention is the most effective way of managing the problem, because the drawback of unwanted garbage is that it ends up in landfill sites. Burying garbage causes environmental problems, contaminating the water table with toxins and the atmosphere with methane gas. Waste incineration also has its drawbacks, discharging dioxins and other hazardous toxins into the air. Use this guide to packaging and products to help you cut down the amount of waste you generate.

PACKAGING
● Use your purchasing power: where possible, buy minimally packaged goods.
● Avoid products wrapped in plastic or presented on a polystyrene tray: plastics contaminated with food cannot be recycled.
● Buy food and products in bulk to reduce packaging.
● Avoid processed meals that often have several layers of packaging to make them attractive to the consumer.
● Refuse the free shopping bags at the checkout: instead, take your own shopping bag or basket.

Buy food loose, where possible, and store in refillable, airtight containers.

- Buy fresh fruits and vegetables loose.
- Buy goods in refillable or returnable containers.
- Drink filtered tap water instead of bottled, to reduce the packaging and transportation costs of bottled water.
- Use metal cutlery and ceramic plates rather than disposable plastic items.

LONG-LIFE PRODUCTS
- Use rechargeable batteries or reusable alkaline batteries that contain no cadmium or mercury.
- Replace conventional light bulbs with low-energy types, some of which last for years.
- Buy a secondhand car instead of a new one.
- Have your shoes reheeled and resoled regularly to get more wear from them instead of throwing them out, and give unwanted shoes and boots to charity.

RECYCLED PRODUCTS
- Buy recycled. Look for products labeled "100 percent recycled"—just "recycled"on the label can mean as little as 1 percent.
- Buy recycled stationery, newspaper, toilet paper, cardboard boxes, food cans, glass bottles, and jars.
- Some garden furniture, flooring, office accessories, fiberfill quilts and fleeces are made from recycled plastic bottles.
- Certain brands of sleeping bag are filled with shredded telephone directories.
- Scrap tires can be recycled into playground surfacing material and carpet backing.
- Old railroad ties can be made into furniture.
- Buy items from secondhand stores if possible.
- Choose biodegradable plant pots made from paper and coir instead of plastic ones.

Buy vegetables in recyclable brown paper bags instead of plastic. This will also allow the produce to breathe.

ALTERNATIVES TO DISPOSABLES
The following guide suggests alternatives to disposable goods made from plastic and bleached paper which use up natural wood and oil resources, involve intensive industrial manufacture, and create waste.

AVOID	USE
Plastic shopping bags	Canvas or string bags or baskets, or reuse plastic bags
Plastic garbage bags	Recycled plastic garbage bags
Paper towels	Dish towels
Disposable cleaning cloths	Cotton cloths or clean rags, or reuse old towels and dish towels
Plastic sponges	Cellulose sponges (biodegradable)
Paper or polystyrene cups and plates	Ceramic plates, or reuse plastic ones
Paper napkins	Cloth napkins
Teabags and coffee filters (bleached)	Loose tea, coffee press
Disposable diapers (bleached)	Cloth diapers
Baby wipes	Damp flannel or cloth
Tissues, cotton balls (bleached)	Biodegradable, unbleached versions, or handkerchiefs
Batteries	AC current, or rechargeable batteries
Nylon pantyhose	Socks, durable leggings, cotton tights
Disposable razors	Straight razor, or refill blades
Ballpoint pens	Refillable ink pens

WHAT TO RECYCLE?

Sorting out items to be recycled is the beginning of the process. Setting up a system where you have a series of storage bins for each category will make the process far simpler. First find out which materials your local facilities accept for recycling and then set up your bins accordingly. Most recyclable items just need a quick rinse to prevent them from smelling while stored. These tips offer practical advice for the beginner, to make recycling easy.

Store newspapers for recycling in a brown paper bag so that both contents and container can be recycled.

PAPER

Every ton of recycled paper saves 15 trees. It is turned into new paper products such as newspapers, printer paper, packaging, books, stationery, toilet paper, and paper towels, or shredded to make animal bedding.

- Save newspapers, magazines, phone books, white envelopes, computer paper, old letters, and paper packaging.
- Staples in paper are acceptable, but remove rubber bands or plastic wrap.
- Store paper flat: it takes up less space.
- Do not include the following in your paper recycling: carbon paper; stickers; cardboard; laminated paper; laminated cardboard.
- Discard plastic-lined paper drink cartons; fast-food wrappers made from plastic; dirty or food-stained paper; tissues or napkins.
- Exclude glossy magazines, which have insoluble glues in the spine. Recycle magazines by offering them to friends or to a doctor's or dentist's waiting room.

PLASTIC

Plastic does not break down in landfill sites; but it can be recycled to make diverse products including clear film for packaging, carpet fibers, patio furniture, agricultural pipes, industrial flooring, garbage bags, and clothespins.

- Recyclable plastic is coded with the recycling symbol (chasing arrows) on the base of the container. However, many local recycling plants do not accept certain types of plastic. If you buy plastic goods, check that they are recyclable.
- Most plastic goods are numbered to grade the different types for recycling: 1 and 2 for containers; 4 for bags; 7 for mixed or layered plastics that are not recyclable. Separate plastics for recycling into bins numbered accordingly.
- Recycle plastic bottles but remove the bottle tops, which are made of a different plastic and require separate recycling.

POLYSTYRENE WASTE

Polystyrene cups, plates, carryout food containers, egg cartons, and plant pots do not biodegrade and cannot be incinerated because they release toxic gases. In some countries, most polystyrene waste is sent to landfill sites, but it can be recycled. Canada and some European countries such as the Netherlands and Germany have a collection system and reprocessing program for polystyrene.

- Avoid using plastic food wrap or buying food in plastic tubs; they are not recyclable once they have been contaminated with food.
- Try to cut down on TV dinners: they are packaged with layers of plastic that are not recyclable.
- Plastic bags are excluded from recycling programs. Store and reuse plastic bags as trash can liners and shopping bags.

ALUMINUM & STEEL

In Western industrialized countries, every 50 million people use 13 billion steel cans each year. Aluminum cans can be recycled to make new cans, and aluminum foil is reprocessed into car engine components.

- Save all empty food cans and pet food cans.
- Save all foil packaging, such as baking and freezing trays, and carryout food containers. Keep in a separate bin from tin cans, since they need a different recycling treatment.
- Do not include empty paint cans or aerosol cans, since they are classed as hazardous waste (see page 84).

Rinse aluminum food cans under the faucet before adding to the recycling bin to prevent them from smelling.

GLASS

Up to 90 percent of reclaimed glass can be recycled to make bottles, glasses, jars, and household objects, such as candlesticks.

- Glass is recycled according to color: green, clear, and brown. Store it in these categories.
- Paper labels can be difficult to remove and may be left on.
- Glass is heavy, so do not overfill containers or they will be unmanageable.
- Store lightbulbs, sheet glass, mirrors, and pyrex separately from bottles and jars, since they have a different composition.

Recycling boxes that fit under a kitchen unit where food is prepared are easy to access and make ergonomic sense.

ORGANIZING RECYCLING

- Plan stackable recycling storage to save space.
- Use plastic boxes for collection: bags break and may leak.
- Choose smaller containers; if they are too large they may become impossibly heavy.
- Place them close to the source of the waste.
- Label the different bins to make sorting easier.

HOUSEHOLD ITEMS

Paper, glass, and aluminum are everyday recyclable items, and large containers at some recycling centers now also allow for the recycling of items such as books and electronic goods. For other recycling tips, see below.

TEXTILES, CLOTHES, & SHOES

- Old curtains, bedding, clothes, and upholstery can be recycled to make car-insulation fibers and furniture fillings.
- Sell unwanted textiles that are still in reasonable condition at a rummage sale, or donate old fabrics to charity.
- Beds and sofas, and soft furnishings of all kinds, including curtains and carpets, can be offered to secondhand dealers, or to charities that pass them on to people in need and community groups.

- Charity shops take wearable clothes and shoes, and even furniture and soft furnishings, for resale to raise funds.
- Wearable clothes and shoes can also be placed in charity clothes drops.
- Tie pairs of shoes or sneakers together before recycling.
- The Nike Corporation shreds old shoes to make athletic mats, which are then donated to good causes (see Resources page 169).

Sort old textiles into a box, and when you have collected a sackful, take them to your local recycling center.

BOOKS & TOYS

- Old schoolbooks can be sent to the developing world: involve children in collecting the books as part of their education, connecting them to the global community (see Resources page 169).
- If you have a large number of secondhand books you no longer want, a charity may be willing to pick them up from your house.
- Toys can be donated to toy libraries or charities that will send them to poorer countries.

ELECTRIC & ELECTRONIC GOODS

Millions of tons of electrical and electronic goods end up in landfill sites every year, but it doesn't have to be this way. With a little forward planning and a change in buying habits, you can cut down on your personal turnover of goods.

- Buy quality equipment that will last, and can be repaired.
- Upgrade your computer rather than buy a new model.
- Find out about organizations that recycle computers, or projects that take unwanted computers from businesses (see Resources page 169).
- Find out whether local schools, technical colleges or charities would like an old computer as a gift.
- When buying a refrigerator, washing machine, dishwasher, or oven, ask the retailer if they organize recycling for scrap and parts. Your local municipality may offer a similar service. If recycling a fridge, make sure it will be drained of CFCs before disposal.
- Some cell phone manufacturers have "take-back" programs that also include phone batteries.
- Landline phones are accepted for recycling by some telephone companies.
- Find out if local community programs and/or commercial organizations have reuse schemes for electrical goods.

PRINTERS & TONER CARTRIDGES

Most people now have a computer and printing facilities at home. However, computer printer cartridges and inks generate a lot of plastic and non-biodegradable toxic waste. Responsible suppliers are addressing this problem by offering recycling facilities for printer inks and toner cartridges.

● Toner cartridges are classified as "difficult waste," but most can be returned to the manufacturer for recycling.
● Buy toner cartridges from manufacturers that have a postage-paid return system for sending empty cartridges back.

● Companies that recycle individual inkjet cartridges and toner cartridges can be found on the internet (*see Resources page 169*).
● Some charities may offer "toner donor" programs. If you register with such a program, the charity will usually provide postage-paid for you to return inks or cartridges for recycling.
● Refillable printer toner cartridges are available: some companies offer refilling services by mail.

RECYCLING FRUIT CRATES

Wooden crates and boxes that have formerly been used to transport fruit and vegetables make ideal containers for items you wish to recycle. Alternatively, you can turn them into attractive and practical storage boxes that can be stacked away neatly, taking up the minimum of room. Make sure they are clean and dry, and paint them in with a nontoxic natural paint or wood stain in a color of your choice.

PACKAGING LEGISLATION

While Germany, Austria, France, and Sweden implement a strict "producer responsibility" policy which drastically reduces packaging materials and actively encourages recycling, Great Britain and the US have not yet adopted this policy. Follow these tips to reduce waste packaging in your home.
• Avoid products that come in "mixed packaging" with, for example, cardboard and bubble-wrap, which are not recyclable.
• Avoid wax and foil-lined cartons, or "tetra pack" (made with paper, polyethylene and foil) since this type of packaging is difficult to recycle.

● Fruit boxes and crates are not designed for domestic use, so the surface of the wood may be rough. Sand smooth before painting or staining, especially if children are going to use them to put away their toys.
● Check for staples and nails: remove staples, and hammer nailheads flush.

1 Apply paint or stain to the sanded surface, using 1–3 coats, as preferred.

2 Use the boxes to store jars, toys, magazines, newspapers, or whatever else you need to keep in order.

ORGANIC WASTE

Making compost—a rich, dark, sweet-smelling, soil-like material created from rotted organic waste—not only helps you grow healthy plants, but is also one of the easiest ways of recycling food and household waste materials, including cardboard and paper. The money it saves you on commercial soil improvers, fertilizers, and mulches is not inconsiderable, and it is a good natural alternative to peat. If you have no outdoor space for making compost, find out if your community offers a composting program for recycling organic household waste.

Feed the soil with rich organic compost to get your plants and vegetables off to a good start.

WHY COMPOST?

Multipurpose compost, sold in garden centers, is not a compost but a growing medium made from sand, coir, peat, and fertilizers. Here are the eco-benefits of real compost.

- It nourishes plants with well-balanced "food."
- It improves the structure of the soil, helping light soils to hold water, and lightening heavy soils.
- It helps control diseases by maintaining healthy plants.

- It reduces pollution by cutting down the need for bonfires to burn leaves and brush.
- It helps to save the local and sometimes rare wildlife on fragile peatland habitats, which are on the brink of extinction.

WHAT TO COMPOST

Not all organic household waste can safely go on the compost pile. Here's what to include:

THE YARD
- Fall leaves
- Plant remains, such as dead cut flowers or bedding plants
- Annual weeds (many perennials can regrow from the tiniest piece of root)
- Hedge clippings and prunings (tough, woody ones should be shredded first)
- Sawdust and wood shavings
- Old straw and hay

- Animal manure (but avoid cat litter or dog feces: *see page 83*)

THE HOME
- Fruit and vegetable peelings
- Teabags and coffee grounds
- Cardboard and paper, shredded
- Wood ash
- Organic household paint (*see page 34*)

Fruit and vegetable peelings make excellent material for the compost heap.

WHAT TO AVOID

- Diseased plants
- Meat and fish scraps, which may attract pests
- Cat litter and dog feces (they contain harmful parasites)
- Disposable diapers (the plastic does not degrade)
- Glossy magazines, which contain toxic glues and formaldehyde
- Coal and coke ash, which are heavy in petrochemicals

COMPOST PILES & BINS

- Compost can be made in a simple pile, but it needs to be covered (*see below*) to keep it warm and moist.
- You can make a simple bin by driving four wooden posts into the ground, then stapling chicken wire to them, leaving one side tied, not stapled, for easy access.
- A compost bin with a volume of about 202 gallons (765 liters) will be sufficient for an average household's organic waste over a year. The ideal ecological material to use is untreated wood.
- Keep your compost bin away from the vegetable garden, since the bugs it attracts (slugs, snails, and earwigs) will not be beneficial to your crop.
- If you are short of space, you can buy a stack-composter that works by using composting worms to turn your waste into a rich liquid manure.

SUCCESSFUL COMPOSTING

- Start filling your bin with the waste material listed on page 82, mixing it each time.
- Cover your compost pile with old carpet, an old blanket, or thick plastic sheeting to warm it up and accelerate the process.
- Try to introduce "compost activators" to the pile. Layering in comfrey leaves, chamomile, and poultry manure will all help to reduce the length of time needed to make rich, dark compost to 12 weeks instead of the more usual year.
- Horse and straw manure, well rotted over a period of 3–6 months, also acts as a natural accelerator.

- Mix grass cuttings in to achieve a good balance of "green" and "brown" material in the heap.
- If the items are dry, water well as you add them, but don't let the heap become soggy.
- Turn your heap every few weeks with a garden fork to aerate it.
- Do not put compost on bare soil in the winter because many of the nutrients will be washed away. Dig it into your beds in spring so that young plants and new growth get the benefit of the feed. Or you can simply spread it as a mulch, and let earthworms carry it into the soil (*see below*).

Spread cut chamomile over the top of your compost to help speed up the natural decomposition process.

WHY MULCH?

Mulching means protecting the soil with a surface layer of organic matter. It keeps moisture in, stops nutrients from leaching out of the soil, prevents wind erosion during winter months, and can be used to suppress weeds during the growing season. It can also be used to feed the soil. Apply it during the fall and early spring. Use about two shovelfuls per square yard. The natural materials used to make mulch include: grass clippings; woodchips; eggshells (for calcium); mushroom compost; and straw and bracken.

LEAF MOLD MULCH

Leaf mold makes a good soil mulch and warm winter cover for the vegetable garden. Pile the leaves into a garbage bag, and poke holes in the sides. Leave to rot for up to 1 year before use. Apply to the soil in autumn and early spring.

HAZARDOUS HOUSEHOLD WASTE

Without realizing it, many of us allow hazardous waste to enter the water supply by disposing of it down sinks or toilets or by placing them directly into the garbage. Some household products are labeled hazardous on the container, and should be treated as such. The following tips explain how to dispose of these hazardous products in a responsible and environmentally responsible manner.

RECYCLABLE WASTE

Several European countries pioneered recycling of both hazardous and reusable waste. Those countries that lag behind can adopt their practices without having to make a huge financial investment. Switzerland and the Netherlands are at the forefront of this movement, while Denmark has a color-coded recycling bin system on the streets and for domestic use. These recycling initiatives are actually an important part of these European countries' economies. The following information explains why safe and responsible disposal is important.

HOUSEHOLD BATTERIES

These contain heavy metals, including zinc, mercuric chloride, lead, and cadmium. There are very few facilities for recycling them in the US, but in Japan, Germany, Switzerland, and the Netherlands batteries are collected separately and disposed of as hazardous waste in "secure" landfill sites. Apart from running equipment off AC current, the only viable option is to use rechargeable batteries, selecting those that contain no mercury or cadmium and that can be recycled once their life is over. Batteries in cellular phones and portable power tools can usually be returned to the manufacturers, often by freepost. Silver oxide batteries for cameras can be given to jewelers to recover silver.

CAR BATTERIES

Encouragingly, there are established systems for reclaiming lead acid batteries used in vehicles, so ask your local garage for information.

AEROSOLS

These can be recycled at some recycling centers but do not crush the can, and make sure that it is empty.

MOTOR OIL

This contains heavy metals and is highly toxic, yet every year when people change their car engine oil at home, they pour this hazardous liquid down drains. Not only is this practice highly environmentally damaging—it kills plants and animals and can render water undrinkable—but it is also illegal. For proper disposal, place used engine oil into a

When changing your car engine oil, be sure to funnel the dirty oil into a large plastic container for disposal.

clean plastic container, label it "used motor oil" and take it to a garage, or the local oil-recycling bank. You should follow the same procedure for disposing of antifreeze, which is equally hazardous.

CARS
Most vehicle parts can be recycled or the metal recovered, but there are still unlicensed dismantlers operating who ignore environmental guidelines and allow hazardous fluids to be discharged into landfill sites along with vehicle metal that could be recycled. Ideally, sell your car to someone else, or ensure that a licensed dismantler scraps it.

SAFE DISPOSAL

Many familiar household products contain hazardous material, so try to replace them with safer products whenever possible. Buy hazardous products in the amount you will need and use them up. Always read the label for guidelines on safe usage and storage. If you are unsure about the hazardous nature of a product, do not put it in the garbage, or empty it down the drain. Contact your local recycling center for specialized advice. Although regulations for safe disposal will vary from region to region, the following provides broad guidelines (*see also Resources page 169*).

● Cosmetics: leave nail polish to harden before putting it in the trash. Take nail polish remover to a disposal facility. Perm solutions may be flushed down the drain with plenty of water.
● Garden herbicides and insecticides: when empty, fill the container one-quarter full with water, put the lid on, and shake. Use rinse water as for full strength applications. Repeat two more times, then dispose of the container. Fertilizer, if it doesn't contain pesticides, may be disposed of with the garbage.
● Moth balls: take to a disposal facility.
● Household products: cleaners containing ammonia, bleach, or detergents may be flushed away with plenty of water. Take oven cleaners to a disposal facility. Flush away drain cleaners with plenty of water. Diluted fabric dyes may be flushed down the drain; take concentrated dyes to a disposal facility. Take stain or spot stain remover to a disposal facility.

● Paints, paint strippers, paint brush cleaner: see page 34 for guidelines.
● Artist and hobby paint: take to a disposal facility.
● Metal polishes: take to a disposal facility, or expose to the air to evaporate the solvents, then put the container in the garbage.
● Wood cleaners, polishes, and waxes: take to a disposal facility.
● Medicines: some pharmacies will accept unwanted medicines; most can be flushed down the toilet. Chemotherapy drugs and antineoplastic medicines must be returned to the dispensing clinic. Take head-lice shampoo to a disposal facility. Return unwanted thermometers to a drugstore.
● Smoke detectors: the sealed unit contains radioactive material. Return old detectors to the manufacturer for safe disposal.
● Business directories: contain nonbiodegradable dye that contaminates other paper in

Batteries and aerosol cans are classed as hazardous waste and should be collected and recycled following your municipality's guidelines.

the recycling process. Check with your local recycling center for details of collection.
● Swimming pool chemicals: take to a disposal facility.

REUSING

Be resourceful and devise creative ways of reusing household materials. Take time to repair worn or broken items to counteract the prevailing culture of built-in obsolescence and disposability. Buying quality goods in the first place is truly a good investment, since they will last longer and do not need to be replaced on such a regular basis. The next step is to care for your possessions—read care labels, study the instruction manuals, and keep machines serviced. If you have no use for something, consider whether a charity shop or someone else might want it. The following suggestions offer some ideas for clever reuse.

GETTING THE HABIT

Being wasteful is only a habit, so being careful about reusing items can become a new habit. Inventing new uses for existing goods will not only save you money, but will also reduce the impact that manufacturing processes have on the environment, and alleviate the problem of waste.

Twisted sheets of newspaper make good kindling for an open fire.

PAPER
- Always use both sides of the paper.
- Use scraps of paper for shopping lists and memos.
- Reuse envelopes, addressing them with recycled labels.
- Offer bulk, unwanted paper to schools and community centers.
- Cut pretty greeting cards in half and reuse them as postcards. Remounted on a plain recycled card, they can look as good as new.
- Christmas, birthdays, and anniversary parties are great fun, but generate disproportionate amounts of waste in terms of present wrapping paper and decorations. Try to unwrap presents carefully, keeping ribbons and smoothing out your favorite wrapping papers so that you can use them again for someone else, rather than just throwing them away.

A remnant of wallpaper can be cut and folded to make an attractive drawer lining that will also help to protect your clothes.

GLASS

● Rinse out old jam jars and reuse them to store foodstuffs, nails, and other small hardware items, or use as a desk organizer or outdoor candle holder. Refill with homemade jam or offer them to beekeepers, who are often grateful for donations of honey jars.

ALUMINUM FOIL

● Reuse foil, which is seldom worn out after using just once: wipe with a damp cloth, dry, and store.

HOUSEHOLD GOODS

● Cut up really old clothes or sheets for cleaning cloths, and use old sheets as floor covers for repairs or decorating.

● Old clothing can be used for your pet's bedding.
● Organize an exchange day with friends and neighbors for goods that you no longer need, or contribute unwanted goods to rummage sales.
● Glass spectacle lenses can be measured, repaired, and cleaned up for reuse by opticians for people in need, or donated to charities to send to countries in the developing world (*see Resources page 169*).

PLASTICS

● Grow seedlings in old yogurt containers.
● Cut the tops off plastic bottles and use them in the garden to protect delicate plants from frost.

Stuff bulky plastic bags into a space-saving tower with holes so that they are easy to access for reuse.

MEND AND SAVE

Repairing broken or damaged items keeps them out of the trash can, prolongs their life, saves you money in the long run, and reduces the cycle of buy, discard, and buy that underpins the relationship between consumerism and production.

● Keep a shelf or drawer stocked with adhesives (for glass, china, wood, and plastic), sandpaper, steel wool, an old toothbrush or small brush (for removing dirt in cracks before mending), and metal polish (not very ecological but it removes scratches from glass surfaces—and even your car).
● When repairing china or glass, first make sure that the edges to be glued are clean.

Make sure you are using the right kind of adhesive for the job. Read the instructions and follow them carefully.
● Keep a small sewing repair kit handy in a drawer that fits into a small box or tin.

EDUCATING CHILDREN

One of the most positive things you can do is to encourage children to reuse and recycle products, so that they consider it a normal and natural part of everyday life. If they do not think of it as difficult, it will soon become habitual for them.

Children quickly appreciate why recycling is necessary, so take time to explain the benefits in simple terms. Many young children are very sensitive and really care about the earth, how animals are treated, and fairness for others who are less fortunate. If they see parents and other family members using recycling bins, buying fair trade goods, and giving unwanted items to charity, they will be encouraged to do the same. Teachers can also convey the same message informally at school.

HEALTHY FOOD

Eating well, and enjoying fresh healthy food in all its variety, is life-enhancing. In the developed world, we are faced with more choices about how and what we eat than ever before. More and more people are choosing to eat organically grown food, believing that it is more nutritious and less contaminated than mainstream food products. There is evidence to suggest that organic foods contain fewer traces of pesticides and fertilizers, and that vegetables and fruits ripened in the sun—instead of grown on a large scale under glass—contain more nutrients. Personally, I prefer to eat organic food because I think it tastes better. For those concerned about animal rights, it is reassuring to know that animal welfare is an important part of the organic farming ethos. Although organic items are a little more expensive, often the food goes farther because it has a lower water content and higher nutritional value.

DEVELOPING AWARENESS

The more awareness we bring to the activity of preparing and eating food, the healthier, safer, and more harmonious our lives will become. How our food is grown, transported, and packaged all have an impact on the environment. Choosing fair trade products helps to ensure basic rights for food producers in less developed countries. Buying fresh food locally is not only healthier but kinder to the environment. Gardeners can play their part, too, in halting the disappearance of traditional fruit and vegetable varieties by growing their own.

An organic vegetable box can be delivered to your door in some areas. Some farms offer this service direct.

Fruit and vegetable juices p90

Key foods to buy organic p94

Natural food additives p96

Kitchen hygiene p106

A GOOD DIET

Although there is much advice about what constitutes a healthy diet, the consensus based on health studies is that we thrive when our diet consists of about 60 percent complex carbohydrates, 25 percent fats, and 15 percent proteins. A good diet is a varied diet, and eating plenty of fresh vegetables—both cooked and raw—and fresh and dried fruits provides us with many of the nutrients, vitamins, and minerals that we need. Whole grains and legumes provide the remainder of the complex carbohydrates. Our protein comes from smaller amounts of lean meat, poultry, and fish, some dairy produce, and seeds and nuts.

Drinking freshly pressed fruit or vegetable juice is another way to increase your fruit and vegetable intake.

"FIVE SERVINGS A DAY"

Current nutritional advice is to eat a minimum of "five servings" of fruit and vegetables daily. It sounds like a lot until you understand that a "serving" in these terms is only the size of a fistful of food. One of the best ways of ensuring that you do so is to eat fresh fruits or vegetables as snacks. Eat these foods as fresh as possible: the longer fruit and vegetables are stored, the greater the loss of nutrients. The following are some useful examples of the equivalent of one serving:

A small portion of fresh vegetable soup is equivalent to one serving, but this generous bowl of soup probably equals three.

- 1 medium-sized apple
- 1 large carrot
- 1 banana
- 4 oz (100 g) cooked or raw vegetables, salad, or fruit
- 1 small handful of dried fruit (around 2 oz/50 g)

SUGAR & FATS

The accepted wisdom among nutritionists is to eat a low-sugar, low-fat diet. Refined sugars are an unnecessary part of our diet: small amounts are fine, but to rely on them for energy leads to malnourishment and obesity. The body manufactures its own sugars from the complex carbohydrates that we eat, and will maintain stamina far better than with a "sugar rush" induced by eating chocolate, cake, or cookies. Try to limit your intake of foods that contain refined sugars and fats to the occasional treat.

ARTIFICIAL SWEETENERS

These are best avoided since the effects of aspartame, acesulfame, and sucralose are not fully known. Use natural sweeteners such as cane juice, fruit juice, or honey instead.

FATTY ACIDS

The right amounts of the right fats are essential for good health. Certain fatty acids are essential for nourishing body tissue (which includes the brain). Linoleic acid (LA), or omega-6, and alpha-linoleic acid (ALA), or omega-3, are especially important for health. Corn, sesame seed, sunflower, safflower, and wheatgerm oils contain LA, and oils derived from flax seed, walnut, hemp seed, soybean, and canola all contain ALA. Seed oils should be unrefined and preferably "cold-pressed" or "virgin" since heat and light can destroy the essential fatty acids they contain. Fish such as salmon, mackerel, and herring contain ALA derivatives that have many positive health benefits, so regular amounts of these fish are important in a balanced diet.

PROBIOTICS

Probiotics are bacteria that keep the intestinal tract healthy. They are found in miso (fermented soy) and yogurt, so include these in your diet.

FATS TO AVOID

The following fats are best left out of your diet, or only used occasionally: saturated and trans-fats found in fatty meat and processed foods; refined vegetable oils; hydrogenated oils such as in margarine; and fats used in fried foods.

MEAL PLANNING

In addition to having a varied diet, some people find huge health benefits from ensuring that their meals are balanced correctly, in line with the "food combining" system devised by Dr. William Howard Hay in the early 20th century. Because proteins and starches are digested differently by the body, Dr. Hay's diet separates these and other foods into compatible and noncompatible groups.

The principles of this diet are to plan your meals so that they are protein-based or starch-based, with neutral foods that can be eaten with either of these two. Starch and sugar should not be eaten with proteins, and fruit is best eaten separately. Root vegetables, such as beets, potatoes, and Jerusalem artichokes, are fine with a carbohydrate meal but not with protein meal due to their high carbohydrate content. For example, eat fish without french fries or bread, but with vegetables and salad instead.

GUIDELINES FOR FOOD COMBINING

● Allow salads, vegetables, and fruits to form the major part of your diet.
● Eat proteins, starches, and fats in small quantities, and never eat them together at the same meal.
● Avoid processed foods, particularly white flour and sugar. Use only wholegrains and unprocessed starches.
● Always leave about four hours between meals so that the digestive process can be completed.
● Refined sugars are not useful, so avoid desserts and candy.
● All green vegetables and salads are neutral foods, and can be combined with protein or carbohydrates.
● Eat melons and citrus fruits on their own.

A small piece of grilled fish served with a large selection of steamed vegetables is good food combining.

ORGANIC FOOD

Concerns over food safety and quality have fueled the growing popularity of organic foods, and many people believe that eating organic is best for their health and well-being. Others are not so convinced and feel that eating a wide range of fresh vegetables and fruits is just as beneficial as eating organic. It isn't, of course, an "either/or" issue: you can eat some organic food and some nonorganic. The fact that organic food can be more expensive may influence your decision, as may the production methods of organic farmers and how much more sustainable and friendly they are for the environment and wildlife.

WHY SHOULD YOU CARE?

If you follow the old adage "you are what you eat," you will accept that our body's cells are made from the food we ingest. If we enjoy fresh, uncontaminated food, this is reflected in our health, vitality, and energy. Pesticides and fertilizers, which kill insects and promote plant growth, affect us with their toxicity in other ways. Processed foods that are required to have a longer shelf-life contain additives and preservatives. Intensive farming methods are also a concern, not only because of animals rights issues but also because the hormones and chemicals that promote animal growth and maintain health find their way into the food they ultimately provide.

Try to buy organically produced cocoa and chocolate, because the plants are susceptible to pests, and nonorganic crops are heavily sprayed.

REASONS FOR EATING ORGANIC FOOD

- Organic farming prevents soil erosion and protects the quality of the soil.
- Organic food grown on soil that has not been depleted by intensive farming methods contains more essential and trace minerals than nonorganic food nutrients—and you can safely eat the skins of fruits and vegetables such as carrots, apples, and potatoes, which are often the most nutritious part.
- Your food is free of most herbicides, pesticides, fungicides, nitrates, fumigants, additives, preservatives, hormones, antibiotics, irradiation, genetically modified organisms, and toxic metals.
- Organic methods promote animal welfare.
- No organically born and reared animal is known to have contracted mad cow disease.
- It is much healthier for children, who are especially vulnerable to the cancer-causing pesticides in food according to many studies. Children may be more at risk because relative to their size, they eat more food than adults, but the range consumed is narrower. In addition, their developing systems may be more sensitive to pesticides.
- It is safer for those involved in food production: a US National Cancer Institute study found that farm workers exposed to herbicides and pesticides have a higher risk of developing cancer than those who have not been exposed.

CHEMICALS IN FOOD

Food grown nonorganically with the aid of pesticides and fertilizers contains traces of toxic chemicals that can cause serious health and environmental problems. Although some of the most toxic chemicals have been banned from food production in developing countries, the fresh produce we import from these countries still contains many of them.

FERTILIZERS & PESTICIDES

Fertilizers are designed to help plants produce luscious and healthy crops, but research has shown that artificial fertilizers reduce the nutritional value of fruits and vegetables, and affect human fertility. Harmful preservatives and cosmetic chemicals may also sprayed onto fresh food to increase their shelf-life and to improve their appearance to the consumer. Pesticides include insecticides, molluscicides (to kill slugs and snails), and nematicides (to kill worms). Other chemical treatments include herbicides, fungicides, fumigants, defoliants, and plant-growth regulators. Residues from these products can remain in the soil for decades and are taken up by deep-rooting vegetables.

ORGANOPHOSPHATES (OPS)

These are the most widely used group of pesticides. They are acutely toxic, affecting the nervous system and disrupting hormone function. High levels of methyl parathion and azinphos methyl have been found on a wide range of fruits and vegetables. The US has now eliminated the use of methyl parathion on certain crops and reduced allowable residues for azinphos methyl.

DIELDRIN

This insecticide accumulates in human body fat and has been linked to reproductive disorders and cancer. It is banned but, where previously in use, it persists in the soil, and is taken up by the roots of some plants, such as winter squash. It may also be found in fish, dairy products, and animal meats.

HEPTACHLOR EPOXIDE

Although this insecticide is banned, residues remain in the soil and are taken up by crops grown in contaminated areas. It is a potent carcinogen.

METHOMYL

An acutely toxic insecticide that is found in many fruits and vegetables, and is listed as an endocrine disrupter.

LINDANE

This insecticide is an endocrine disrupter and has been linked to breast cancer and anemia. It is applied in spray form to treat a number of food crops, and is also used to control ticks on livestock. It is banned in some countries, and restricted in others.

MALEIC HYDRAZIDE

This is sprayed onto onions and potatoes to stop them from

Fresh fruits and vegetables may look healthy but many have been grown using toxic pesticides and fertilizers. Tomatoes are a good example.

sprouting. It contains minute quantities of a known toxin, hydrazine, which may leach into water supplies, and is toxic to aquatic life.

FOOD WAXES

Fruits and vegetables may be coated with one of a number of waxes to maintain freshness and improve their appearance. Paraffin wax, a petrochemical derivative, may interfere with digestion and the absorption of vitamins. Other coatings include carnauba wax—the same wax that is used on cars and floors—and shellac.

FORMALDEHYDE

Fresh mushrooms are frequently fumigated with this toxin to give them a longer shelf-life in the supermarket.

Certain fruits and vegetables are best bought or grown organically, since they may harbor higher levels of toxic residues than other foods.

FOODS VULNERABLE TO RESIDUES

If you are concerned about the safety level of some of the food you eat, there are certain fruits and vegetables that retain more chemical residues than others. While stating that "legal limits do not define safety," a 1999 analysis of US government data on pesticide residues in foods supplied a toxicity index of pesticide contamination, giving a breakdown of the levels, listed below. Check this list to see which foods it is best to buy organic.

TOXICITY INDEX

HIGH	MEDIUM	LOWER
Peaches	Apples	Apricots
Squash	Bananas	Chocolate
	Grapes	Eggs
	Green beans	Fish
	Milk	Grains
	Peas	Lettuce
	Spinach	Oranges
	Strawberries	Meat

REMOVING RESIDUES

When eating nonorganic fruits and vegetables, it is recommended that you wash them thoroughly to remove as many chemical residues as possible, and that you peel fruits and root vegetables— experts recommend always peeling the skins of peaches, apples, pears, and grapes. Washing fruits and vegetables with dishwashing liquid is said to be very effective in removing surface residues, but make sure this is a "soft chemistry" variety and rinse the items well in water afterward.

ORGANIC CERTIFICATION

Certified organic growers have to follow strict guidelines for food production. For example, they are not allowed to use sewage sludge to enrich the soil, whereas commercial growers are permitted to do so. By law, foods can only be sold as "organic" if they have been certified by official, regulatory bodies, which vary from country to country.

ORGANIC MEAT & FISH

Eating organic meat and fish whenever possible means that you will be furthering animal rights and also, by buying lesser-known breeds, supporting biodiversity.

WHY CHOOSE ORGANIC?

Eating meat raises a number of environmental and ethical issues, some of which can be avoided by choosing organic.
● Intensively reared animals are often kept in dark, crowded conditions, and are fed drugs such as growth-stimulating hormones, steroids, sulfa drugs, colorings and flavorings.
● Milk from dairy cattle, and cheese made from it, may contain DDT residues, antibiotics, hormones such as

bovine growth hormone, and mastitis bacteria. It may also be homogenized, which can lead to heart disease in humans.

● More than half the world's antibiotics are used to promote growth in animals reared for meat.

● A high proportion of all poultry and meat products produced from intensively farmed meat may be infected with salmonella, E. coli, or campylobacter.

● Unlike intensively reared animals, organic livestock spend much of their time outdoors, grazing on organic pastures. The animals are raised in closed, self-regenerating herds, and many are kept in family groups.

● Organic animals are not given unnecessary medication, and wherever possible are treated with natural remedies. Animals are allowed to mature naturally, without the aid of growth-promoting agents .

● If you eat a lot of meat, try to cut down on the amount. Two thirds of the worlds' agricultural land is used for raising livestock, which could otherwise be under crop cultivation with far higher food yields.

FREE–RANGE EGGS

The public is becoming increasingly aware of the appalling conditions in which factory chickens are kept. Although "barn chickens" and "barn-laid" eggs might sound like a more natural option, birds raised this way are still reared in highly artificial conditions, crammed by the thousand into vast sheds. For ethical and health reasons, always try to buy free-range chickens and eggs—organic too, if at all possible.

Eggs, fish, milk, grains, and chocolate may store medium to low levels of toxins, and if possible are best bought organic for ethical as well as health reasons.

EATING FRESH FISH

Farmed fish—usually salmon and trout—are kept in restricted tanks, in water cleaned with chemicals. They are fed on a diet of rich processed foods to build up their body fat. Living in confined quarters, they are prone to lice, for which they are treated with antibiotics. Buy organic fish when you shop and eat out.

● Wild fish, if caught in coastal waters, may be contaminated with industrial pollution. Shellfish, in particular, can be highly polluted because they live in coastal habitats.

● Larger fish contain more contaminants and should be avoided, especially by pregnant women, because they may contain high levels of methylmercury, which can harm an unborn child's nervous system. Swordfish, marlin, shark, king mackerel, and tilefish are the worst offenders.

● Largely herbivorous fish such as tilapia, catfish, red and sockeye salmon, and wild trout are less likely to be contaminated, as are deep-water fish such as sardines.

● When cleaning the fish, remove as much surface fat as possible, since this is where the bulk of the chemical contaminants are stored.

● The way the fish is cooked can help to reduce the traces of chemicals in the body fat, skin, and muscle tissue: grilling, baking, and steaming allow the juices and fats to run off, whereas frying and making soups reserve the fat.

READING THE LABEL

Foods contain additives for several reasons: to replace the nutritional value lost in processing; to enhance their texture or appearance; and to offer a longer shelf-life, or to facilitate the preparation of the processed food. It is not always possible to tell from reading the food product label whether the additives come from natural or chemical sources, since this is not a legal requirement. The best advice I can offer to the consumer is to choose a product labeled as "natural," although labeling is not necessarily 100 percent accurate .

FOOD ADDITIVES

Producers do not have to declare whether pesticides have been used in the cultivation of fresh fruits and vegetables, and the law does not require many additives in processed foods to be labeled as such. The fact that substances are "approved" by government agencies does not always mean that they are safe, since the long-term effects may not have been fully tested.

IRRADIATION

Some foods are irradiated with a dose of radiation about 60 million times that of a chest X-ray. This is to kill insects and bacteria, and to prevent sprouting and slow rotting. It destroys at least 10 percent of the vitamin content, and alters the chemical structure of the food. No long-term safety studies have been carried out, although irradiation is suspected of causing leukemia and other cancers in humans, and kidney disease. In many countries, all irradiated food must be labeled as such: look for the logo, and, where possible, try to avoid all irradiated foodstuffs.

NATURAL ADDITIVES

The following additives come from natural plant and animal sources and are a safe alternative to chemical additives and colorings. Look for them in the ingredients list on the label.

- Acetic acid (vinegar)
- Sodium chloride (salt)
- Albumen (from egg white)
- Annatto (an extract from a rainforest tree)
- Beta-carotene (from carrots)
- Citric acid (from citrus fruits)
- Dextrose (from corn sugar)
- Guar gum (from a seed grown in India)
- Gum tragacanth (from a thorny shrub native to the Middle East)
- Lactic acid (from whey, cornstarch, potatoes, and molasses)
- Lecithin (a substance occurring naturally in eggs, soybeans, and corn)

Agar-agar, carrageenan, dulse, and aginates from seaweed contain valuable minerals and flavor food naturally.

ADDITIVES TO AVOID

Read packaging carefully and try to avoid the following.

SULFITES

These additives are used in foods to prevent spoiling and discoloration, and are listed as sulfur dioxide, sodium sulfite, sodium and potassium bisulfite or metabisulfite. They can trigger severe allergic reactions, including nausea and vomiting, breathing difficulties, and abdominal pain. Asthmatics are especially susceptible. Sulfites are found in wine, shellfish, fruits and vegetables, salad dressings, sauces, and corn syrup. They may be used in self-service salad bars to keep food looking fresh. In the US, foods to be eaten raw may not be treated with sulfites.

NITRATES & NITRITES

These additives are used to enhance color and inhibit the growth of the botulism bacteria in cured meats (especially pork), fish and cheese, sausages, luncheon meats, and hot dogs. A percentage of nitrates convert to nitrites once ingested, which may then combine with amines (proteins in food) to form carcinogenic nitrosamines. However, there is as yet no compelling evidence that eating nitrates or nitrites poses a risk to humans.

ARTIFICIAL COLORS & FLAVORINGS

Almost all artificial colorings have been shown to be carcinogenic in animals. The observations of doctors and parents have been that when artificial colorings and flavorings are avoided, children's hyperactivity and other behavioral problems improve significantly.

MSG

Monosodium glutamate is a flavor enhancer often used in Chinese restaurant food. It can cause headaches, cold sweats, and heart palpitations. Studies show that MSG can cause brain damage and female sterility in animals.

EDTA

Ethylenediaminetetraacetic acid is used as a preservative in processed foods, and may have toxic effects. Symptoms recorded by those with high exposure to it include dizziness, headaches, sneezing, nausea, and asthma attacks.

Salt and sugar are natural additives. Use them in moderation and avoid processed foods, which contain high quantities of both.

E-NUMBERS

There is a complete list of e-numbers—European Union permitted additives—available on the internet (*see Resources page 169*). The ones listed here have been linked to health problems, including asthma.

E 100–180 (coloring agents)
E 102 (the yellow coloring tartrazine, which is linked to allergies and adverse reactions)
E 200–290 (preservatives)
E 300–322 (antioxidants)
E 400–495 (emulsifiers and stabilizers)
E 420–421 (sweeteners)
E 173 (aluminum, which has been linked to senile dementia and Alzheimer's disease)

GENETICALLY MODIFIED (GM) FOODS

Genetically engineering food means manipulating DNA to increase yield and strengthen resistance to disease. In plants this helps to control pests and weeds and to enhance nutritional value. However, many people are concerned about the impact GM crops could have on wildlife because they disturb the natural ecological balance, and about the transfer of genetic modifications to wild plant species. The long-term effects on humans of eating GM foods is not yet known. If you want to avoid them, look for "GM-free" or "no GMOs" labels on foods.

WHAT WE DRINK

Water is vital to good health: after all, the human body is made up of over 70 percent water. Although the water that comes out of your faucet is treated to make it as safe as possible to drink (*see page 15*), these measures by no means remove all contaminants. In some countries (the United States, Australia, New Zealand, and parts of Europe), the water is also fluoridated to prevent tooth decay, but there are concerns about the long-term health effects of fluoridation.

CONTAMINANTS IN THE WATER SUPPLY

According to the Worldwatch Institute, it is more important now than ever before to protect the water supply from chemical abuse. Groundwater pollution is effectively permanent. It is not uncommon for the contaminants listed below to be found in public water supplies. Between them, these contaminants have been found to cause birth defects; reproductive system damage; cancer; liver, kidney and nervous system damage; and gastroenteric diseases. But it isn't all bad news—over 95 percent of these chemicals can be removed by using water filters.

WATER DISINFECTANTS
The most widely used is chlorine, but chloramine and chlorine dioxide, weaker forms of chlorine, may also be used. They are all known irritants. Of particular concern is the reaction of chlorine with organic matter in the water to produce disinfectant by-products such as trihalomethanes (including chloroform), dangerous compounds that have been linked to cancer.

VOLATILE ORGANIC COMPOUNDS (VOCS)
These derive mainly from industrial chemicals and solvents (e.g., benzene, toluene, vinyl chloride), and also from household cleaning products.

TRACE METALS
These include heavy metals such as lead, mercury, arsenic, aluminum, cadmium, copper, chromium, and the radiological contaminant radon.

SYNTHETIC ORGANIC CHEMICALS
Drinking water may contain many synthetic organic chemicals (*see page 93*). High levels of nitrates from fertilizers are a concern; they are linked to a number of health risks.

MICROBES
Two harmful microbes found in drinking water are the parasites *Cryptosporidium* and *Giardia*; both cause gastric illness.

HOW SAFE IS BOTTLED WATER?

European standards for factory bottled water are lower than for tap water. Federal rules specify no protection of bottled water sources, although they do have water quality standards for tap water.

● Disinfection to eliminate contaminants is common, adding extra chemicals such as chlorine, which can create by-products.
● Bottled water may not be fresh: in many countries there is no legal requirement to put an expiration date on the label.
● Many manufacturers use plastic bottles that leach polymers into the water, are not degradable, and sit in landfill sites.
● Fluoride levels can be five times higher than in tap water.

FILTER YOUR WATER

Health experts recommend drinking 2–4 pints (1–2 liters) of water per day. Water company data will tell you the quality of our water as it leaves the treatment plant but not as it comes out of your tap, so it makes sense to filter it.

ASSESSING WATER QUALITY

Find out the answers to these questions to help you decide what kind of water purification system you need (*see below*).
● Where does your water come from?
● Are you near industrial sites that emit toxic waste, or agricultural land that uses pesticides and fertilizers?
● Is your water carried into your home by lead piping?
● Is chlorine used to disinfect it? Is it fluoridated?

Herbal infusions use boiling water and are a purer way of drinking tap water.

CARBON FILTRATION

All activated carbon filtration systems—water-pitcher filters, countertop and undersink filters—will remove chlorine and its by-products, organic chemicals, and VOCs, and improve the taste of your water. They may include an ion-exchange resin that will sift out heavy metals such as lead and aluminum. They will not remove fluoride, nitrates, or microbes. However, systems with solid carbon block filters (often the plumbed-in variety) that have a very small pore size will filter out certain microbes.

REVERSE OSMOSIS

The most effective systems filter water through activated carbon and then a semi-permeable membrane that rejects minerals, trace metals, fluoride, nitrates, microbes, and a range of other impurities, while improving flavor.

COFFEE & TEA

Use unbleached coffee filter papers for preference, or opt for white, oxygen-cleansed ones.

Tea and coffee are both popular alternatives to drinking a glass of water. But remember, both contain caffeine and are mildly diuretic.

● Tea plantations use many pesticides, some of them very toxic and banned in the West.
● Many tea bags are bleached using chlorine, and may leach dioxins into your tea. Use loose leaf teas and a teapot instead.
● Green tea is healthier than black tea because it is not fermented, and so contains numerous vitamins and minerals. Medical research shows that green tea prevents tooth decay, reduces halitosis, and boosts the immune system against the flu, some cancers, and heart disease.

● Many coffee plantations use pesticides that are banned in the US and Europe. These pollute local water supplies and damage the health of the plantation workers.
● Instant coffee may contain artificial flavors.
● Decaffeinated coffee may be processed with the solvents hexane, a component of which is known to cause nerve damage, and methylene chloride, which is also found in paint remover and is a probable human carcinogen. Choose water-processed brands.

FOOD SUPPLIERS

Food buying has become increasingly centered on the supermarket, since it is an easy and convenient way to shop. Because most people prefer to shop for a week's food supply in one trip, and many people live a long way from the nearest store, supermarket shopping is geared around the car—an unecological factor in more ways than simple use of gas. One of the attractions of the supermarket is the enormous choice on the shelves. However, many of the goods will have been transported from all over the world, and, to arrive "fresh," will have used up electricity for refrigeration, preservatives, and aviation fuel. In addition supermarkets factor in a staggering margin of waste: huge quantities of perishable foods are disposed of once their shelf-life is over.

HOW TO SHOP ECOLOGICALLY

Use the supermarket when you need to, but also consider some of the alternatives listed here. Smaller food outlets will tend to specialize, offering quality over quantity.

Plan to buy locally produced foods in season, when they are plentiful, offer the best quality , and are inexpensive.

SHOP LOCALLY
If possible, walk or cycle to the store instead of taking the car, and use farmers' markets and specialty stores. This may save time by avoiding traffic jams and long supermarket checkout lines. It also saves gas and delivery costs, keeps local people in business, and supports the community. This kind of shopping is more personal. Shopping little and often means less waste and fresher food.

BUY LOCAL PRODUCE
Farmers' markets are taking an increasing share of the food business, and local producers still sell produce and make cheeses or sell cream from local dairy farms. There are no middlemen involved, so their prices are often lower.

PROMOTE BIODIVERSITY
Choose old-fashioned or unusual varieties of fruits and vegetables, and buy meat from farmers who raise rare breed livestock.

ORGANIC BOX DELIVERY
There are many local organic home delivery services now available. You simply call, fax, or email your order to the supplier, and it arrives

on your doorstep at the arranged hour. This saves you time and fuel, and it is much more economical for one van to deliver to many addresses. Your local supermarket may even have such a program. If you do join a delivery service, ask for organic and GM-free products—businesses respond to consumer demand.

FAIR TRADE GOODS

Whenever possible, buy food produce displaying the "Fair Trade" label (*see Resources page 169*). A number of products, such as coffee, tea, chocolate, bananas, sugar, honey, cookies, cocoa powder, orange juice, granola, rice, and dried fruits are all available, and the range is expanding all the time.

ORGANIC SUPERMARKETS

Increasingly, there are a number of specialized organic supermarkets opening in some areas. Although they are more expensive than regular supermarkets, you can be sure that all the produce has been carefully sourced from high-quality organic suppliers.

READ THE LABEL

When shopping for food, always read the label carefully (*see pages 96–97*). Select items that are low in or free from additives and preservatives and synthetic food colorants, are not highly packaged, or are packaged in recyclable material such as paper rather than plastic. Ask for unbleached coffee filters, tissues, toilet paper,

and diapers that are chlorine-free. Consumer demand is making these products much more common.

Demand for unusual varieties of popular fruits and vegetables (here, sprouting broccoli) ensure biodiversity.

SHOPPING FOR SEASONAL FRUITS AND VEGETABLES

Generally speaking, you will get the best flavor when buying in season. This at-a-glance table will help you see the best time of year to buy certain fruits and vegetables to ensure that they are fresh: there will be variations according to local produce in particular climates, and in some cases produce may be imported.

WINTER	SPRING	Carrots	Spinach
Beets	Artichokes	Cauliflower	Sweet peppers
Brussels sprouts	Asparagus	Cherries	Tomatoes
Cabbage	Cauliflower	Corn	Zucchini
Cauliflower	Chicory	Corn salad	
Celery	Mushrooms	Cucumbers	FALL
Jerusalem artichokes	New potatoes	Fava beans	Apples
Leeks	Radishes	French beans	Beets
Onions	Shallots	Garlic	Broccoli
Parsnips	Sorrel	Herbs	Brussels sprouts
Potatoes	Watercress	Lettuce	Cabbage
Rutabagas		New potatoes	Celery
Winter squash	SUMMER	Peaches	Fennel
	Apples	Peas	Pears
	Apricots	Pole beans	Plums
	Artichokes	Snow peas	Spinach
	Bok choy	Soft berries	Squash

FOOD PACKAGING

In spite of the fact that it is a legal requirement that packaging should not harm health or affect food quality, the following information points out where packaging issues are still a problem.

LEAD-SOLDERED CANS

Although lead-soldered cans for food are banned, old or illegally imported lead-soldered cans may still occasionally find their way onto shelves. These cans are easy to recognize because they have a top and bottom rim, and a soldered side seam that has small dents along it. (Lead-free cans are either seamless or welded with a dark paint line along the seam.) The lead leaches into the food, which can lead to neurological damage. Behavioral problems in children, such as hyperactivity, have been associated with lead content in food.

Fresh produce bought direct from a food co-op is not sealed in plastic, which has health and packaging advantages.

PLASTIC PACKAGING

Plastic-coated cans may leach plastic molecules into the foods they contain, while processed foods are frequently packaged in layers of plastic.

Chemicals in plastics may also migrate into food when heated, which is often the case with microwave convenience foods. The health effects of plastic residues in food are unknown.

CHOOSING WINE & BEER

There is evidence that moderate amounts of wine and beer are good for your health, and may help to prevent heart disease and strokes. However, as with food, nonorganic wines and beers may contain a range of additives and contaminants.

WINE
- There is no legal requirement to list the ingredients that go into wine, so it is a good idea to choose brands that voluntarily do so.
- Wines themselves often contain up to 20 additives to enhance their taste, flavor, and color.
- The sulfites sometimes added to inhibit oxidation and spoilage in nonorganic wines can cause allergic reactions. However, sulfite is formed naturally during the fermentation process, so it cannot be avoided completely.
- Grapes for nonorganic winemaking are commonly treated with about a dozen applications of pesticides in the growing season. Buying wine made with organic grapes ensures a pesticide-free product.
- Organic vineyards maintain a healthy balance in the soil.
- Biodynamic viticulture is an organic approach that uses special homeopathic sprays and the movements of the planets in the cultivation process.

BEER
- As with wines, nonorganic beers are made from hops sprayed with chemicals, and have artificial flavorings and colorings added.
- Organic beers are available. Some are additive-free, and will be labeled as such.
- Buying locally brewed draft beer saves on the transportation, processing, and bottling that bottled beers undergo.
- Try brewing your own beer. It is fun and saves money.

PLANNING YOUR SHOPPING

The following tips are intended to help you plan your shopping more efficiently and help build up a pantry of essential items so that you do not have to waste energy on unnecessary trips to the grocery.

- Buy nonperishable goods in bulk: rice, beans, pasta, flour, and seeds, toilet paper, canned goods, and cleaning products all fall into this category. Bulk-buying cuts down on packaging, saves money, and reduces the number of shopping trips you make.
- Make sure dried foods are stored in a cool, dry, pest-free environment to keep them in good condition.
- Keep a running shopping list, adding to it when you are aware that items are getting low. Make sure your whole family is involved in this to make managing the household simpler. Using a shopping list means that you will not be tempted to buy foods that you don't need, which will cut down on waste.
- Some perishable goods such as bread, milk, and butter can be frozen, so store them in bulk in the freezer. Freezing sliced bread keeps it fresh, and you can remove it one slice at a time for toasting.
- Consider sharing trips to the supermarket with a friend or neighbor—it will halve your fuel costs as well as help to reduce pollution.

Essential cooking ingredients such as flour can be stored in bulk. Once opened, store in an airtight glass jar.

WILD FOODS

Throughout the year it is possible to gather wild produce from many natural habitats, and so make the most of "food for free."

- A suitable field guide to wild plants will help you to find and identify the many edible herbs and leafy plants that can be harvested wild. In the fall, make the most of fruits and nuts that grow wild in fields, hedges, and woodland.
- Pick wild foods as far away from main roads as possible, to avoid contamination from exhaust fumes.
- If you are unsure that you have correctly identified a wild food, it is best to leave the plant alone. Some wild plants are poisonous.
- Always get the property owner's permission before you pick foods from any public or private land.

Always check with an expert before eating wild mushrooms you have found. Chanterelle mushrooms, shown here, are safe to eat, and are easy to identify by their distinctive yellow gills.

GROW YOUR OWN

You don't need to be an experienced gardener to grow your own organic vegetables and fruits. Just by following some basic guidelines you can grow fresh seasonal food, safe in the knowledge that they are free of chemical residues. Surprising amounts can be grown in a small space, and a neat vegetable patch can be as attractive as a flower border.

Pea plants will climb up bamboo canes and produce beautiful flowers.

CHOOSING A SITE

For successful results and good harvest yields, take time to choose the right position in your garden for growing fresh produce, following the guidelines below.

● Choose a sunny site that is not overshadowed by tall trees so that your crop is not in shade, which may inhibit growth.
● Choose a sheltered site that is not exposed to winds.
● Check the soil type with a soil test kit (*see Resources page 169*): vegetables do not grow well in acid soil. If your soil is on the acid side, you can make it more alkaline by applying ground limestone.
● Ideally, the soil needs to be dark and crumbly to at least the depth of your shovel: if it is heavy clay, you will need to lighten and improve it by adding layers of organic compost to create new topsoil.

For best results, begin this process in the fall so that the soil is ready for planting the following spring (*see below*).
● Vegetables need plenty of water to grow. Make sure that you have easy access to a garden hose or—better still—use a rain barrel to collect fresh rainwater (*see page 15*).

PREPARING THE GROUND

Leeks prefer a well-drained, relatively fertile soil, but do not overfertilize.

Whatever soil type you have, vegetables are hungry plants. Feed the soil with well-rotted manure in the fall and spring and take time to prepare the site before planting.

● To clear the ground, break up the soil with a fork to aerate it, and clear it of weeds.
● Cover the ground with black plastic or a mulch to prevent more weeds from growing before you plant.
● On difficult or poor soils, create a raised bed for growing vegetables, and fill with organic compost to improve the soil quality. Use gravel boards to contain the new soil in the beds.

● Mix manure or compost into the top 8 in (20 cm) of the soil.
● Dig in or top-dress with your own household compost (*see pages 82–83*), using two wheelbarrow loads for every 12 square yards (10 square meters).
● Leaf mold is much lower in nutrients than manure, so it is excellent for growing root vegetables such as carrots and parsnips, which prefer less rich soil conditions.

WHAT VEGETABLES TO GROW

By growing your own vegetables organically, you will have nutrient-rich, healthy food delivered straight to your table at a fraction of the cost of commercial produce—and nothing beats the taste of freshly picked vegetables. The following list will help you plan your vegetable garden.

EASY VEGETABLES	CLIMBERS	FOR RICH SOILS	IN LIGHT SHADE
Jerusalem artichokes	Climbing French beans	Artichokes	(sown in midsummer)
Lettuces	Cucumbers	Brussels sprouts	Arugula
Onions and shallots	Peas	Corn	Chicory
Pole beans		Cabbage	Endive
Potatoes	FOR SMALL SPACES	Kale	Jerusalem artichokes
Pumpkins and	Baby carrots, beets,	Leeks	Lettuces
squashes	and turnips	Potatoes	Mustard and watercress
Spinach	Green onions	Pumpkins	Peas
Tomatoes	Lettuce	Squashes and zucchini	Radishes
Zucchini	Radishes	Tomatoes	Spinach

SOWING & PLANTING

You can grow vegetables from seed, or from young plants that you buy from garden centers or from mail-order catalogs. Follow the instructions on the seed packets carefully: planting too early, in cold or wet soil, may stop seeds from germinating, and tender young plants can be damaged by late frosts. Some plants, such as zucchini, do best sown in pots under glass early in the season and then planted out when a strong root system is established.

Carrots are grown from seed directly in the ground; they thrive in a sandy soil.

CROP ROTATION

Crop rotation is a key aspect of organic soil management. The principle is never to grow the same crop family in the same place in consecutive years. Rotating crops prevents pests and diseases from becoming concentrated in one area, and ensures that the nutrient requirements of different crop families are met. The main crop families are: brassicas, such as cabbages, Brussels sprouts, and rutabagas; root vegetables, such as potatoes and onions; and legumes and fruits, such as peas, beans, and zucchini.

SUCCESSION PLANTING

With fast-growing crops such as lettuces and green onions, you can plant at least two and sometimes three crops in succession over the season so that you have a continuous supply of the fresh vegetables. For example, a spring planting will be ready in summer, a summer one in the fall.

GARDENER'S DIARY

Keeping a diary is a helpful way of reminding yourself of when to sow and harvest, what varieties grew well, and where and what crops succeeded or failed: your personal experience is the best guide to planning what to grow in the year ahead.

PREPARING FOOD

The kitchen is the heart of the home, and keeping it clean and fresh the natural way is paramount. As well as ensuring basic cleanliness, there are many common sense and natural tips for hygienic food preparation that will create a safe environment and avoid the health risks associated with contamination. Bacteria can contaminate all kinds of foods, causing violent stomach upsets, diarrhea, vomiting, and headaches, and sometimes more acute illness.

KEEPING THE KITCHEN CLEAN

A clean, tidy kitchen is not only desirable for health, but also creates a more pleasant environment in which to enjoy cooking. To ensure basic kitchen hygiene, follow the simple guidelines below.

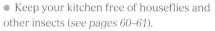

If wooden worktops become pungent, rub them with a cut lemon and the odor will disappear.

- Keep your kitchen free of houseflies and other insects (*see pages 60–61*).
- Avoid open shelving: it attracts dust. Keep kitchen equipment in cupboards and drawers.
- Keep pets off work surfaces and tables: they carry bacteria that can spread disease.
- Reserve the kitchen sink for chores connected with food only: germs left in the sink from clearing up household messes can easily contaminate food.
- Use separate cloths for different purposes to avoid cross-contamination: floor cloths should not be used to clean kitchen surfaces; dishtowels are for drying dishes, and towels for hands.
- A dishwasher gets dishes cleaner and sanitizes them. It is also more economical with water than handwashing.
- Clean out your oven and stove, refrigerator, and freezer regularly (*see page 53*).
- Dispose of kitchen waste regularly. Empty it as often as you need to, and sprinkle baking soda into the trash can to reduce odors.

Leave hand-washed glasses to dry naturally on a clean cloth. This is more hygienic than wiping them dry.

HANDLING FOOD

Maintaining adequate hygiene while handling food is crucial in preventing food-borne infections. There is nothing difficult about good hygiene practices—most are just common sense. Get into the habit of following them, and you will find they soon become second nature.

PREPARATION

- If you have cuts or scratches on your hands, use rubber gloves while preparing foods, to keep bacteria from crossing from cuts to food.
- Always wash your hands with hot water and soap and dry them thoroughly on a clean towel before handling food.
- Wash all fruits and vegetables: rinse or scrub under running water before use, especially if they have been grown with pesticides and fertilizers.
- Where the food type allows, cook food from frozen rather than defrosting it to reduce the health risk of bacteria spreading during the defrosting process.
- Clean up kitchen work surfaces as you cook to keep food preparation areas as hygienic as possible.

COOKING

- Cook foods at as high a temperature as possible, and for an adequate length of time, to neutralize harmful bacteria. The same applies to reheating leftovers.
- Always cook meat thoroughly, until the juices run clear (use a thermometer if you are unsure, or according to the instructions in a good cookbook.)

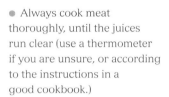

Thaw frozen foods in the refrigerator rather than at room temperature to prevent bacteria from multiplying.

SAFE COOKING: POTS & PANS

Use glass or terra-cotta dishes, and cast iron, porcelain-enamel coated, or anodized aluminum pans. Foods cooked in aluminum react with it to form aluminum salts, which dissolve when exposed to acids, such as those in tomatoes. These salts have been connected with Alzheimer's disease, dementia, and impaired motor-visual coordination. The anodizing process seals aluminum by dipping it into a hot acid bath. Stainless steel may leach toxic metals such as chromium or nickel, and scratched plastic-coated pans should not be used because they contaminate food with plastic molecules.

REFRIGERATING & FREEZING

- Keep the refrigerator temperature at around 39° F (4° C), and your freezer at 0° F (-18° C). When opening a compartment door, do so for as short a time as possible to stop cold air from escaping, and to save energy.
- Chill or freeze food rapidly, in small quantities.
- The door of the fridge is the least cold part, so do not store meat or dairy produce there.

Instead, use it for opened pickle jars, soft drinks and wine, and jams.
- Fresh food should be refrigerated as soon as possible after buying to prevent any existing bacteria from multiplying. The exception is fruit, which needs to be left out to ripen, and gourmet cheeses, whose bacterial activity (and flavor) is killed off by refrigeration.

CLEANUP & LEFTOVERS

- Thoroughly clean cutting boards after use, to prevent cross-contamination between meat, fish, vegetables, and fruit. Use a natural surface cleaner (*see page 52*), or rub with a cut lemon. To be extra-safe, use different cutting boards and utensils for meat, fish, and vegetables or fruit.
- Chill leftovers immediately: botulism can develop if cooked food is allowed to remain at room temperature overnight—as could happen with, say, a slightly warm, leftover baked potato, or vegetables wrapped tightly in foil.

STORING & COOKING

Plastic wrap has revolutionized the way food is packaged and stored. Food is kept fresher for longer because the plastic food wrap stops oxygen from reaching food, preventing

spoilage. However, plasticizers in some food wraps may migrate into food, which has raised health concerns. Healthy cooking, such as steaming and grilling, is also energy-efficient cooking. Cooking can account for up to 10 percent of your total energy costs, so it makes sense to develop good cooking practices.

ALTERNATIVES TO PLASTIC

The jury is still out on the effect of plastics on storing food. Some plastic wraps and containers contain the plasticizer di-(2-ethylhexyl) adipate, or DEHA, which leaches into food, and especially into high-fat food such as cheese and meat. It is a known hormone disrupter and health hazard, although safety levels are still being researched. Food storage containers labeled "polyethylene" do not contain DEHA and the Food and Drug Administration has affirmed the safety of polycarbonate used in food packaging. This does not, however, guarantee its safety. The fact is that plastics can leach into food, and you may be unwittingly ingesting molecules of plastic. The following guidelines suggest some useful alternatives for storing fresh food, as well as ways to use plastic wrap safely.

SAFE SOLUTIONS

● Use glass jars and containers instead of plastic ones. Save jam, honey, and pickle jars of all sizes, preferably ones with metal, not plastic, lids.
● Some natural food stores offer cellophane bags rather than plastic ones, so save these for storing food at home.
● When you do put plastic wrap over food, make sure that the plastic does not touch the food directly or remain in contact with it for long periods, to avoid contamination.
● Avoid microwaving foods covered with plastic wrap, or food stored in margarine tubs or cottage cheese cartons that are not heat-stable at high temperatures. These plastics can melt or warp, causing toxic chemicals to leach into the food as it cooks.

Wrap produce such as cheese, meat, fish, and poultry in wax paper, rather than plastic wrap, since it is free of toxins.

ENERGY-SAVING COOKING

When choosing an oven, opt for a fan, or convection, oven, which uses one-third less energy than standard ovens. Self-cleaning ovens, which have extra insulation, also consume less energy, but don't use the self-cleaning feature more than once a month. Cooking for short periods of time on top of the stove is the most energy-efficient of all.

- Cooking in bulk for the freezer is energy-efficient and means that you can make the best use of seasonal produce. However, do not freeze dishes containing zucchini, mushrooms, tomatoes, squash, or summer berries: they lose flavor and texture when frozen due to their high water content.
- Chest freezers are more economical than upright models, and freezers function more efficiently when defrosted regularly. A freezer kept in a cool garage uses less energy to keep cold.
- The most energy-efficient method of cooking is with a stack-steamer. You can cook fish and vegetables in it at the same time—and quickly. You can also save fuel by turning the heat off before the end of the cooking time, since the steam continues to rise off the hot water.
- Cover pots and pans with a lid to reduce cooking time and save energy.
- Use the right size of electric ring or gas burner for your pan—too large a plate or ring wastes energy.
- Cook as many items as possible in the oven at once, to reduce the number of dishes that need to be cooked separately.
- Grilling meat uses far less heat than roasting or baking.
- Raw foods require only your own energy to prepare them: salads make healthy meals.
- Microwaving food is quick and not energy-intensive, although the safety or

Eating raw foods is good for you, and saves on fuel consumption too.

otherwise of exposure to microwave emissions is not yet established.
- Keep your teakettle free of lime, since furred-up kettles take longer to boil and use up more energy.

POWER OUTAGES

During a power outage, a full freezer will continue to keep food frozen for as long as two days—one day if it is half-full. A refrigerator will continue to keep food chilled for about 4–5 hours, depending on the ambient temperature. Keep the door closed during the blackout. Throw out any meat, fish, milk, poultry, or leftovers beyond that time.

Fresh vegetables cut into attractive julienne strips cook more quickly and save energy.

PERSONAL CARE

Personal care products based on natural and—increasingly—organic ingredients constitute an expanding segment of the beauty market. People are more aware than ever of health issues, animal rights, and environmental concerns when buying cosmetics and toiletries.

PRODUCT MANUFACTURING

The beauty industry is big business and every year 100,000 tons of chemicals are used to make products. Most cosmetics contain additives and preservatives, and they may also include genetically modified ingredients. Some of these contents may be absorbed directly into the bloodstream through the skin during application, and then accumulate in the body tissue. Over 99 percent of oils used in cosmetics are based on petrochemicals, or on chemically extracted and refined plant oils that have been bleached and deodorized, their vitamins removed. There is increasingly convincing evidence that regular long-term applications of such products can constitute a potentially serious health risk.

NATURAL BEAUTY

Often, products can be labeled "natural" provided at least 1 percent of their ingredients are from natural sources. Ingredients are often listed in small print, or even sealed inside the packaging, so that they cannot be read before you buy the product. You do not have to buy all your beauty care items, however: to be really sure of what you are putting on your body, there are simple ways of making your own products with pure and natural ingredients.

Toothpastes made with natural ingredients such as fennel and eucalyptus are now available.

Natural skin treats p116

Body care p119

Foot cream recipe p123

Natural deodorants p125

UNDERSTANDING LABELS

The cosmetics and toiletries industry is only partially regulated. The European Union prohibits the use of over 700 ingredients, while the INCI (International Nomenclature of Cosmetic Ingredients) lists restricted chemicals, yet of the 3,000 registered chemicals companies may legally use in their products, only limited research has been carried out on many of them. Furthermore, legislation on labeling is not universal, and does not apply to some soaps, toothpastes, deodorants, sunscreens, and shampoos. American law requires that the ingredients, but not the finished cosmetic product, be tested for safety before they are released to the marketplace.

Check the contents of soaps before purchase—many contain artificial fragrances, colors, and preservatives.

CHEMICALS TO AVOID

The following ingredients found in beauty products are best avoided or used only occasionally. Check the product label first before buying or using.

PETROCHEMICAL-BASED PRODUCTS
Products based on petrochemicals are widely used in cosmetics. Mineral oils, petrolatum (also known as mineral oil jelly), paraffin, and any ingredient that has the prefix propyl-, methyl-, or ethe- are used in products to "hydrate" the skin. However, because they cannot be absorbed through the skin but sit on the surface, in the process they block the skin's natural function of respiration, inhibiting its ability to eliminate toxins. Petrolatum may cause drying and premature aging of the skin, and strip the

Most natural toothpastes do not use sodium lauryl sulfate, a foaming agent that is an irritant to mucous membranes.

skin of its lubricating oils. Propylene glycol is used to improve foundations and moisturizers: it is also found in antifreeze. It is known to cause cancer in rats. Benzyl alcohol (used in both ballpoint pens and perfume) is an irritant to skin and mucous membranes.

SODIUM LAURYL SULFATE (SLS)
This detergent and foaming agent is found in engine degreasers and harsh cleansing solutions. It is used in bath and shower gels and shampoos, cleansers, and most toothpastes. It can cause skin rashes, hair loss, and eye damage.

DEA, TEA, & MEA
Diethanolaminooleamide, triethanolamine, and monoethanolamine are ammonia derivatives found in foams, shower gels, body lotions, moisturizers, and facial cleaners. Their chemical function is to bind oil and water together and act as detergents. They are known allergens.

PPD
Paraphenylene-diamine, used to produce the black color in hair dyes, can cause allergic reactions and is linked to certain cancers.

PARABENS

Methylparaben and propylparaben are petrochemical-based preservatives used to extend the shelf-life of water-based products and inhibit bacterial growth. They are irritants, yet are found in virtually all toiletries, some toothpastes, and deodorants. They mimic estrogens and have been linked to breast and testicular cancer, prostate disorders, and sperm abnormalities.

FORMALDEHYDE

This chemical toxin is found in cosmetic preservatives. As a cosmetic ingredient, it is not easy to recognize, since it is associated with the additives 2-bromo-2-nitropropane, 3-diol Diazolidinyl urea, DMDM hydantoin, or quaternium-15. It is widely used in shampoos and handwashes, and some nail hardeners. In Sweden and Japan, its use in cosmetics has been banned.

Organic or homemade creams and lotions avoid the use of potentially harmful synthetic ingredients.

DBP & DEP

Dibutylphthalate and diethylphthalate are toxic and highly allergenic chemicals that cause birth defects in rats, yet may be used in skin creams to enhance absorption and as emollients and humidifiers. In nail polish and mascara, they are used to create a flexible film.

ARTIFICIAL COLORS

Known as FD&C Blue 1, Green 3, D&C Red 33, and FD&C Yellow 5 and 6, these artificial colors are potential carcinogens and can damage blood platelets and bone marrow. Carmine can cause allergic reactions.

KATHON GC

This preservative is thought to damage cell growth in ways that may lead to cancer. It is often found listed on shampoos and hair conditioners.

AHAs & BHAs

Alpha-hydroxy acids and beta-hydroxy acids are used as moisturizers in skin creams, dandruff shampoos, and foundations with sunscreens. Little research has been done on them, but they are suspected of increasing cell turnover and decreasing the thickness of the outer skin, making it more sensitive to the sun's rays.

LANOLIN

Although this natural emollient for softening and moisturizing the skin derives from sheep's wool, it can be contaminated in its cosmetic grade. Known contaminants include pesticides such as DDT, lindane, and dieldrin. Creams and lipsticks with lanolin can cause acne.

UNDERSTAND THE JARGON

• "Natural" has no legal or scientific definition. To be labeled as such, a product need contain only 1 percent natural ingredients.
• "Naturally inspired" is equally unspecific.
• "Organic" is the only definition that actually means "chemical-free."
• "Hypoallergenic" is an equally meaningless term because allergies are individual: what this actually means is that the most common allergens, such as fragrance, lanolin, cocoa butter, cornstarch, and cottonseed oils, are removed from the product.
• "Dermatologically tested" has no approved definition and may mean sanctioned by a dermatologist with no national or legal recognition.

PERSULFATE SALTS

These act as boosting agents in hair bleaches and have been linked to occupational asthma among hairdressers. They may also be present in over-the-counter bleaching products.

CHEMICAL UV FILTERS

Sunscreen chemicals such as octyl methoxycinnamate and octyl dimethyl PABA can cause allergic reactions, eczema, rashes, and swellings and may contribute to skin aging.

ARTIFICIAL FRAGRANCES

(see page 124)

SKIN CARE

About 60 percent of any substance applied directly to the skin surface is readily absorbed, so our bodies may take in up to 4.4 lb (2 kg) chemicals every year through this largest organ of the body. Since the effects of many of the chemicals added to toiletries and cosmetics are either unknown or toxic, it makes sense to use skin care products that are derived from natural ingredients. Many organic beauty products use only natural pigments and preservatives, and natural oils from plants grown without pesticides or artificial fertilizers (*see Resources page 170*).

Fragrance-free, natural skin cream is available from good health stores. Add a few drops of essential oil to scent it.

IS IT NATURAL?

Most of us are familiar with natural beauty ingredients such as almond oil, witch hazel, and rose water. However, the labels of natural products often list more mysterious items such as capyrlic or capric triglyceride. Equally, some people may be concerned about using products derived from animal sources. Certain items, such as glycerine or stearic acid, may come from either an animal or a plant source.

ALLANTOIN
A by-product of uric acid obtained from animals. A plant-based alternative is made from comfrey root; it protects, softens, and heals.

COCONUT DERIVATIVES
The coconut is a rich source of ingredients for natural skin care products. Coconut-based cleansers include cocomide DEA, cocamidopropyl betaine, and glyceryl cocate. Many animal-derived ingredients can also be made from coconut. These include the emulsifier and emollients caprylic/capric triglyceride, cetyl alcohol, and cetearyl alcohol.

EMULSIFYING WAX
A wax used to disperse the oil and water in ointments. This is usually made from animal fats, but vegetable-derived forms are available.

GLYCERINE
Obtained from oils and fats, this is an excellent moisturizer and emollient. Vegetable glycerine is available, but most is made from animal fat as a by-product of soap manufacturing. Glyceryl stearate is derived from glycerine and stearic acid (*see opposite*). It is used in beauty products to soothe and soften, and is an effective emulsifier.

POTASSIUM SORBATE
Also known as K-sorbate, this plant-based preservative is derived from sorbic acid and is used in small amounts as an antimicrobial and antifungal agent in cosmetics.

SODIUM BENZOATE
A food-grade preservative that occurs naturally in many plants. It is also antiseptic.

STEARIC ACID
This is most commonly derived from the fat of sheep or cattle, but a vegetable source from the palm or coconut is also available. It soothes, softens, and emulsifies. Stearyl alcohol is prepared from cetyl alcohol and stearic acid and fulfills a similar emulsifying role.

TOCOPHEROL
Commonly known as vitamin E, this antioxidant fights free radicals and improves skin condition. It also acts as a natural preservative. It may appear on the label as D-alpha tocopherol.

IMPROVING SKIN CONDITION

For a naturally healthy complexion, you do not have to resort to a cocktail of products. Enjoying a good diet rich in fresh fruits and vegetables, drinking plenty of water, getting regular exercise, and sleeping well all do wonders for improving the tone and appearance of the skin. Simply follow the guidelines outlined below.

- Follow a healthy diet of fresh organic ingredients (*see pages 90–91*) to give the skin the nutrients and natural oils on which it thrives.
- Get regular, moderate exercise—just brisk walking several times a week in the fresh air makes a substantial difference to your circulation and metabolism, improving the appearance of the skin.
- Do facial exercises: tensing and relaxing cheek muscles helps to improve skin tone.
- Try meditation, relaxation, and breathing exercises to relax the face and oxygenate the bloodstream.
- Don't underestimate the benefits of regular, restful sleep. Get plenty of it.
- Buy natural oils and skin care products based on 100 percent organic ingredients.
- Don't smoke: cigarettes dehydrate the skin and encourage wrinkles.
- Avoid excess alcohol—it dehydrates the skin, strips cells of vital moisture and causes premature aging.
- Avoid too much caffeine, which depletes the skin of some vitamins and minerals.
- Excess salt will overload the kidneys and lead to fluid retention. It can contribute to dark circles under the eyes and cellulite on the arms and legs.
- Skin blemishes and disorders such as acne are often linked to a diet too rich in refined sugar.
- Avoid petroleum-based mineral oil products, which may dry out the skin.
- Get away from the city when possible: man-made chemicals in urban and industrial areas pollute the skin and body as well as the environment.

Drink plenty of filtered water (*see page 99*), at least 2 pints (1 liter) a day. Human beings are made up of over 70 percent water, and the skin is the largest organ of the body. It is thirsty.

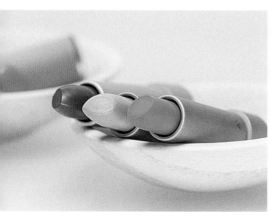

Natural lipsticks are free of chemical coloring pigments and fragrances, and are available using ingredients such as beeswax, mineral pigments, and essential oils.

MAKEUP FOR HEALTH

Perhaps the most toxic of all cosmetic products is lipstick, because it is applied regularly to the thinner skin on the lips and so is easily absorbed. Commercially produced lipsticks may contain PVP (polyvinylpyrrolidone), saccharin, and artificial colors and fragrances (*see page 124*).

Mascara can also be a problem since it may contain formaldehyde, alcohol, DBP, and some plastic resins that can cause irritation, redness, burning, and swelling. Foundation also contains artificial colors and fragrances. Buy makeup made with natural mineral pigments and organic materials (*see Resources page 170*).

HOMEMADE SKIN TREATMENTS

A whole range of fresh, edible ingredients from your pantry and refrigerator can be used to make natural and effective beauty treatments that are free of chemicals.

Apple cider vinegar, rose water, almond oil, vegetable glycerine, avocado, green clay, and yogurt are all you need to keep your skin clean, soft, and supple.

- Use plain natural organic yogurt as a daily skin cleanser. Apply with your fingertips, then rinse off with lukewarm water.
- Organic apple cider vinegar makes a superb skin toner. Moisten a cotton ball with vinegar and dab it on to the skin. Rinse with water.
- Rose water also makes a good skin toner, especially for mature skins. Moisten a cotton ball and dab the rose water onto the skin.
- Mix equal parts of vegetable glycerine, available from most drugstores, and water, for a softening skin moisturizer.
- Buy pure, untreated organic lanolin from a natural health store and apply a small amount to dry skin once or twice a week: this rich oil is extracted from sheep's wool and nourishes the skin. Some people are mildly allergic to lanolin, so do not continue to use it if you find that it irritates your skin.
- If your skin is very dry, dab pure almond oil, or peach, avocado, or even a light olive oil onto the face at least once or twice a week. This will replenish the skin's natural oils and soften and moisturize it.
- Cut the top off a capsule of vitamin E and apply to the delicate skin under the eyes to soften and smooth it. This can be used at night or in the morning.

REGENERATING GREEN CLAY MASK

Green clay (*see Resources page 170*) is one of nature's best ingredients for a facial: this biomineral is a powerful agent of regeneration and leaves the skin feeling elastic, enriched, and fresh. Simply mix 2 tablespoons of green clay powder with enough filtered water to produce a smooth, creamy consistency. Apply the clay all over your face, and lie down to rest and to allow the nutrients to sink deeply into the skin. After 10–15 minutes, the clay will have hardened. Wipe it off gently with a soft damp sponge, and dab the skin with rose water on a cotton ball. Afterward, apply a natural oil if your skin needs moisturizing. Use this natural regenerating treatment once or twice a month.

STEAM FACIAL
This is excellent for deep-cleansing the skin. Stir a handful of dried herbs—calendula, chamomile, lavender, and rosemary are all good for the skin—into a bowl of hot water. Sit over the bowl with a towel over your head for about five minutes, then splash your face with cool water.

AVOCADO FACIAL

This leaves your face feeling wonderfully soft and refreshed.

YOU WILL NEED
2 Tbsp avocado
1 tsp runny honey
3–4 drops cider vinegar

Wrap a towel around your shoulders to protect your clothes, and tie back your hair to keep it off your face. Apply the mixture, avoiding the area around the eyes, and lie down for about 10–15 minutes to allow the mask to soak in and work. Then wipe off with a soft, damp cloth, rinse gently in warm water, and apply some rose water as a finishing touch to soften and smooth the skin.

1 Cut the avocado flesh into small pieces, and place in a bowl. Stir in the honey, then add the vinegar.

2 Mash the mixture with a fork until you have a creamy, smooth paste. Apply it to your face for 10–15 minutes.

OUT IN THE SUN

Getting enough sunshine is essential for physical and mental health because it aids the production of vitamin D: studies show that women who live in sunnier climates have 30–40 percent less breast cancer than those in northern regions, and that those who remain indoors out of the sun are also more likely to develop breast cancer than sun-loving women. However, on the downside, it is generally agreed that overexposure to strong sunlight can increase the risk of skin cancer. Research is continuing into the efficacy of sunscreens, but there is serious evidence that they may only protect against basal-cell or squamous cell carcinomas, and they may also contribute to the aging of the skin. Some sunscreens contain chemicals that mimic the effects of estrogens and have caused developmental problems in rats.

NATURAL SUNSCREENS

● Taking vitamin C (2 grams per day) and vitamin E (1,000 iu per day) may help protect against sunburn, according to the American Academy of Dermatology.
● Look for products that contain the UV filter oryzanol, which occurs naturally in rice bran and has enough UV absorption to be incorporated into skincare products. It is further enhanced by the addition of vitamin E to the product and can offer some UV protection. It is also a known antioxidant. (*See Resources page 170.*)
● People with the lightest skin, hair, and eyes are at greatest risk of contracting skin cancer, so if that applies to you, don't expose yourself to the sun for long periods. Wear a hat or a scarf in strong sun, or stay in the shade.
● If you get sunburned, mix a solution of baking soda and water to make a thin paste and dab onto the affected parts.
● Although some sunshine is good for you, you should avoid exposure between 10 am and 4 pm during the summer months, when the sun is at its strongest.

BODY CARE

You can avoid the hazards linked to the chemical constituents in "off-the-shelf" products for body care and personal hygiene by buying the natural organic alternatives that are now available (*see Resources page 170*). You can also make your baths and showers luxurious and aromatic using natural ingredients that are chemical-free, cost very little, and have no adverse impact on the environment. To complete the experience, use unbleached cotton towels and bathmats, and soft terry-cloth robes—then take time out to pamper yourself.

BATHS & SHOWERS

Bathing is not just about keeping clean. The whole ritual can be healing, calming, and rejuvenating, especially with the help of the right natural products.

BATHING SUGGESTIONS

The basic constituents of bubble bath are detergent and artificial fragrance. These ingredients may cause skin irritations and even vaginal and urinary tract infections. Here are some fragrant and relaxing natural alternatives to add to your bath water:

● 4 pints (2 liters) organic whole milk or buttermilk (Cleopatra's recipe for a perfect skin).

● A dash of olive oil, almond oil, or avocado oil, plus up to 5 drops fragrant essential oils or a mixture of your favorite natural fragrances, to create whatever mood you want (see pages 124–125 for essential oil ideas).

● 1 cup Epsom salts (not more than twice a week), to soften the skin beautifully and gently detoxify the body.

● A few slices of lemon to soften and bleach the skin.

● A handful of fragrant dried herbs and spices (lavender, rosemary, bay, marjoram, cloves, cardamom, allspice, cinnamon) tied in a muslin bag and soaked in the hot water to give out a fabulous fragrance.

Make your own bath oil by adding essential oils to a vegetable oil base (about 6 drops per 1 tablespoon), mixing together well. Pour into the bath and agitate the water to disperse.

SOAP

Soap is not considered to be a cosmetic, so manufacturers are not required to list its ingredients. Basic soap is usually made from animal fats, lye (sodium hydroxide), and glycerine. "Antibacterial" and "deodorant" soaps, however, can contain a host of harmful chemicals, including triclosan. Soaps may contain artificial fragrances, colors, and preservatives. Vegetable-based soaps are your best bet. They are widely available and will be clearly labeled. They are plain, unscented, and uncolored, and made from natural vegetable sources such as olive or almond oil, or vegetable glycerine.

AFTER-BATH TREATS

● To moisturize dry skin, apply a small amount of vegetable oil such as sweet almond or apricot kernel oil. Scent with a few drops of essential oil.
● For a refreshing body splash, add 3 tsp aloe vera gel, 3 tsp witch hazel, and 5 drops essential oil of your choice to ½ cup (125 ml) spring water in an atomizer. Shake before use. If you store in a cool place, it should keep for about two weeks.
● Try mixing orris root and cornstarch in equal parts for an effective powder (see also page 123).

ORAL CARE

Some toothpastes contain fluoride, sodium lauryl sulfate, PVP, saccharin, artificial flavorings, and colorings. Mouthwashes often contain ethanol, artificial colors, and ammonia, and may be labeled unsafe to swallow. For natural dental hygiene try:

● Baking soda—a dentist-approved tooth cleaner and a good plaque-fighter.
● Toothpastes based on natural ingredients that are chemical-free (see Resources page 170).
● Cold mint tea as a mouthwash.

Treat yourself to organic cotton towels and bathmats, and terry-cloth robes that contain no chemical dyes.

COTTON & TOILET PAPER

Formaldehyde, artificial fragrance, and dyes are all present in many brands of toilet tissues, which are also likely to have been bleached with chlorine and to contain dioxins, one of the most toxic chemicals. Colored toilet paper contain dyes based on artificial colors. Try to avoid these products and go for the following alternatives instead.
• Choose organic wool and recycled toilet paper that are dioxin-safe and chemical-free (see Resources page 170).
• Try to buy unscented, undyed toilet paper.

FEMININE HYGIENE

Ever since Toxic Shock Syndrome was linked to tampons, the use of certain rayons and polyesters has been banned. However, viscose rayon is still used in tampons and opinion is divided as to its toxic effect. The sterile whiteness of sanitary products may be deceptively reassuring because chlorine bleaching releases organochlorines such as dioxins. An alternative process, elemental chlorine-free bleaching (ECF), while safer, may still release minute traces of dioxins.

BUYING FEMININE HYGIENE PRODUCTS

● Purchase tampons labelled "no superabsorbent fibers."
● Use certified biodegradable organic cotton tampons, unbleached—or, as a second-best option, bleached using a chlorine-free method.
● Use sanitary pads instead of tampons, buying natural, organic, unbleached, non-perfumed varieties without plastic backings because these do not biodegrade (see Resources page 170).
● Try to find reusable cotton pads, which are becoming more widely available (see Resources page 170).

HAIR CARE

There are many chemical ingredients—often unlisted and sometimes not fully tested—in hair care products, so it is wise to buy organic, or to make your own shampoos, conditioners, and rinses using food ingredients such as lemon, cider vinegar, eggs, and herbs such as soapwort and lemon verbena. If you have permed or colored hair, make sure that your stylist uses ammonia-free products.

SHAMPOOS & CONDITIONERS

Commercial shampoos often contain Quaternium-15, which releases formaldehyde, and sodium lauryl sulfate (*see pages 112–113*). Dandruff shampoos can be particularly problematic, and may include selenium sulfide (linked to damage of internal organs) or resorcinol (may cause irritation to the eyes and skin). Shampoos may also contain the liquid plastic polymer PVP, detergents, and artificial colors and fragrances. Try to use an organic shampoo based on plant materials, or try the following alternatives.

Brushing the hair stimulates the scalp and massages it at the same time. Choose a brush that is gentle on the scalp for best results.

• Instead of using shampoo, beat an egg and massage it into the scalp. Rinse in warm water, and use the juice of half a lemon in the final rinse for added shine.

• If you have dandruff, massage pure apple juice into the scalp, leave for several minutes, then rinse off. Or mix

SOAPWORT SHAMPOO

This is suitable for all hair types. Soapwort (*Saponaria officinalis*) contains saponins, which produce a lather similar to soap. Lemon verbena gives this shampoo a delicious citrus fragrance and catnip promotes healthy hair growth. This recipe makes enough for 6–7 shampoos, and keeps 8–10 days if stored in a cool, dark place.

NATURAL HEAD LICE TREATMENT

Head lice infestation is common among children: however, prescription products and over-the-counter remedies rely on highly toxic pesticides. Instead, use an olive, neem, or coconut oil shampoo—these oils kill lice. Rinse with hot water, shampoo a second time, rinse again, then comb out the hair with a nit comb, rinsing out the comb in hot water after each sweep. Give the hair a final rinse in a bowl of hot water and cider vinegar (2 pints/1 liter water to 1 cup/250 ml vinegar.) Dry the hair, then check it again. Remove remaining nits or eggs with double-sided tape or tweezers. Repeat at least twice a week until the infestation has gone.

2 teaspoons of cider vinegar in 1 cup water and massage in.

• Rub baking soda into wet hair after shampooing, massaging it in well. Rinse out. Baking soda makes a fabulous conditioner, leaving your hair beautifully soft.

• Add cider vinegar to the final rinse to add shine.

YOU WILL NEED:

1½ Tbsp dried soapwort root, chopped

1 pint (500 ml) water

2 tsp dried lemon verbena

2 tsp dried catnip

Simmer the soapwort in water for 20 minutes. Remove from the heat, add the herbs, and cool. Strain into a bottle.

NATURAL LEMON HAIRSPRAY

Hairsprays and mousses may contain the plastic polymer PVP, formaldehyde, artificial fragrance, and alcohol, which can cause skin reactions and irritation to both the eyes and nose. Sprays may contain aerosol propellants using CFCs that damage the ozone layer. The following recipe offers a natural alternative:

YOU WILL NEED
1 lemon (or 1 orange if hair
  is very dry), chopped
1 pint (500 ml) water
1 Tbsp vodka

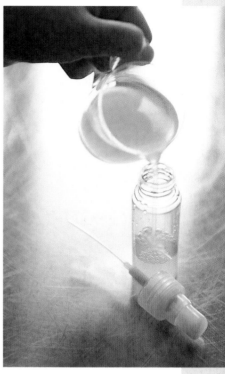

This natural hairspray relies on vodka as a preservative, which gives it a shelf-life of up to four weeks. If you keep it in the refrigerator, it should last a little longer. The spray leaves your hair feeling soft and smelling aromatic, as well as keeping it in place. For flyaway hair, you could also try an infusion of dried rosemary. Add a tablespoon of the herb to the same amount of water and simmer for 10 minutes, then strain, cool, and use.

1 Place the lemon and the water in a pan and bring to a boil. Simmer until reduced by half. Cool, then strain.

2 Add the vodka to the mixture to preserve it, then pour into a fine sprayer bottle and store in a cool place.

HAIR COLORINGS

Research into hair dyes is ongoing. In 2001, a study by the University of Southern California found that women who use permanent dyes at least once a month for one year or longer were more at risk of bladder cancer than normal. Earlier studies have found that long-serving hairstylists ran three times the normal risk of bladder and breast cancers after working with chemical hair dyes. Dark-colored, permanent dyes have been singled out for particular concern. Manufactured hair dyes are known to contain up to 20 chemicals, some of which have not been fully tested for safety and are exempt from legislation. Try these natural hair colorants instead.

● Organic hair colorings based on plant ingredients such as marigold, hibiscus, indigo, and henna are available, so seek out a hair stylist who uses them.
● Use henna to darken or highlight hair, but make sure that it is "pure."
● Have highlights ("foils") put into your hair instead of full hair color: this way the dye does not touch the scalp and penetrate the skin.
● Cold black tea and coffee make wonderful hair rinses for dark hair, both to strengthen color and to hide gray hairs. In a large bowl, pour 1 quart (1 liter) of boiling water over 3 teabags or 3 tablespoons of coffee grounds and leave until cold. Strain off and keep in the refrigerator, where it will keep for up to two weeks. Apply to dry hair and allow to dry. Reapply after each wash.
● Cold chamomile tea can be used in a similar way to highlight blonde hair.

HAND & FOOT CARE

The fashionable emphasis on manicures and pedicures in recent years has brought more people into frequent contact with numerous harsh chemicals found in nail polish and nail polish remover, many of which pose health problems. Ideally, learn to love your hands and feet in their natural state, saving polished nails for special occasions. Use the suggestions here to promote naturally soft skin and healthy, shiny nails.

NATURAL HAND CARE

It is a fairly straightforward process to make your own moisturizing hand oil or to find products in supermarkets and health food stores made from organic natural ingredients (*see Resources page 170*). Here are some homemade recipes to try out.

- Add a dash of almond oil or even plain olive oil to a sinkful of water when you wash your hands, to soften them.
- Massage a few drops of almond oil into dry hands.
- For a scented oil, add a few drops of patchouli, lemon, and lavender essential oil to ¼ cup (60 ml) of almond or jojoba oil.
- Mix equal quantities of coconut oil and vegetable glycerine in a small bottle and rub well into your hands.
- Mix 1 teaspoon honey with 2 teaspoons almond oil or olive oil and add 2 drops of lemon essential oil. Rub in well.

NAIL POLISH

The problem with nail polish is that many contain harmful chemicals such as toluene and other solvents, as well as formaldehyde resin. These substances may cause nose and throat irritations, rashes, headaches, nausea, and asthma. The worst allergic reactions are caused by the plasticizer dibutyl phthalate (DBP), which is known to cause birth defects in animals, and is especially dangerous to the male reproductive system. It is used as a coating agent in nail polishes, topcoats, and hardeners to prevent the polish from cracking, but it leaches into your skin whenever you wash your hands. In addition, nail polish remover contains acetone, a powerful solvent derived from petroleum. To limit your exposure to these chemicals, follow the guidelines below.

- Buy nail products that avoid these chemicals (*see Resources page 170*).
- If you use nail color on your toenails, use a safe water-based paint, or a polish containing as few chemicals as possible (*see Resources page 170*).
- Avoid nail hardeners and strengthen your nails and stimulate the circulation by rubbing in walnut, almond, or neem oil, scented with one or two drops of frankincense. This is also an effective cuticle softener: after massaging it in, just ease the cuticles back.

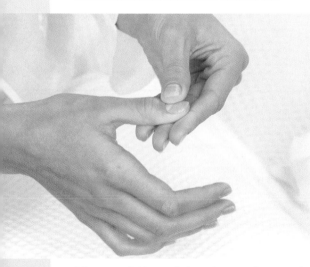

Bring a natural shine to nails by applying a small amount of vegetable or neem oil, then buffing with a nail buffer.

NATURAL FOOT CARE

Feet are often neglected and respond well to a little pampering. Caring for your feet couldn't be simpler if you use the natural products described here.

- Remove rough or dead skin by rubbing with pumice stone (natural volcanic silicate).
- Massage small amounts of almond oil into toenails to strengthen them and keep them from drying out.
- Treat your feet to a refreshing massage with 4 teaspoons (20 ml) of almond oil mixed with 6 drops of peppermint essential oil.

FOOT CREAM

This light, scented cream will keep for about six months if stored in a cool, dark place.

YOU WILL NEED
¼ cup (60 g) natural cream base (*see Resources page 170*)
6 drops apricot kernel oil
6 drops frankincense essential oil
6 drops geranium essential oil
6 drops benzoin essential oil

The cream and apricot oil will moisturize the feet and prevent dry skin, while the essential oils add fragrance.

1 Place the natural cream base in a bowl and add 6 drops each of the essential oils.

2 Whisk together with a small wooden spatula and transfer into a small glass container with a lid.

3 Massage the cream into the feet after a bath, while the skin is still damp.

TALCUM POWDER

Some people like to apply talcum powder to their feet after bathing. Talc is made from magnesium trisilicate, a mineral obtained from the mining of talc rocks. It contains minute fibers that are easily inhaled, and is closely related in structure to asbestos. A 1993 National Toxicology program carried out in the United States showed that talc caused tumors in the ovaries and lungs of rats. Instead of using talcum powder, dust your feet (and other parts of the body) with cornstarch to absorb moisture.

FRAGRANCES

Fragrance is either natural or synthetic, and is found in a wide range of personal products. Natural scents such as jasmine are derived from plants. Artificial ones are manufactured in a laboratory from synthetic chemicals. Their production creates toxic waste, and many artificial fragrances present a recognized hazard to health, so are best avoided.

SYNTHETIC FRAGRANCES

Of the 5,000 chemicals used in perfumes, about 95 percent are made from petrochemicals. Typically, one fragrance will include hundreds of chemicals. These include benzene derivatives and aldehydes, which are strongly scented synthetics that are classified as hazardous waste. Most ingredients are not disclosed on the label, and are covered by the generic terms "parfum" or "fragrance." Over time they accumulate in body tissue, and the resulting toxicity can cause headaches, lethargy, skin sensitivity, asthma, inability to concentrate, and nausea. More serious reactions can include birth defects, central nervous system disorders, and cancer.

NATURAL FRAGRANCES

Plant oils are extracted and distilled to produce "essential oils" that make ideal natural fragrances. They come in three grades: clinical, absolute, or pure; normal or perfume grade, which may also be labeled as "extract" or "tincture," and which have been diluted with alcohol and/or plasticizers to make them resilient and easier to handle; and food grade. Many essential oils on the market are adulterated with synthetic fragrance, and/or diluted with base oil. The only way to be certain of buying pure essential oils is to buy them from a reputable retail outlet (see Resources page 170).

Certified organic oils are available and will be free of pesticides, fertilizers, GMOs, and any other adulterants.

USING ESSENTIAL OILS

Pure-grade oils are very potent and should be used carefully as scent, according to instructions, usually mixed with a base oil or water, and never ingested. Here are some guidelines for using essential oils safely and effectively. Keep them out of reach of children.

● In bathwater: add 5–8 drops of your chosen oil or oils, and agitate the water to distribute.
● To perfume a room: put 4–5 drops into a small amount of water in a vaporizer and light the candle underneath. Refill when the water level runs low.
● As perfume: add 10 drops of your chosen oil to a tablespoon of a base oil such as almond, jojoba, wheatgerm, or evening primrose, and dab on the neck and wrists as with regular perfumes.
● For massage: add 10–12 drops of essential oil to 4 teaspoons of base oil, choosing suitable oils for each massage. Store in a cool dark place.

THE PROPERTIES OF ESSENTIAL OILS

Different oils have a range of mood-enhancing benefits and can be useful for treating the symptoms of fatigue, stress, and depression. Smell the oils before purchase to see which appeal to you. Do not use in pregnancy, since some can be harmful (*see page 130*).

● Uplifting: geranium, orange
● Intimate: sandalwood, patchouli, jasmine
● Relaxing: neroli, lavender, vetiver
● Calming: sandalwood, sage, lavender, chamomile, neroli
● Energizing: rosemary, pine, lemon, orange

● To relieve anxiety: basil, bergamot, geranium, lavender
● For mild shock: chamomile, melissa, neroli, peppermint
● For depression: bergamot, clary sage, neroli, chamomile, juniper, lavender
● For mental fatigue: basil, peppermint, rosemary, pine

NATURAL DEODORANTS

The primary active ingredient in most deodorant products is aluminum chlorohydrate, which stops wetness but may block and infect underarm skin follicles. Another active ingredient, triclosan, used for its antibacterial properties, can cause liver damage. Deodorant products may also contain ammonia, formaldehyde, talc, and artificial fragrance.

● Use baking soda as a natural deodorant: it's fantastically effective. Just pat on a little with the fingertips after bathing or showering while the skin is still slightly damp. If your skin finds baking soda slightly abrasive, mix with a little cornstarch to soften it and make it feel silky.
● Buy deodorants that use natural ingredients (*see Resources page 170*).
● Use crystalline deodorant stones available from health stores (*see Resources page 170*).

Dampen a crystalline deodorant stone under the faucet, then gently rub the stone on the skin. Baking soda is another inexpensive but effective deodorant.

NATURAL AFTERSHAVE

¼ cup (60 ml) rose water
½ cup (125 ml) witch hazel
4 teaspoons vodka (as a preservative)
12 drops benzoin essential oil
4–5 drops each rosemary and geranium essential oils

Put the ingredients into a small glass bottle and shake well. This natural aftershave will keep indefinitely.

AFTERSHAVE

Most commercial aftershaves contain a high synthetic alcohol content, which makes them very drying to the skin. The following natural alternatives are just as effective.

● Buy aftershave that uses only natural ingredients (*see Resources page 170*).
● Plain witch hazel, available from most drugstores, mixed with an equal quantity of rose water, is a soothing astringent.
● For mature, dry skins, add a little vegetable oil to the witch hazel and rose water astringent; about 1 teaspoon to a 5 fl oz (150 ml) bottle of mixture. Almond oil and apricot kernel oil are both suitable and very moisturizing. Shake the bottle every time you use it to disperse the ingredients, especially the oil.

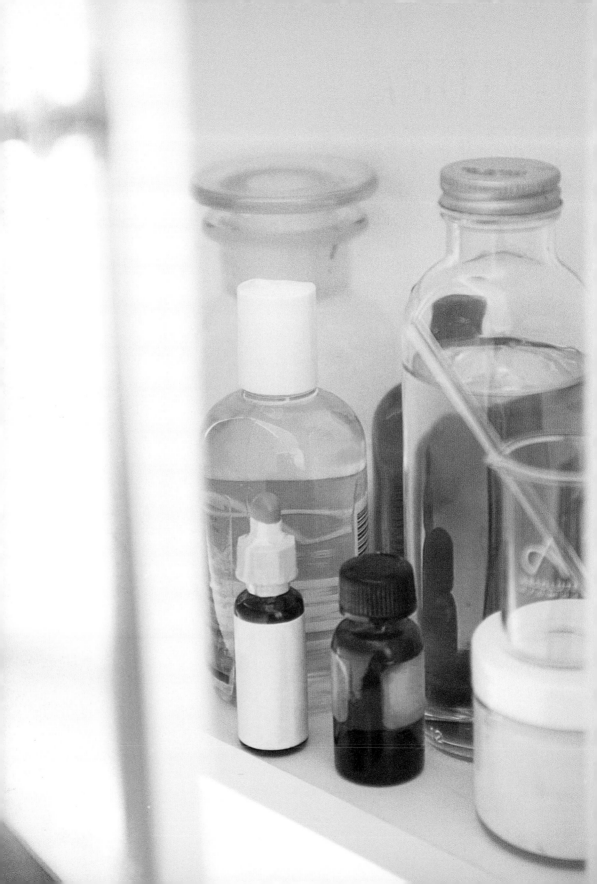

NATURAL REMEDIES

For common ailments, it is not always necessary to pay a visit to the doctor or to buy over-the-counter remedies at the pharmacy. There are many natural cures and holistic remedies that avoid the use of drugs and leave you free of side effects. Homeopathy is a valuable "alternative" medicine that bases treatment on an analysis of your personal profile. Acupuncture has been proven to relieve many ailments, herbalism is a powerful form of medicine, and aromatherapy and massage treat a number of complaints successfully. Osteopaths and chiropractors are now endorsed by conventional medical practitioners, and the Alexander Technique has helped many people with back and neck problems, among other complaints.

STAYING HEALTHY

You can do a great deal to prevent problems from arising in the first place by taking up various forms of bodywork: yoga, Pilates, and T'ai Chi all offer positive health benefits. Yoga is renowned for its relaxing and balancing effects, as well as for toning the body, and it also strengthens the immune system. Pilates keeps the skeletal–muscular system strong, and T'ai Chi maintains a balance of physical and mental fitness. To ease anxiety and depression, and to relieve stress, meditation has been proved to be an effective aid.

Keep a range of natural remedies in your medicine cabinet to deal with minor ailments that can be treated safely at home.

Hangover cure p128

Garlic antiseptic p129

Chamomile tea p130

Simple meditation p133

COMMON AILMENTS

A surprising range of everyday ailments can be treated successfully with food plants such as onions (antibiotic), garlic (antiseptic and antibiotic), and lemon (antioxidant). Many cooking ingredients, such as vinegar, baking soda, salt, honey, and oats, also form the basis of natural remedies. Herbs such as thyme (antiseptic and antifungal) and lavender (a carminative and an antidepressant), and spices such as cloves (antibacterial) and ginger (antispasmodic) offer safe, cheap, and easy-to-use remedies. Remember also that water is one of nature's greatest healers: when you are sick, always drink plenty of filtered water to flush the toxins out of your system.

THE NATURAL MEDICINE CHEST

Common ailments—from colds and sore throats to insect bites—can all be treated successfully without recourse to medicinal drugs. With just a handful of everyday ingredients, you will have the basis for a natural medicine chest and first aid kit.

COUGHS & COLDS
● To soothe a cough, place 1 teaspoon of chopped root ginger (an antispasmodic), 1–2 tablespoons of honey, and a squeeze of lemon juice in a mug of boiling water, and drink 3–4 times a day.
● A cup of hot water containing 2 teaspoons of cider vinegar makes a good decongestant for a cough.
● For a cold, finely chop a few cloves of garlic (or the same amount of raw onion), cover with honey and leave for 2–3 hours, then take teaspoonfuls throughout the day.
● Echinacea is an excellent remedy for a cold, plus soluble vitamin C (up to 500 mg per day).

CHILBLAINS
● Mix 1 teaspoon of cayenne or chili powder with 1 tablespoon of base oil (*see page 124*) and rub into the affected area; this improves the circulation and relieves inflammation.

EARACHE
● Warm a little olive oil. Prick a garlic clove with a pin and leave to soak in the oil for a few minutes. Pour a little of the infused oil into the ear and plug with cotton balls.

For a hangover, blend together banana, soy milk, and fruit juice. Drink this mixture to help line the stomach and absorb toxins produced by alcohol consumption.

For headaches, soak cotton pads in 1 cup (250 ml) water and 1 teaspoon of dried mint, and place over the eyes.

HANGOVERS

● Blend 3 small red chili peppers with 1 pint (500 ml) tomato juice and a dash of soy sauce. Drink as much as you can. This releases natural painkillers into the body.

● Blend 1 peeled banana with 1 pint (500 ml) soy milk and 2 tablespoons of fruit juice of your choice. Chill the mixture, and drink.

● Eat two apples first thing in the morning. This will help to replace lost vitamins and reduce the effects of dehydration.

HOMEMADE GINGER ALE FOR NAUSEA

Grate about 6 oz (175 g) fresh ginger root, place it in a pan with 1 pint (500 ml) water, and bring to the boil. Simmer for 5 minutes, then leave to stand for 24 hours. Strain through muslin, return the juice to a pan and add 1¼ cups (300 ml) honey. Simmer for 5 minutes, then cool and bottle. Store in the fridge. Take 1 tablespoon of the mixture in a glass of soda water as required.

HEADACHES

● Make a ginger poultice to relieve head tension. Mix 2 tablespoons of ground ginger with a little water and warm gently in a pan. Spread onto a cotton pad and press onto the forehead. Lie down in a quiet, dark room while you allow the treatment to work.

● Drink a tea made from 1 teaspoon each of chopped lemon grass, fennel seeds, and cardamom. Lie down with a scarf over your eyes and rest.

● Peppermint, rosemary, or sage teas are all helpful in relieving headaches.

INSECT BITES & STINGS

● Mix 1 teaspoon of baking soda and a little water or vinegar into a paste, and apply directly to the sting.

● Rub a few drops of pure lavender essential oil directly on to the affected area.

● Rub the cut side of an onion on to a wasp- or beesting.

● Catnip has been found to be an effective insect—and especially mosquito—repellent: rub fresh leaves over exposed skin, or buy extract of catnip.

SORE THROAT

● A simple mixture of hot fresh lemon juice and honey is one of the best remedies for a sore throat.

● Make a salt water solution with 2 tablespoons of salt and 1 cup (250 ml) warm water. Use as a gargle.

● Heat 1 tablespoon each of honey and brown sugar with 3 tablespoons of cider vinegar. Add a peeled clove of garlic and leave to infuse. Let cool and gargle.

STOMACH PROBLEMS

● Baking soda acts as a gentle antacid in cases of indigestion or heartburn. Mix 2 teaspoons of baking soda with ¼ cup (60 ml) of water; stir.

● Drink fresh lemon or lime juice mixed with a little water for stomach ache.

● Ginger has a soothing effect on the digestive system and is useful for travel sickness and morning sickness in pregnancy: drink ginger tea or chew a little piece of the root.

● A cup of black tea is very effective for soothing an upset stomach.

A peeled garlic clove rubbed directly on to a cut will prevent infection.

SMALL WOUNDS & CUTS

● Garlic is antiseptic, and onion antibacterial: apply either to a small cut to keep it clean and germ-free.

● Lavender essential oil can be applied straight to burns or cuts. It helps heals them quickly, preventing scarring.

THE HERBAL MEDICINE CHEST

There are plenty of natural remedies based on plants and herbs that are available to treat and cure most of the minor complaints that affect us. Like conventional drugs, these are produced commercially, but they do not contain added synthetic chemicals. If your home medicine cabinet is filled with over-the-counter drugs and medications, it is worth knowing that many manufactured drugs contain artificial colorings and flavorings, preservatives, alcohol, and sugars. Antacids, for example, which are used to treat symptoms of heartburn and indigestion, may contain aluminum compounds, which have been associated with the onset of Alzheimer's disease—so replace these synthetic remedies with the herbal ones described below.

Treat insomnia or indigestion with a soothing cup of fresh chamomile tea.

USING HERBS SAFELY

Herbal remedies may come from natural sources, and have fewer, if any, of the side effects of conventional drugs. They should still be treated with care, however, since high concentrations of plant substances can be as toxic as ordinary medicines.

- Read the directions for use carefully and never exceed the stated dose.
- Do not take more than two internal herbal remedies at the same time, or one internal and one external.
- If symptoms persist, consult a doctor.

- Never give infants under six months internal medicines without professional advice.
- During the first three months of pregnancy all medicines—herbal included—should be avoided completely, including essential oils. Always get professional advice if you

wish to use herbal remedies or essential oils after the first trimester.
- Never ingest essential oils, and dilute for external use except where specified.
- If you are on medication, ask your doctor if it is safe to take a herbal remedy.

HERBS DURING PREGNANCY

Most culinary herbs are safe to eat during pregnancy. The following herbs are important exceptions, however. You must avoid them at all costs, either in food or medicinally, since they can stimulate the muscles of the uterus and result in a miscarriage.

- Blue cohosh (*Caulophyllum thalictroides*)
- Goldenseal (*Hydrastis canadensis*)
- Juniper (*Juniperus communis*)
- Pennyroyal (*Mentha pulegium*)
- Sage (*Salvia officinalis*)
- Yarrow (*Achillea millefolium*)

WARNING
The following nine essential oils are not recommended for external use during pregnancy: basil, chamomile, juniper, lavender, marjoram, myrrh, pennyroyal, sage, and thyme.

NATURAL REMEDIES TO STOCK

The herbal remedies listed here should be available from most health food stores and some drugstores. Always read the instructions on the packaging, and take particular note of any cautions. Always check with a doctor before taking a herbal remedy if you have any serious medical condition.

PREPARATION	USE
ALOE VERA	
Cream	Minor burns and scalds, sunburn, stretch marks, warts, wounds and grazes, eczema
Lotion	Use as gently soothing, astringent skin cream
ARNICA	
Cream	Bruises, sprains, aching muscles
Homeopathic tablets	Emotional shock, injury, pain, and trauma
CALENDULA	
Cream	Acne, boils, athlete's foot, bites and stings, diaper rash, bruises, minor wounds, and swellings
CHAMOMILE	
Oil	Diaper rash: 3 drops German chamomile in 6 tsp almond oil
Cream	Sore and itchy skin, bites and stings, sore nipples, eczema, and muscle spasms
Tea	Insomnia, indigestion, morning sickness, baby colic (use German chamomile)
CLOVE	
Essential oil	For toothache: 1–2 drops on cotton ball, dabbed onto sore area
COMFREY	
Ointment	Bruises, acne, boils, fractures and wounds, fungal skin infections, psoriasis, stiff and aching joints
ECHINACEA	
Tablets or tincture	Stimulates immune system when under attack, used for colds, the flu, coughs, and fevers. Also mild asthma, and cold sores
GARLIC	
Capsules	Increases resistance to infection: use for colds and the flu, coughs, and bronchitis. Helps to lower blood pressure. Use for cold sores, and digestive infections
HYPERICUM	
Cream	Cramps, neuralgia, cold sores, back pain, stiff and aching joints and muscles
Oil	Minor wounds and burns

PREPARATION	USE
LAVENDER	
Essential oil	For back pain, irritability, asthma, headaches: 5–6 drops in 4 tsp (20 ml) base oil. For insect stings and bites, use undiluted. For insomnia, stiff and aching joints: 8–10 drops in bath water
MEADOWSWEET	
Tea	Stomach acidity, heartburn, and diarrhea
Tablets	Rheumatic aches
NEEM	
Oil	Head lice, skin rashes, ringworm. Also a powerful insect repellent.
Cream	Eczema, psoriasis, and acne
SLIPPERY ELM	
Capsules	Coughs, bronchitis
Powder	Acidity, indigestion
Tablets	Diarrhea, irritable bowel syndrome, haemorrhoids
TEA TREE	
Essential oil	For stings, burns, wounds, skin infection, ringworm, athlete's foot, warts and corns, acne and boils: 4–5 drops per 3 tsp (15 ml) base oil. For vaginal thrush: 2–3 drops oil in 1 tsp olive oil on a tampon, insert for 2–3 hours at a time; and 8–10 drops in bath water with a cup of cider vinegar
THYME	
Essential oil	For scabies, bites and stings, sciatica and rheumatic pains, ringworm, athlete's foot, and thrush: 3–4 drops in 1 tsp base oil
VALERIAN & HOPS	
Tablets	Insomnia; calming in times of stress, tension, and anxiety
WHITE WILLOW	
Tablets	Arthritis, rheumatic pain, back pain, stiff knees and hips, high fevers. Also reduces night sweats and hot flushes in menopause
WITCH HAZEL	
Distilled	Insect stings, sore skin, rashes, broken and varicose veins, bruises, and eczema

HEALING THROUGH BODYWORK

Taking up the practices of yoga and meditation can do much to prevent as well as to cure minor body ailments, while improving your quality of life at the same time. Yoga leads to a better balance of body, mind, and spirit, and the stillness of meditation brings calm, clarity, and a sense of perspective to life issues. Neither practice is difficult: anyone is capable, at any age, and in any condition. Also, yoga and meditation exercises do not have to be particularly demanding: doing just a little on a regular basis will make a difference to your general level of fitness and your sense of well-being. Invest in comfortable, loose-fitting clothes in natural fabrics for your yoga practice and aim to allocate a time in your day so that yoga becomes a habit. Establish a routine so that practicing becomes a part of your everyday life: the benefits are huge.

If you have been practicing yoga for a while and are quite supple, perform this long back stretch to increase neck and spine flexibility and open up the chest.

YOGA

Yoga is a philosophy that originated in northern India around 5,000 years ago. The combination of physical work, mental focus, and breathing exercises has an impact on many aspects of your being, although yoga as now practiced in the West concentrates mainly on the physical element. Through a series of exercises, known as asanas, yoga increases strength and stamina, suppleness and flexibility, improves posture and concentration, reduces stress, brings deep relaxation, and promotes a sense of well-being and balance. The asanas should be practiced in coordination with the in- and out-breath. Find a teacher to help you adopt the correct postures, and invest in a good yoga book (*see Resources page 177*).

This simple side stretch will improve your balance and increase the strength in your arms and legs, as well as stretching and toning your waist. Hold for a few minutes, then repeat the same stretch on the left side of your body.

GUIDELINES FOR YOGA PRACTICE

- Practice in a quiet, warm room away from distractions such as the telephone.
- Wear loose clothing so that you can stretch, and perform the exercises in bare feet.
- Always allow three hours to elapse after eating a full meal, or two hours after a light one, before practicing yoga.
- If you have any specific medical problems, inform a qualified yoga teacher—there may be specific asanas that will benefit your medical problem (or ones to avoid).
- Do not attempt advanced postures such as the headstand until you are practiced at yoga: you could damage your back and neck muscles and joints.
- Remember that yoga is not a competition, so work at your own pace and level of flexibility.

MEDITATION

Practices of meditation derive from many cultures, and there are numerous techniques. Whichever method you choose, the aim is to heighten your awareness of the present moment and to leave you with a calm, expansive mind and a feeling of peace. Research has shown that mediation can help relieve stress, high blood pressure, cardiac disease, chronic pain, psoriasis, and even some cancers, including breast and prostate cancer. Immune function improves, too, so a regular practice of "sitting" can be not only enjoyable but also improve your health.

To put it simply, meditation may be defined as "stopping and breathing." Stopping means stopping the mind from engaging with its chattering thoughts (the ancient Indian texts call it the "monkey-mind"), so for most of us that means stilling the body, too.

You can meditate on the train, or for a few moments at work. However, for most people the way to start is to find a quiet place to sit, perhaps with a candle and some incense, in a clean, warm, and uncluttered room. You can sit cross-legged on the floor, or kneel unaided or with the help of a kneeling stool. If this is uncomfortable, sit on an upright chair with your back supported. In both cases, keep your spine upright but relaxed, your hands resting in your lap, and your face relaxed. You can close your eyes or keep them open.

A SIMPLE MEDITATION

- Sit comfortably on the floor or a chair.
- Make sure your shoulders, neck, and jaw are relaxed, and your body soft.
- Become aware of your breathing, noticing the rise and fall of the abdomen on each inhalation and exhalation.
- Keep your attention focused on the breath: if it strays, say to yourself "breathing in" as you inhale and "breathing out" as you exhale, to help focus the mind.
- Build up this practice from 5 minutes or so until you can easily maintain it for 20 minutes. As with any skill, it's a question of practice, of acquiring a kind of "fitness" for mental focus, and of learning the habit of quietness.

Sit still with your palms in your lap, your back straight, and your body relaxed, and concentrate on your breathing.

BABY CARE

It is natural for parents to want to provide the best possible start in life for a new baby. Infants are especially susceptible to pollutants in the environment and often react negatively to synthetic chemicals: in the past decade there has been a doubling of asthmatic conditions in children under five, and an increase in allergies in children. In the home, children may be exposed to hormone disrupters in certain types of plastics, pesticides and fertilizers in food, tobacco smoke, cadmium and other heavy metals in house dust, untested chemicals in toiletries, and paints and other household furnishing fibers that "outgas" chemical fumes. Keeping the home free of as many of these substances as possible, and making sure that it is clean, will go a long way to ensuring the health and safety of babies and young children.

Healthy baby food p136

Diaper choices p138

ORGANICS FOR CHILDREN

We can make a substantial contribution to counteracting the negative impact of such household pollutants. Follow the advice offered in this chapter and feed your children on wholesome home cooking made from organic ingredients, avoid plastics by selecting natural furnishing and bedding materials such as wood, wool, cotton, leather, and metal, and dress them in clothes made from 100 percent natural fibers. Decorate their bedroom with nontoxic paints and finishes, and so provide them with a room that is free of synthetics and chemicals and has a greatly improved air quality. You may not find all these child-friendly products in the average store just yet, but there is plenty available by ordering through the internet or by mail order.

Organic bedding p140

Natural fibers such as organic wool and cotton will provide your baby with an allergy-free, nontoxic start in life.

Cleaning toys p141

FEEDING YOUNG CHILDREN

Since the majority of milk formulas and baby foods are not organic, babies fed on these may be exposed to varying levels of pesticides and other chemical residues such as PCBs and dioxins. Of the 400 baby foods products tested by an independent watchdog on food issues, 70 percent were bulked out with low-nutrient starches. As a young mother, I disliked the taste and smell of manufactured baby foods and had no reason to suppose that my baby would react differently. As soon as she was weaned onto solids, I used to purée the fresh food that my husband and I were eating—avoiding hot spices and olives but including small amounts of garlic—and she thrived, growing up into a healthy child and adult with a love for and an interest in food.

The best start in life that you can give your baby is to breast-feed, and to go on to wholesome, home-cooked meals.

WHY BREAST-FEED?

Breast milk is nature's baby food and, as such, it contains every nutrient your baby needs for its development. Even the manufacturers of formula milk recognize that it is a "poor relative" of the real thing. Here are some reasons why breast-feeding is good both for your baby and for you.

● Breast-feeding strengthens a baby's immune system: breast-fed babies tend to get fewer gastric and respiratory problems, eczema or diabetes, and go to the doctor less frequently than bottle-fed babies. There is also less risk of Sudden Infant Death Syndrome.
● Breast-feeding creates a unique bond between mother and baby.
● Breast-feeding is labor-saving and convenient.

KEYS TO SUCCESSFUL BREAST-FEEDING

● Make sure you get adequate nourishment by eating a healthy, balanced organic diet (*see pages 90–91*).
● Avoid caffeine, alcohol, prescription drugs, spicy foods, and foods containing chemical additives: these will contaminate your milk and be passed on to your baby.
● Eat little and often to keep your energy levels up.
● Get as much rest as possible.
● Drink at least 4 pints (2 liters) of water per day to make up the liquid you lose.
● Consult your doctor or midwife, or a support group (*see Resources page 173*) on any problems with breast-feeding.

BOTTLE FEEDING

If you decide not to breast-feed, or are unable to for any reason, there are a few organic milk formulas available on the market (*see Resources page 173*). The majority of milk formulas are not organic and may contain preservatives and other chemicals. Always read the label before buying. Do not attempt to make your own formula milk from cow's milk and honey: babies should not be fed honey until they are over 12 months old, and cow's milk is designed for calves, not humans—it can give babies anemia and severe intestinal bleeding. Use glass rather than plastic bottles: plastic leaches out into the milk.

HEALTHY OPTIONS

Growing infants are especially vulnerable to chemicals in food and water: they need relatively large amounts of food for their body size, and their blood, liver, and kidneys are not able to fully excrete waste materials, so residues are stored in the body. Evidence suggests that babies' nervous systems are especially vulnerable to neurotoxins during the rapid growth from birth to one year old, and similarly the immune system and endocrine glands are not fully developed and damage may occur. Babies are sensitive to taste, and many lifelong habits are acquired in early life: make sure that they are good ones. Feed your baby homemade, organic food to encourage the habit of eating well, rather than relying on processed foods.

- Buy organic, and spare your baby exposure to pesticide and fertilizer residues.
- Check the labels on all foods from baby through toddler to the next stages of childhood: due to consumer pressure, some baby-food manufacturers have stopped using genetically modified foods in their products.
- Avoid all additives and preservatives, stabilizers, emulsifiers, antioxidants, thickeners, processed starches and sugars, flavor enhancers, sweeteners, and colorings because they have been linked to a range of health problems, including allergic asthma, eczema, and even cancer. Some additives not permitted in baby and toddler foods are nonetheless found in "family foods" that you may feed to your toddler.
- Avoid plastic cups and tableware to decrease exposure to PVCs.
- Sugar is often added to baby foods and leads to an unhealthy dependency on sweetness, as well as causing long-term illness. Obesity among children is increasing at an alarming rate, and sugar has been implicated in some cancers, liver disease, eye and skin problems, and diabetes.

TOP TIP

Invest in a juicer and make your own fruit drinks for children, using organic fruit.

Purée vegetables such as fresh peas and spinach to feed your baby, to help develop good eating habits in later life.

REMOVING FOOD STAINS

Babies often regurgitate milk and puréed foods. To remove the stain and the odor, wipe up the stain with water, then sprinkle it with baking soda. Allow time for the baking soda to be absorbed before washing.

CARING FOR TEETH

Go easy with fruit juices, which contain natural acid that can destroy the enamel on your child's teeth if consumed in large quantities. They often contain large amounts of sugar, too, which increase the risk of developing cavities. Nonorganic fruit juices also contain traces of pesticides.

Dilute fruit juice with either water or yogurt to reduce the fruit sugars to which your child's teeth are exposed.

DIAPERS & SKIN CARE

A baby's skin is soft, thin, and delicate and must be treated with the utmost care. It can more readily absorb chemicals that may be present in various products, ranging from disposable diapers to baby creams and skin lotions. In addition, the environmental impact of disposable diapers is considerable, not only in their manufacture, but also as a major contributor to household waste, and thus to air and water pollution.

CHOOSING & USING DIAPERS

Reusable diapers are available in organic cotton. Some have integral tying string, so don't need pins. Diaper liners can also be used, plus woolen diaper covers, which will keep your baby warm in cold weather and cool when it is hot.

As a baby, your child will use about 5,000 diapers, and approximately 4 percent of all household waste consists of soiled diapers. The pros and cons of disposable versus cloth diapers are outlined below.

CLOTH DIAPERS

● Cloth diapers are much more absorbent than their disposable equivalents.
● Folded cloth diapers are awkward to use, but fitted versions are now available.
● Although the initial cost of buying cloth diapers is higher, in the long run it comes to less than half of what you pay out on disposables, even after taking laundering into account.
● Cloth diapers can be used for subsequent babies, or can be recycled.
● Washing cloth diapers is far better for the environment than throwing away several nonbiodegradable disposables on a daily basis. There are diaper services in most cities (*see Resources page 173*) that will launder diapers for you. These services use 32 percent less energy than home washing, and 41 percent less water because of their bulk loads and commercial machines.

DISPOSABLES

● Disposable diapers are made from synthetic fibers that contain deodorizing chemicals, bleaches, and highly toxic dioxins that are all harmful to the environment. These cause skin rashes on sensitive baby skin. Diaper rash was practically unknown before 1950, when disposable diapers were introduced.
● Worldwide, literally millions of disposables are used per day, and end up in landfill sites where they remain for years— they may take 10 years or more to decompose.
● Millions of trees per year are cut down to produce just the absorbent paper "fluff" in disposable diapers.

USING CLOTH DIAPERS

- Use 100 percent organic cotton diapers.
- Buy enough to allow for laundering and drying: three dozen should be adequate.
- Invest in washable gauze diaper liners that make cleaning easier, rather than disposable paper ones.
- Buy at least two pails with lids, a supply of borax and/or baking soda, and "soft chemistry" laundry detergent for presoaking soiled diapers before laundering.
- Let your baby go without diapers as often as possible to expose its skin to the fresh air.
- Do not feel guilty about using the occasional disposable when convenient.

CLEANING CLOTH DIAPERS

Rinse wet diapers and dispose of solid matter down the toilet. Place the diapers in a pail with a borax or baking soda solution, and leave to soak for 6–8 hours or overnight. Drain the soaking solution down the toilet. Machine-wash the diapers on a hot cycle with a double rinse. Dry outside if possible: sunshine is a natural bleach and disinfectant. If you have to tumble-dry, it will help to sterilize the diapers.

To soak cloth diapers, you will need a bucket with a lid. Half fill the bucket with cold water and stir in 3–4 tablespoons of borax or baking soda, to deodorize and reduce staining.

BABY SKIN CARE

Because baby skin is so delicate and sensitive, avoid using strong soaps and shampoos made for adults on your baby. Additives such as artificial colors, fragrances, and preservatives can cause irritation and allergic reactions. Choose plant-based, natural, organic oils and creams (*see Resources page 173*). These products are not tested on animals, are biodegradable, and can be guaranteed to be free of synthetics and petrochemicals.

- Never use soap products on a baby's face—the skin here is more sensitive than elsewhere.
- Use lotions, oils, and powders that come from natural and organic sources, such as almond oil and cocoa butter.
- Dry your baby with a soft cotton towel and avoid talcum powder. Inhalation of talc has been linked to serious illness and even death.

- Buy diaper cream containing ingredients such as red clover, a natural anti-inflammatory.
- Use shampoo containing chamomile oil, which is gentle for baby hair.
- Treat skin rashes with calendula cream.
- For diaper rash, mix 3 drops of German chamomile oil with 2 tablespoons of almond oil and rub on the affected area.

Chemical-free baby toiletries, including baby toothpaste, are now available from health food stores.

CLOTHES, BEDDING, & TOYS

The chances are that your new baby will move into a newly decorated room. If it is your first crib, it may have a new mattress and bedding. Be aware that new paint, carpet, vinyl wallpaper, synthetic mattresses, and no-iron sheets may all "outgas" chemical fumes. To give your new baby the best start in life, keep these toxins to a minimum by choosing natural fibers and decorating products where possible. If your local stores do not supply what you want, there are plenty of mail-order outlets that do (*see Resources page 173*).

BABY CLOTHES

Babies grow so fast that their clothes never get much wear, and so remain in good condition. Why not save a small fortune by exchanging with friends, or buying secondhand in stores or through local newspaper advertisements?

● When buying clothing new, avoid synthetic fibers and formaldehyde finishes.
● Make sure that sleepwear is not treated with flameproof chemicals that your baby will inhale during sleep. Buy natural fabrics instead—wool, cotton, linen, and hemp (*see Resources page 173*). These are less flammable than synthetics and so will minimize any fire hazards to which babies and young children might be exposed.
● If possible, buy clothes made from natural fibers that have been organically produced, and so contain no chemical residues.

BEDDING

Fibers that "breathe" will help your child rest more comfortably and reduce exposure to toxins during sleep. Opening the bedroom window to let in plenty of fresh air is also beneficial.

● Choose a mattress carefully. Most mattresses, whether for adults or for babies, are filled with polyurethane foam, covered with polyester, and treated with flameproof chemicals. In addition,

Organic cotton baby clothes, towels, and bed sets are free of synthetic chemical finishes or treatments.

many crib mattresses have an extra plastic covering for waterproofing. Babies spend many more hours in their beds asleep than adults, and have no choice but to inhale the gases emitted by these substances for protracted periods. You are unlikely to find what you want in most stores, so try mail–order companies that sell mattresses with natural and even organic coverings and fillings in cotton or wool (*see Resources page 173*).

● Bed sheets and covers are also available in natural and organic fibers, and are no more labor-intensive than synthetic bedlinen with no–iron finishes. Cotton sheets and pillowcases do not need ironing if the washing instructions are followed correctly, and they are hung out to dry outside, then smoothed flat before folding.

● If possible, buy your baby a wooden crib made from sustainable wood.

TOYS

The prevalence of plastic in children's toys is overwhelming. It may seem that there is no choice but to surround your children with playthings that "outgas" and turn the playroom into a toxic zone. Many children's toys are made from PVC—polyvinyl chloride—otherwise known as vinyl, whose manufacture and disposal creates dioxins, highly toxic substances.

Soft vinyl toys may contain phthalates, which are banned in some European countries. These chemicals may leak from the toy when sucked, chewed, squeezed, or even just held. The European Science Committee has advised that phthalates cause liver, kidney, and testicular damage and may affect hormones and lead to reduced fertility in later life.

● Plastic toys are non-biodegradable and eventually increase the amount of plastic in landfill sites.

● To avoid plastics, give your babies and children toys made from natural materials such as wood, cotton, wool, fleece, paper, leather, and metal.

● Toys made from natural materials tend to last longer and can be recycled by donating them to charity or to friends with children.

● Join the local toy library and borrow toys and books: this gives your child more variety and saves money.

● Make your own playthings with your children from simple everyday objects (little boxes, jars, desk supplies, cardboard tubes), as well as natural objects such as seashells and pine cones, and stock up with natural paints to decorate them with.

● Save your old clothes for a dress-up box.

● Save paper for your children to draw on, and magazines for them to make collages with.

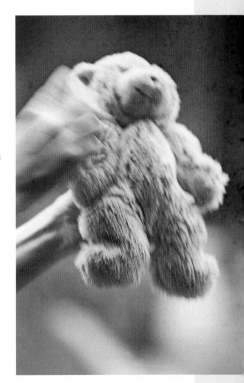

CLEANING TOYS

● To clean soiled plastic or wooden toys, dissolve 2 heaping tablespoons of baking soda in 1 pint (500 ml) warm water. Either submerge the toy and soak it, or wipe it clean, then rinse in cold water and leave to dry naturally.

● To clean a soft toy, place in a plastic bag with some baking soda, seal it and shake vigorously from time to time over a period of several hours. Brush the baking soda out of the plush with a stiff brush, and the toy will look like new.

A dusting of baking soda eliminates odors and removes stains from soiled stuffed toys.

KEEPING PETS

Pets provide great affection and companionship, but animals kept in the home will also raise greater health and hygiene issues than, say, ponies, potbellied pigs, ducks or geese, which are kept outdoors. In this chapter, the focus is on caring for dogs and cats, because they are the animals that the majority of people wish to keep in their home. There are guidelines on how to maintain a clean, allergy-free environment without resorting to strong chemicals. Advice is also given on how to prevent unwanted fur hair loss by regular grooming, and to remove fluff from carpets and soft furnishings, together with ways pet owners can maintain high standards of hygiene by keeping pets off beds and furniture.

PEST CONTROL

During the warmer summer months, pests such as fleas and ticks are picked up on the coats of animals. Rather than relying on chemical flea treatments, pests can be controlled naturally using simple recipes based on essential oils. Pet urine and excreta can also be a problem in the home, especially with young animals. Contact with excreta is especially harmful to children, so it must be cleaned up safely in the home, yard, and public places. The odors and stains resulting from urine and excreta can be treated naturally, too.

RESPONSIBLE BUYS

Before buying a pet, bear in mind that there are thousands of animals in shelters that need homes. If you are choosing a bird, reptile, or tropical fish, make sure that it has been bred in captivity and has not been taken from the wild (*see Resources pages 174*).

A small, wire-haired dog like this Border terrier needs regular grooming to prevent it from shedding unwanted hairs in the home.

Pet foods p145

Vitamin supplements p145

Healthy coat p147

Removing pet hairs p156

143

FEEDING YOUR PET

Many of the pet foods on the market make great claims to be "complete," but do not take into account that dogs, and to some extent cats, benefit from plant nutrients. Before domestication, these plant nutrients would have been available in the wild when eating the entrails of prey that had grazed on pasture. Commercial pet foods lack this natural diversity and compensate by introducing chemical additives, which are thought by some vets to trigger allergies and weaken the immune system.

Holistic vets recognize that the best diet for dogs and cats is principally raw organic meat, plus some vegetable scraps and minimal supplements. Pets on this varied diet have fewer digestive problems, and are less susceptible to parasites, skin ailments, and a buildup of tartar on teeth.

Keep leftover vegetables to feed to your dog as a healthy addition to its diet.

PET FOOD FACTS

Although convenient for pet owners, canned or dried animal foods may not necessarily be good for your pet or the environment.

The following facts will help you to make an informed decision about the foods available and help you to decide for yourself.

- Pet foods contain a wide range of chemicals. These include pesticides, nitrates, lead, synthetic preservatives, and artificial flavorings and colorings.
- All pet foods are made up from livestock carcasses, and are high in animal fats.

- They contain salt and high levels of sugar to make them more palatable.
- About three-quarters of the contents of canned pet food is water.
- Canned pet foods may contain lead from the soldering of the cans (see page 79).

- Dry cat foods have been linked to kidney problems in cats on this diet, especially if they don't drink enough water. A balanced diet of different types of food is best for the health of your cat. If your cat has a bladder disorder, you may want to avoid dry cat food.

DIETARY IMPROVEMENTS

The following dietary program works very well for my pets. However, not all vets would support such a feeding program. Always consult either your own vet or a qualified holistic vet before following a homemade diet for your pet.

- Feed your dog one-third raw meat or fish to two-thirds vegetables and cereals.
- Cooked brown rice is very nutritious, as are nuts and seeds and all vegetables.
- For cats, create a diet consisting of three-quarters raw meat or fish, mixed with

vegetables, cooked grains (for example, barley or millet), and oats soaked in milk. This should result in a calmer nature, fewer infestations, and improved resistance to infection.
- Ask for kidney, liver, heart, and tripe at the meat counter of your grocery store.

- Fish is an excellent protein for dogs and cats, and the essential fatty acids Omega-3 and Omega-6 in fish will boost your pet's immune system.
- To save money, buy meat bones in bulk and freeze them.
- Dilute cats' milk with water.
- Do not give cats cream: it is too rich for them and gives them indigestion.
- Let cats and dogs graze on herbs and grasses. Parsley is a digestive tonic, dandelion a liver toner, and yard grass cleanses the lymphatic system.

Let your pet enjoy a varied diet that includes raw meat and vegetables as an alternative to canned and dried foods.

VITAMIN SUPPLEMENTS

The following supplements help treat a host of pet complaints and are suitable for both cats and dogs. Add the capsules to your pet's food to make pill-taking more palatable.

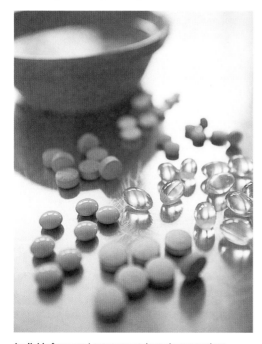

Available from good pet stores and veterinary practices, vitamin supplements should be taken as directed.

BREWERS' YEAST
This soothes nerves in animals as it does in humans, and also works as a flea deterrent. Give 25 mg per 11 lb (5 kg) bodyweight.

COD LIVER OIL
This eases stiff joints and skin problems in both humans and animals. Give 1 capsule or teaspoon per day.

GARLIC CAPSULES
To deter parasites and act as a natural antiseptic, give 1 garlic capsule or clove in food daily.

SEAWEED
This supplement has benefits for cats and dogs including: a shinier coat; improved alertness; healthier teeth and gums, and better bowel function. Give according to packet instructions.

SUNFLOWER OIL
To prevent dry, flaky skin, add 1 teaspoon of sunflower oil to your pet's food each day.

WHEATGERM OIL
This calms skin complaints, the nervous system, and encourages healthy reproduction. Give your pet 2 teaspoons per day, in food.

PEST CONTROL

The pesticides used in animal pest-control products are strong chemicals, leaving dogs, cats, and small mammals exposed to toxins. Impregnated flea collars can cause contact dermatitis, and give off chemical fumes that you, your children, and your pet inhale. You and your family will also come into contact with the chemicals in pet flea sprays and shampoos, among which may be organophosphate and carbamate compounds, with active ingredients such as the nerve poisons propoxur (very toxic orally), diazinon (linked to dozens of pet deaths and also toxic to bees), and carbaryl (a potential human carcinogen). The pesticides amitraz and permethrin are suspected endocrine disrupters. Pets treated with these chemicals may have symptoms such as vomiting, depression, lethargy, diarrhea, loss of appetite, and itchy skin.

FLEAS

Although we are encouraged to believe by pharmaceutical companies that strong chemical sprays are the only hygienic way to prevent or rid domestic animals of a flea infestation, there are many natural alternatives that were in common usage before the introduction of chemical products. The following tips explain how to control pests the natural way to keep your home free of toxins.

HOMEMADE CAT FLEA COLLAR

This simple recipe uses a blend of hydrosols or hydrolats, also known as herbal waters (*see Resources page 174*), to make a fragrant cat collar that repels fleas. I make one for my cat every summer and it is very effective. Use hydrosols rather than essential oils for cats because they metabolize them more effectively. When you have mixed the alcohol, hydrosols, and garlic oil together in a small bowl, soak the felt collar in the liquid until it has absorbed it all. Allow the collar to dry, then put it around your pet's neck. The flea-repellent effect will last for about four weeks before you need to treat the collar again.

YOU WILL NEED
Soft felt cat collar
2 teaspoons pure alcohol (vodka will do)
1 tablespoon rosemary hydrosol
1 tablespoon lemon verbena hydrosol
1 tablespoon lavender hydrosol
1 tablespoon pennyroyal hydrosol
oil squeezed from 4 garlic capsules

A felt cat collar soaked in herbal hydrosols and garlic is repellent to fleas and will keep your cat free of infestations.

OTHER NATURAL FLEA DETERRENTS

● Pet flea combs are available from most pet stores. They are fine-toothed so that they can trap adult fleas, but they also pick out the dried blood and flea feces in pet fur on which the larvae feed. After combing, dunk any fleas that are caught on the comb into warm soapy water to kill them. Flush the used soapy water down the toilet to avoid further infestation.

● When bathing pets, make a rinse out of pennyroyal or wormwood herb tea (do not use these herbs on pregnant pets). Make the infusion strong and allow it to cool before use.

● Pennyroyal or wormwood powder is also available from some vets; they are not recommended for pregnant pets. Sprinkle the powder on to your pet's coat and then rub it in vigorously. Leave for 10–15 minutes before bathing the animal.

● Add brewer's yeast powder or capsules—about 25 mg per 11 lb (5 kg) bodyweight—to your pet's food daily during an infestation to deter fleas.

● Add 1 garlic capsule to your pet's food each day to deter fleas and prevent roundworm.

● Add 1 teaspoon of cider vinegar to your pet's drinking water on a daily basis.

● Make up a blend of 5 drops of tea tree oil to 2 teaspoons of sunflower oil, and massage this into your dog's coat: it is antiseptic, soothes itchy skins, and deters fleas.

● To remove fleas from pet bedding, wash it regularly.

● Regular vacuuming, especially of pets' sleeping areas, sucks up flea eggs and helps to prevent reinfestation.

● Try using an electric flea trap as an alternative to chemical sprays. This works by emitting gentle heat that attracts fleas and traps them on sticky paper.

● Treat pet rabbits and guinea pigs with a non-organophosphate insecticide.

TICKS

If your pet picks up a tick, do not attempt to pull it out of your animal's coat: half of it will be left in the skin and can cause infection. Apply a drop of kerosene or olive oil and the tick should "back out."

HOMEMADE DOG FLEA MASSAGE OIL

This is the mixture I use on my dog at the height of summer flea infestation: increase or double the quantities for larger dogs. Omit the pennyroyal oil if your dog is pregnant.

YOU WILL NEED

2 teaspoons of sunflower oil
3 drops orange oil
3 drops citronella oil
3 drops lemon oil
3 drops tea tree oil
1 drop pennyroyal oil (use with extreme caution as in high doses it can be extremely toxic)

Mix together the sunflower oil and essential oils in a glass bowl and gently massage the mixture into your dog's coat, using your fingertips. Your pet should enjoy the massage and the attention, and will smell wonderful. Perform this treatment every other day until the fleas subside.

1 Mix together the essential oils in a small glass dish, taking care to add no more than 1 drop of pennyroyal oil.

2 Add the sunflower oil to act as a base for the essential oils. Massage the blend into your dog's fur.

PET HEALTH

Part of the responsibility of keeping pets is to make sure that they are healthy. They need regular checkups and a program of vaccinations to boost their immune systems. Vet bills can be expensive, so find a reputable pet insurance program that offers comprehensive cover. However, some people believe that pets do not need to be vaccinated as often as the drug companies recommend. Trials show that only a small percentage of animals vaccinated are really protected against fatal diseases, and that hygiene and nutrition have contributed as much to disease control as vaccination programs. Also, as with humans, vaccines may cause side effects in pets.

Homeopathic treatment and alternative medicine is also available for pets: it has a good record for behavioral, emotional and stress problems, travel sickness, nasal problems, colitis, allergies, long-term diarrhea, and arthritis. Chronic skin problems and eye and ear infections are better remedied with drugs. If you have several pets, keep a natural first aid kit at home to treat your animals for minor complaints—not only will this avoid trips to the vet, which can be stressful for pets, but it will also save on vet bills.

FIRST AID

Like human homeopathic remedies, those for pets are based on natural plant, animal, and mineral substances. If possible, keep a medicine box of the following homeopathic remedies for treating minor ailments. Store them in a cool, dry place. To treat your pet, use the pipette to place 2–3 drops of the remedy in the animal's mouth. Try not to allow the pipette to touch the animal and contaminate the remedy. In acute cases, dose your pet every 20–30 minutes, in less acute cases, every 1–2 hours, and in chronic conditions 2–3 times a day. If your pet's symptoms persist, seek professional advice.

- Arnica: shock, bruising, or swelling; for soothing before and after an operation or birth trauma; for eye injuries.
- Aconite: shock, trauma (first aid after a car accident, for example); for fights with other animals, during thunderstorms or fireworks; for difficult birthing; fever if thirsty and restless; sunburn if onset is acute and animal is restless.
- Apis: bee or wasp stings.
- Arsenicum: acute diarrhea or vomiting.
- Belladonna: temperature, fever, and inflammation.
- Hypericum: animal bites.
- Heparsulph: infected wounds, burst abscesses, and wound pain.
- Rhus tox: arthritis, joint sprains, and stiffness in the mornings; for working dogs before and after going out.
- Sulfur: itchy skin (you can also buy small blocks of solid sulfur to place in your pet's water bowl, where they will leach into the water. These blocks of sulfur are available from good pet stores).
- Symphytum: to promote healing of broken bones.

> **TOP TIP**
>
> To give your dog medicine, grasp its upper jaw with one hand to prevent biting. Hold the pipette in your free hand and place the liquid at the back of the dog's tongue.

ALLERGIES

Like humans, domestic animals can suffer acute allergic reactions to chemicals and solvents such as formaldehyde that are used in carpet production. Many pets are also adversely affected by air fresheners and other chemical cleaning sprays.

- Avoid proprietary brands of pet shampoos: they are likely to contain strong chemicals that cause allergies. Use organic pet shampoos instead.
- Avoid spray-on or dust-on carpet cleaners, which may cause severe skin problems on contact with your pet's belly.
- Using "soft chemistry" floor cleaners and bleaches will reduce the amount of toxic chemicals that your pet is likely to come into contact with.
- When recarpeting or putting down a new floor, choose natural, untreated materials (see pages 42–43).
- Use natural air fresheners in your home (see page 49).

COAT & SKIN CARE

Keeping your dog or cat well-groomed will remove dead skin cells and dirt from the fur and prevent skin problems from developing. Long-haired pets will need daily grooming and short-haired types weekly brushing to keep in condition.

GROOMING YOUR PET

- If you have the outdoor space, groom your pet outside to prevent hairs, skin particles, and dirt from being released into your home environment.
- During times of year when flea infestation is at its height, groom daily with a flea comb if possible (see page 147).
- To ensure complete removal of fleas and mites, wash your pet's brush and comb immediately after grooming, and leave them in a warm place to dry.

1 Calm your dog and encourage it to sit or stand still before you begin grooming.

2 Using a soft bristle brush, take long, gentle strokes and groom the animal from head to tail. Rhythmic movements will help to keep your pet relaxed.

PET HYGIENE

Following these basic guidelines will not only keep your home free of pet odors and pests, but will also do much to improve your pet's health. Trials show that hygiene contributes as much to disease control in animals as repeat vaccinations do. It will add to your personal enjoyment of your home, too, as well as protecting family and visitors from the potential hazards of exposure to animal parasites. Train your dog at as young an age as possible not to jump on furniture—remember that they are pack animals who need to know who is top dog! Cats are more difficult, but give them their own comfortable sleeping area and encourage them to lie there, rather than on chairs, sofas, or beds, or shut doors to rooms you do not want them to enter.

A quick and effortless way to remove pet hairs from upholstery is with a tape roller.

INSIDE THE HOME

As well as fleas, there are other diseases that humans can catch from pets, including roundworms, hookworms, and tapeworms, which are all transmittable from pets to their owners. This advice will keep the home you share with your pets germ-free.

DE-WORM REGULARLY
To eliminate parasites (roundworms), de-worm your pets regularly according to size.

WASH YOUR HANDS
Never touch a dog or cat while eating, and wash hands before meals and snacks if you have been petting animals.

PET BEDDING
Pets carry bacteria that can make humans sick: keep pet bedding, dishes, and toys out of the kitchen, and away from cooking utensils or work surfaces. Sprinkle dried pennyroyal or wormwood into your pet's bed to keep it flea-free. Vacuuming around the bedding daily will pick up fleas

at adult and egg stage: empty the contents of the bag afterward and put in a lidded outdoor trash can. Wash your pet's bedding regularly.

VACUUM CARPETS
Vacuum carpets regularly to avoid the accumulation of pet hairs, especially if you have young children who spend a lot of their time on the floor.

CAT LITTER TRAYS
Two potentially serious infections, toxoplasmosis and toxocariasis (*see opposite*), can be caught from cat feces. Keep soiled litter trays away from children and pregnant women, and wash your hands after emptying.

STORING PET FOOD
Keep opened cans of pet food in the refrigerator and cover with a reusable, plastic lid to prevent odors from contaminating other fresh foods in the fridge.

FLIES

It is important to keep houseflies and other insects out of the house, and away from food, since they may carry fecal matter from your pets' droppings. To deter flies, grow herbs like rue (citrin) or tansy and hang bunches of them in living areas. A tub of mint by the kitchen door is also effective.

ELIMINATING ODORS

If a cat urinates or sprays in the house, first wash the area immediately with an enzyme-free laundry detergent, and rinse thoroughly with cool water. By eliminating the smell completely you will prevent the animal from returning to the same spot to repeat the offense. Baking soda will also reduce odors when sprinkled into a cat litter tray.

If the cages of small mammals such as hamsters, guinea pigs, and ferrets smell bad, sprinkle a layer of baking soda under the bedding every time you clean out the cage.

If a puppy wets the carpet, soak the area at once with soda water, then mop up with a wet cloth, redampen with soda water and wipe clean.

DOG FOULING

Million of gallons of dog urine and tons of dog feces are deposited on our city streets every day. The feces of both dogs and cats contain a roundworm called *Toxocara*. This can infect humans with a disease called toxocariasis that can cause blindness or partial loss of vision. Children are the ones most obviously at risk, and must be taught as early as possible not to go near or touch pet excreta.

Sprinkle baking soda or borax on carpets and allow it to soak up the moisture and deodorize the patch.

• Have a poop-scoop handy for cleaning up messes in the yard, and for when you take your dog out in public places.

• De-worm your pet regularly to ensure that its feces are free of parasites. Look out for little white worms, like rice grains, in feces in the summer. These flea tapeworms can be passed on to children and must be gotten rid of.

• Take a supply of small plastic bags for poop-scooping when you walk the dog in the street or the park; simply put your hand into the bag like a glove, pick up the feces, pull the neck of the bag back over your hand and twist the top closed. Many parks and municipalities provide special garbage cans for disposing of dog feces.

• Pregnant women should wear rubber gloves if they have to clean up dog or cat feces, because of the risk of toxocariasis and toxoplasmosis.

• Clean up pet feces as soon as possible, and use a mild disinfectant such as "soft chemistry" bleach on the area to kill off any worm eggs.

Never allow your pet on areas where children play: children can pick up roundworms from dog feces, which gives them toxocariasis, causing cysts in the eyes and even blindness.

WORKING AT HOME

When you are setting up a workstation at home it is worth giving some careful thought to the office environment: it will contribute to the quality of your work output, as well as to your health. Make the most of whatever space you can put aside for a home office and invest in natural materials and the best possible equipment, and it will pay dividends. Try also to create a well-ventilated room with clean air for your health and well-being, and invest in effective task lighting to prevent eyestrain.

STRESS RELIEF

Long hours at work induce stress, so build regular stretches and exercise into your daily schedule. Your work will improve as a result: the brain needs rest as much as it does stimulation, and it also needs oxygen, so a brisk walk or exercise in the fresh air will improve concentration and motivation. Working at home can be both more productive and enjoyable when you look after your body. A well-designed chair and workstation is integral to this, so take time to plan the layout of your work area.

RECYCLING OFFICE EQUIPMENT

Running a home office that is environmentally friendly makes sense: buy recycled or recyclable equipment, and organize recycling bins for waste materials. Use as many nontoxic products as possible, and minimize the amount of energy spent on lighting and heating. Use your purchasing power in your choice of office supplies, and become an ethical consumer.

Create a comfortable, well-planned home office with good lighting, restful colors, and privacy.

Cleaning the keyboard p156

Keeping your desk neat p157

Sitting correctly p159

Spending ethically p161

DESIGNING A HOME OFFICE

A well-designed home office is also an efficient and energy-saving one. Start by measuring the dimensions of the room, and make a floor plan that includes the position of the windows (and therefore the direction of natural light) and the position of electric and telephone sockets. Then plan out how to maximize your space. For example, an L-shaped desk placed in a corner ensures good access to reference items placed on shelves on the walls above the desk. Bear the following design points in mind to help you arrive at a successful solution.

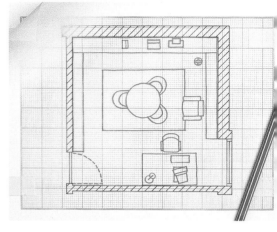

SPACE

To make working at home a pleasure rather than a source of frustration, spend time planning the space and consider the following points for a satisfactory result.

For the most efficient arrangement, draw a scale plan of the room, then plot the layout of furniture and fixtures to make best use of the available space and light.

● Position the main work surface near natural light, but not in direct sunlight. Organize directional lights to suit your specific work tasks (*see opposite*).
● Ask a professional electrician to install extra electric sockets to ensure that your power supply is sufficient for your needs.
● Install a second phone line if you need a modem connection, or broadband service to access the internet at high speeds.
● Plan holes for equipment cables in work surfaces to tuck wires neatly out of sight.
● Choose a soft rather than hard natural flooring material to absorb sound.
● Plan a storage area using storage cubes under work surfaces, drawers and shelving, filing cabinets and

cupboards, so that all items can be put away to create a clutter-free work environment. Store filing trays and boxes on deep shelves in order to keep your work surface clear.
● Keep equipment and files that you use most frequently within easy reach (on shelves above and below the worktop) and place less frequently used items farther away.
● Keep worktops free of equipment such as telephones and faxes. Position these to one side so that you have space to spread out paperwork.
● The colors you choose for the office are thought to affect performance. Reds and oranges are stimulating, soft blues boost imagination and creativity, and yellow is a lively color and is associated with mental clarity.

AIR QUALITY

According to various academic studies, photocopiers, computers, fax machines, and printers release ozone, which can exacerbate allergic reactions and make asthma worse. Ozone causes a significant reduction in lung function, yet levels close to electrical equipment in office buildings often exceed World Health Organization exposure limits. Also, office products such as adhesives and sealants contain hydrocarbon solvents that are dangerously toxic. As a general rule, choose office items made from hard rather than soft plastics, which tend to "outgas" for long periods, sometimes with no warning smell.

ENVIRONMENT

A working environment that is comfortable and relaxed, with good levels of natural daylight, will be both more pleasant to work in and better for your productivity. Here are some hints and tips for creating that environment.

- Make your home office a strictly no-smoking zone.
- Ventilate the room well with plenty of fresh air, and/or an extractor fan.
- Install an ionizer: the balance of positive and negative ions in the atmosphere is disturbed by electronic equipment.
- Use soy-based or other nontoxic inks for printing (see Resources page 175).
- Use water-based marker pens and correction fluid.
- Install office furniture that will not "outgas" and toxify the atmosphere: buy secondhand or choose natural materials other than plastics, and avoid pressed-wood products (see page 11). Solid wood worktops are both practical and beautiful.
- Make sure your photocopier is the "dry copy" variety and does not use volatile toners that give off strong vapors of ammonia, ethanol, and kerosene (in fact, only old or secondhand copiers are likely to do so). Maintain your copier correctly, and place it near a window to ensure good ventilation. The same applies to fax machines and laser printers. If your photocopier gives off chlorine or sulfur smells, have it serviced.
- Power your office with electricity from renewable sources. Set your heating at a constant temperature, lowering it toward the end of the working day. An ambient temperature of around 68–74°F (20–23.5°C) in winter (73–78°F/23–26°C in summer) is most likely to keep you alert, but remember that your body temperature drops if you sit still for long periods of time.

LIGHTING

The Applied Psychology Unit at Cambridge University in England has shown that good lighting leads to increased efficiency in the workplace. Here's how to achieve it.

- Make the best use possible of whatever natural light is available. If your office is in an attic room under the roof eaves, consider installing a skylight or dormer window, which will give a wonderful, even light all day long.
- To save energy, install energy-efficient light bulbs, using daylight bulbs or compact fluorescent lighting (see page 21), not regular fluorescent strips that can contribute to eyestrain, headaches, and stress.
- Arrange task lighting carefully for work areas.
- Lighting costs can account for 25 percent of business electricity bills, so energy-saving bulbs can cut costs significantly. A large company cut its lighting use by up to 90 percent in this way, and within two years they had a 53 percent return on their investment.
- Install occupancy sensors that turn off lights when no one is in the room, or do this manually.

If possible, situate your desk next to a large window so that you can gain maximum benefit from natural light throughout the working day.

CHOOSING EQUIPMENT

When you purchase new office equipment, find out whether it has been tested and certified to produce only low emissions. Printers and copiers can be sources of ozone and VOCs. Also bear in mind the following points.

COMPUTERS & PHOTOCOPIERS

● To save power, use the computer standby facility.
● Use a screensaver to save energy when your computer is not in constant use.
● Buy a printer that prints on both sides of the paper.
● Buy a copier with a duplex function (one that will photocopy on both sides of the paper).

● Buy a photocopier whose parts can be recovered and reused: in 1998 the Xerox Corporation recycled or refurbished more than 79,000 tons of old machines.
● Buy remanufactured or refillable toner cartridges for your copier.
● Do not sit too close to the copier, to avoid inhaling fumes.

OFFICE TELEPHONES

● Purchase a telephone from one of the few companies that remanufactures new phones from recycled parts, (see Resources page 175).
● Consider setting up a business contract with a telephone company that not only offers savings on phone calls and Internet use but also donates some of its company profits to ethical and environmental causes (see Resources page 175).

MAINTAINING EQUIPMENT

Clean out dust and other dirt particles from between the keyboards with a damp cotton swab dipped in baking soda.

Looking after your office machines carefully will give them a longer and more efficient working life, which in turn will help reduce the mountains of obsolete appliances that are difficult to recycle and often end up in landfill sites.

● Buy "soft chemistry" cleaners in bulk for office use (see Resources page 175).
● Wipe the computer screen clean with an antistatic cloth to keep it dust-free and to prevent eye strain.
● Wipe the office telephone clean, especially the receiver, with a "soft chemistry" lemon-based cleaner (see Resources page 175).
● To clean computer keyboards and telephone keypads, first unplug them, and then clean them with a dry, soft bristle brush, rubbing the bristles against your hand first to create static electricity, which will attract the dust to the bristles.
● Dirt that collects on the computer mouse pad can get inside the mouse and stop it from working correctly. Keep the mouse pad clean by wrapping some adhesive tape, sticky side out, around your fingertips, and swiping them over the surface of the pad.

CHOOSING STATIONERY

Recycled stationery supplies are now mainstream products, and no longer difficult to obtain. Many companies offer a mail-order service, and buying in bulk is not only cheaper but saves on packaging too.

- Use recycled, unbleached stationery for your correspondence: it requires no raw material, cuts energy consumption, and reduces air and water pollution by up to 50 percent.
- Some laser printer paper contains a melted plastic toner and is not valuable for recycling because it does not make quality paper the second time around. Buy plain, uncoated laser printer paper if possible.
- Think before you print a document: reread and check the spelling to avoid running out innumerable versions that waste paper.

- Look for recycled office supplies such as scissors and pencils (*see Resources page 175*).
- Buy recyclable fax paper, mailing labels, files and folders, flip charts, storage boxes, and sticky notes.
- Buy refillable highlighter pens, and ink pens that use cornstarch (*see Resources page 175*).
- Buy office supplies in bulk where possible to reduce packaging and transportation costs: consider sharing an order of office supplies with a friend or colleague. Buying in bulk is cheaper, too.

Keep a good supply of recycled address labels so that you can reuse any size of envelope that you receive.

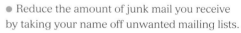

- Reduce the amount of junk mail you receive by taking your name off unwanted mailing lists.
- Reduce or eliminate the use of colored paper, since it is more difficult to recycle.
- Use shredded waste paper for protective packaging rather than plastic bubble-wrap.
- Take a canvas bag with you when buying office supplies, rather than accepting a plastic shopping bag.
- Use both sides of the paper for rough drafts.
- Use scrap paper for lists and memos.
- Put aside a space to store used envelopes, boxes, and padded bags for reuse.
- Use string to tie packages rather than large quantities of plastic packaging tape.
- Reuse files and binders, relabeling them for their new function.
- Recycle all your waste paper.
- Do research on-line or in libraries rather than ordering hard-copy material.

Instead of buying plastic desk-organizers for pens, paper clips, and other desk accessories, improvise with recycled cans, glassware, and coffee mugs.

CREATING A WORKSTATION

Using computers for long, unbroken periods of time has been shown to cause serious eyestrain, skin problems, headaches, repetitive strain injury (RSI), and high levels of stress, as well as muscular aches and pains (*see below*). Computers generate low levels of radiation, and the positively charged field around a computer neutralizes negative ions in the atmosphere. High concentrations of positive ions are associated with respiratory problems, fatigue, headaches, irritability, and metabolic disorders. Studies at Columbia University in New York have shown that people who work with VDUs all day have more physical and mental health problems.

Attach a screen-shield to a computer screen to reduce exposure to electric field radiation.

WORKING AT A COMPUTER

Computers are part of modern life and there is no avoiding them; however, how and how much we use them will make a considerable difference to any detrimental effects they may have on us or on our working environment.

● Spend no more than four hours a day seated in front of a computer looking at the screen.
● Take a break to exercise and stretch the body every 30 minutes: exercise boosts energy levels, and the break from concentration can refresh the mind.
● Take a relaxing "eye-break" every 10 minutes: gaze into the distance, or let your eyes wander around the room.
● Use a laptop with a LCD (liquid crystal display) screen, which operates on a lower voltage, and extends its radiation less far.
● Sit as far away as possible from the screen—at least 30 in (75 cm) from the front of the computer.
● An antiglare screen will also shield you from the electric fields (VLF/ELF) in electromagnetic (EMF) radiation and eliminate static.
● To reduce glare, diffused office lighting is best. Make sure that light is not shining directly onto your screen. Task lighting can be designed to illuminate your worktop without reflecting in the screen.
● Have a mobile keyboard so that you can alter its position regularly, and thus avoid repetitive strain on your wrists.

Use a towel for support rather than letting your wrists rest on the hard edge of the desk, which can be uncomfortable.

SEATING ARRANGEMENTS

A chair that supports you properly while you work is one of the most important items that you can invest in. Sitting at a PC positioned at the wrong height for your chair can strain the neck badly, and an ill-designed seat can strain your spine. A keyboard at the wrong height can create shoulder, elbow, and wrist problems.

- Invest in a quality chair with an adjustable lumbar support: your alignment changes throughout the day. Buy one with multiple adjustments for pelvic, lumbar, and shoulder support.
- Arrange your workstation so that your eyeline is level with the top of the computer monitor. The worktop height should be arranged so that your arms are relaxed, making a 90° angle with the keyboard. Your feet should be flat on the floor, and your knees bent at a 90° angle. The keyboard should be slightly slanted and wrists supported.
- Take short breaks from the PC in order to stretch and relieve stresses on the body. Working for long, unrelieved periods on a keyboard can cause repetitive strain injury (carpal tunnel syndrome), which is excruciatingly painful and debilitating. The only cure for it is rest, so it is best to avoid it in the first place.

TAKE CARE OF YOUR BODY

Take up yoga and go to a class at least once a week to help you stretch and relax. Go for regular walks. Take a short break to stretch and breathe deeply every 30 minutes.

1. Interlock your fingers and stretch your arms over your head, palms upward. Lean back in the chair, stretch up to the ceiling, and take several deep breaths.

2. Stretch the arms out to the side of your body and point the fingers up to the ceiling. Take several deep breaths. This opens up the carpal tunnel in the wrists and helps prevent strain.

RELAXATION TECHNIQUES

Close your eyes. Massage the bridge of the nose with your index finger, working in small circles in both directions. Pinch the bridge of the nose several times. Press the fingertips gently over the closed lids. Press into the inner corners of the eyes to release tension. Massage the cheekbones with the fingertips, using a series of small circular movements.

A chair with adjustment levers to alter the height of the seat and back position will offer the best comfort and support.

MONEY MATTERS

Becoming an ethical consumer is part and parcel of questioning where things originate, and how the global economy works and how it affects individual communities. Knowledge is power, and with a little economic information, thought, and reorganization, we can make sure that our purchasing habits have a positive rather than a detrimental effect on the world around us. One of those ways is by buying products that carry the "Fair Trade" label.

Carpet production is one area where fair trade benefits the workers—look for the Rugmark label on hand-woven rugs as a sign that they are fairly traded.

FAIR TRADE

The vast bulk of worldwide trade is controlled by multinational companies. Individual farmers and workers, particularly in developing countries, find it increasingly difficult to produce their goods independently of this system, in which profits go to the company and not to the workers, and working conditions and wages are beyond the workers' control.

There are now alternative trading organizations around the globe that campaign for human rights issues and give small producers access to Western markets, enabling them to sell a wide range of goods, including coffee beans and clothes. Local people group together to form cooperatives and earn a reasonable return on their products. They are guaranteed fair wages, decent working conditions, fair prices for their goods, and job security. Look for the distinctive black-and-white "Fair Trade" label: some goods can be found in the supermarket, health food stores, and coffee shops. Most fair trade programs are ecologically sound, being small and efficient enterprises that use local resources and cause little pollution. Profits tend to be reinvested into the community, building health clinics and supporting other community projects.

ETHICAL INVESTMENT

This is not a new idea: ethical investment has been practiced since the nineteenth century, when wealthy religious groups sought to ensure that their money was not used to fund tobacco, gambling, or alcohol production or to support those that manufactured arms.

Many major financial companies have responded to consumer demand by creating socially responsible investment funds. These funds aim to avoid harmful enterprises, while others actively support ethical ventures. There are numerous organizations that will invest your money in socially responsible ways, and financial advisers who specialize in these areas (see Resources page 175). Research and analysis has shown that in the long term, ethical investment funds perform just as well, if not better, than other mutual funds, since the fund managers have in-depth knowledge of the companies and why they have ethical status.

FINANCIAL INVESTMENT

● Get independent financial advice: the commission charged on investments is the same if you buy the product direct, so take this opportunity to get ethical investment advice as part of the financial service.

● Discuss your ethical viewpoint with your financial adviser in order to obtain the best product from your standpoint: environmental investment is complex and varies widely in performance.

● Consider a portfolio that may include both ethical and regular investments, in order to make the most of your savings and spread your risk.

● If your financial adviser charges a fee, make sure that the commission is fed back into your investment: you should never have to pay both a fee and a commission.

CREDIT UNIONS

● If you are unhappy with banking systems, use a local credit union where you can save and borrow money at low rates of interest in a cooperative, non-profit organization (*Resources page 175*).

● Apply for a Greenpeace credit card (PVC-free and biodegradable), knowing that a small percentage of your everyday spending power will go to good causes.

● Join a local exchange and trading program where members exchange and share goods and services with each other. No money changes hands, and it builds up community ties as well as

Buying fruits and vegetables that are grown locally makes good money sense.

being a practical way of pooling resources and minimizing environmental impact: for example, by sharing tools.

MORTGAGES

● Some banks and savings and loans offer "green" mortgages, as well as providing free, energy-efficiency building surveys. Others are dedicated to improving the environment by promoting sustainable housing, energy-efficient homes, and restoration of old buildings. Some government programs also provide subsidies and low-cost loans for building restoration.

INSURANCE

● Some insurance brokers offer ethical household, travel and commercial insurance: consult an adviser or search the internet.

Support small farmers and businesses by buying goods direct from the producer so that you know their origin.

RESOURCES

One of the best ways of obtaining the most up-to-date and relevant information about the nontoxic household products on the market and the environmental issues discussed in this book is through the Internet. Even if you do not have a website address for a relevant site, simply type a key word into a search engine and it should come up with several results that match your request. Most good websites offer links to other sites that may prove surprisingly useful. So whether you want to know more about recycling matters, or house interiors, or even everyday domestic tasks, go online, or contact the associations and companies listed below by email, telephone, or letter.

HOME BASICS

Aerias, LLC
1337 Capital Circle, Suite G
Atlanta, GA 30067
Tel: (678) 931–2290
Email: info@aerias.org
www.aerias.org
For information on indoor air quality.

Building For Health Materials Center
P.O. Box 113, Carbondale, CO 81623
Tel: (800) 292–4838
Email: crose@sopris.net
buildingforhealth.com/bhchome.html
For natural building materials, such as eco-lumber, natural paints, flooring, and air and water filtration systems.

BYO Natural Furniture
Tel: (415) 454–9948
www.tamalpais.com/htmlpages/BYO/byo.html
For information on how to build your own natural furniture.

Caroma USA, Inc. (Canada)
61 Hazelton Avenue, Toronto
ON M5R2E3, Canada

Tel: (416) 925–5556
Email: gsheargold@caromausa.com
www.caromausa.com

Caroma USA, Inc. (US)
1669 Brighton Beach Road,
Menasha, WI 54952
Tel: (920) 830–3461
Email: jkaras@caromausa.com
www.caromausa.com
For dual-flush toilet systems and compost toilets.

EcoBusinessLinks Environmental Directory
www.ecobusinesslinks.com/index.htm
For information on environmentally responsible practices in building and living. "Environmental Directory" of companies that manufacture eco-friendly products, such as natural building supplies and insulation, eco-furniture, and organic paints.

Electrowind/Eifco (Canada)
P.O. Box 713, 2 Taggart Street
Guelph, ON N1H 6L3, Canada
Tel: (800) 265–8340 or (519) 836–2280
Email: service@electro-wind.com
www.electrowind.com/Product/products.htm
For paper-based insulation products.

Environmental Protection Agency
www.epa.gov
Information on asbestos in the home; for
information on asbestos removal contractors,
call the EPA at 202–554–1404.

Georgia Pacific Corporation
133 Peachtree Street, N.E.
Atlanta, GA 30303
Tel: (404) 652–4000
www.gp.com
For paper-based insulation products.

GreenHomeBuilding.com
P.O. Box 632, Crestone, CO 81131
Tel: (719) 256–4279
Email: kelly@greenhomebuilding.com
www.greenhomebuilding.com/about_us.htm
For information on natural building.

Health Goods
P.O. Box 6463
Manchester, NH 03108–6463
Tel: (888) 666–7761
Email: info@healthgoods.com
www.healthgoods.com
For a variety of products, including air and
water control products and home testing kits.

Jon-Don
400 Medinah Road,
Roselle, IL 60172
Tel: (800) 400–9473
Email: jdsales@jondon.com
www.jondon.com
For domestic hygrometers.

Midwest Composites, Inc.
869 E. Schaumburg Road #154
Schaumburg, IL 60194
Tel: (847) 301–2030
Email: allen@clearlight.com
www.clearlight.com/
midwestcomposites/index.html
For paper-based insulation products.

National Safety Council
1121 Spring Lake Drive,
Itasca, IL 60143
Tel: (630) 285–1121
www.nsc.org
For information on air quality and hazardous
chemicals.

Natural Building Colloquium
www.networkearth.org/naturalbuilding/
colloquium.html
For information on natural building.

Real Goods
360 Interlocken Blvd., Suite 300
Broomfield, CO 80021–3440
Tel: (800) 919–2400
www.realgoods.com/renew
For graywater bypass systems, water-saving
showerheads, compost toilets, and many other
energy-efficient products.

Radon Information Center
1936 Butler Bridge Road
Fletcher, NC 28732–9365
Tel: (800) AIR-CHEK
www.radon.com
For information on radon testing.

Sinan Company
P.O. Box 857, Davis, CA 95616
Tel: (530) 753–3104
Email: sinan@dcn.davis.ca.us
www.dcn.davis.ca.us/go/sinan/
For natural building materials, such as paints,
wood finishes, metalworks, and carpets.

Sun-Mar Corporation
5035 North Service Road
Unit C9, Burlington
ON L7L 5V2, Canada
Tel: (905) 332 1314
www.sun-mar.com
For low-flush toilet systems and compost
toilets.

Sustainable Architecture, Building, and Culture
P.O. Box 30085, Santa Barbara, CA 93130
www.sustainableabc.com
For information on natural building materials and techniques.

● For natural nontoxic paints and finishes, see DECORATING & FURNISHING.

SAVING ENERGY

Creative Energy Technologies
CET Solar Store, 65 Route 106
North Springfield, VT
Tel: (888) 305–0278
Email: info@cetsolar.com
www.cetsolar.com
For solar-powered hot water systems and a variety of other solar-powered systems, appliances, and products.

Crest–Center for Renewable Energy and Sustainable Technology
1612 K Street, N.W.
Suite 202
Washington, DC 20006
Email: info@repp.org
www.crest.org
For information on renewable energy , efficiency, and sustainable development.

EcoBusinessLinks Environmental Directory
www.ecobusinesslinks.com/ecotourism.htm
"Environmental Directory" of eco-tourism travel guides and agents.

Energy Star—U.S. Environmental Protection Agency
Tel: (888) STAR-YES
www.energystar.gov/default.shtml
For information on energy—and cost-efficient practices.

Green Wave
P.O. Box 1850
Middleburg
VA 20118
Tel: (877) 730–8255
Email: talkback@greenwave.com
www.greenwave.com/products
For energy-saving appliances.

Innovative Insulation, Inc.
6200 W. Pioneer Parkway
Arlington
TX 76013
Tel: (800) 825–0123
Email: insulation@earthlink.net
www.radiantbarrier.com/contact.html
For reflective foil insulation for roof rafters.

International Federation of Automotive Engineering Societies
www.fisita.com/
For information on energy-efficient automotive transportation and low-sulfur diesel.

Noli Control Systems
P.M.B. 168
1060–D Avenida de Los Arboles
Thousand Oaks
CA 91362
Tel: (805) 492–8381
Email: info@nolico.com
www.nolico.com/saveenergy/esp_home.htm
For energy-saving lightbulbs.

Office of Energy Efficiency
Natural Resources Canada
580 Booth Street, 18th Floor
Ottawa
ON K1A 0E4
Canada
www.oee.nrcan.gc.ca
Consumer information, guides to business and industry agencies, workshops, and special events.

Office of Energy Efficiency and Renewable Energy—U.S. Department of Energy
www.eren.doe.gov/consumerinfo
For general information on saving and recycling energy.

Northern Power Systems
182 Mad River Park
PO Box 999, Waitsfield, VT 05673
Tel: (802) 496–2955
Email: contact@northernpower.com
www.northernpower.com
For information on wind and solar energy.

Pacific Biodiesel
285 Hukilike Street, B103
Kahului, HI 96732
Tel: (808) 877–3144
www.biodiesel.com
For organically produced diesel fuels.

Sears
Tel: (800) 349–4358
www.sears.com
For energy-efficient appliances.

Sinan Company
P.O. Box 857, Davis, CA 95616–0857
Tel: (530) 753–3104
Email: sinan@dcn.davis.ca.us
www.dcn.davis.ca.us/go/sinan
For natural insulation materials.

Solar Access Renewable Energy
3 Elm Street, Peterborough, NH 03458
Tel: (877) 650–1782
www.solaraccess.com
For information on the solar industry and renewable energy.

Ultratouch: Natural Cotton Fiber Insulation
The Crestone Mart, 182 Galena Ave.
Crestone, CO 81131
Tel: (719) 256–4670
Email: crestonemart@hotmail.com

www.nhe.net/naturalcottoninsulation
For natural insulation materials.

● For natural insulation materials, see HOME BASICS.

DECORATING & FURNISHING

Auro Natural Paints and Finishes
1340-G Industrial Avenue
Petaluma, CA 94952
Tel: (888) 302–9352
Email: info@aurousa.com
www.aurousa.com
For natural paints, primers, stains, finishes, adhesives, carpets, tiles, cleaners, and more.

Earth Runnings
PO Box 3027, Taos, NM 87571
Email: earthrun@newmex.com
www.earthrunnings.com
For mainly hemp (but also some organic cotton) bed linens, table linens, yoga mats, meditation cushions and stuffed animals.

Eco-Planet Internet Store-EcoChoices
P.O. Box 1491, Glendora, CA 91740
Email: service@ecochoices.com
ecochoices.com
For natural beds, mattresses, bedding, pillows, furniture, cork flooring, wool carpet, sofas, armchairs, hemp slipcovers, and hammocks.

Environmental Interiors
P.O. Box 27026, Seattle
WA 98125–1426
Tel: (206) 418–8120
Email: info@envirointeriors.com
www.envirointeriors.com
For natural building materials, furnishings, linens, wall and floor treatments, and air and water quality treatments.

Fair Trade Federation, Inc.
1612 K Street NW, Suite 600
Washington, DC 20006
Tel: (202) 872–5329
Email: info@fairtradefederation.org
www.fairtradefederation.com
*For information on Fair Trade organizations
from which to buy organic goods, such as
hand-crafted rugs and blankets.*

HempStores.com
www.hempstores.com
*For locating stores in the US and Canada that
sell hemp products.*

Miller Bros. Paint and Decorating
P.O. Box 12210, 4343 Montgomery Road
Cincinnati, OH 45212
Tel: (877) 531–1517
Email: info@millerbrospaint.com
www.millerbrospaint.com/b2n.htm
*For "Back to Nature" products such as water-
based, solvent-free paint and varnish
removers, and lead abatement products.*

National Paint and Coatings Association
www.paint.org
*For advice on disposing of leftover paint in an
environmentally safe way.*

Nirvana Safe Haven
3441 Golden Rain Road, Suite 3
Walnut Creek, CA 94595
Tel: (800) 968–9355
Email: daliya@nontoxic.com
www.nontoxic.com/purewoolcarpets
For information on natural carpets.

Nitty Gritty Reproductions
170 King Street East
Toronto, ON M5A 1J4
Canada
Tel: (416) 364 1393
www.nittygritty.ca
Milk-painted handcrafted furniture and

*agents for the Canadian Old Fashioned Milk
Paint Company.*

Organic Matters
707 South First Street
PO Box 598, La Conner, WA 98257
Tel: (800) 843–9069 Email: om@organic-
matters.com
www.organic-matters.com
*For organic bedding, blankets, clothing, rugs,
and soaps.*

OrganicMattresses.com
Lifekind® Products
PO Box 1774,
Grass Valley, CA 95945
(800) 284–4983
www.organicmattresses.com
*For organic cotton beds, mattresses, futons,
blankets, sheets, pillows, and towels.*

Sage Creek Naturals
7976 Tugwell Road
Sooke, BC, VOS-1NO
Tel: (866) 598–1400 (US and Canada)
Email: wholesale@sagecreeknaturals.com
www.sagecreeknaturals.com
*For organic cotton baby clothing and bedding,
and house linens.*

Tekiah Hammocks
439 Valley Drive, N.W.
Floyd, VA 24091
(540) 745–5835
www.hemphammocks.com
For quality hemp and "envirope" hammocks.

Trade Partners UK-USA
British Trade Office, British Consulate-
General, 845 Third Avenue, 9th Floor
New York, NY 10022
Tel: (212) 745–0495
www.tradepartnersuk-usa.com
*For water-based, solvent-free coatings
removal products.*

Under the Canopy
12926 Hyland Circle,
Boca Raton, FL 33428
(888) CANOPY-9
www.underthecanopy.com
For organic bed and bath items, and fabrics (cotton, hemp, wool, silk, linen, and ramie).

● For listings of paints, finishes, and natural furnishings, see HOME BASICS.

CLEANING THE HOME

Abundant Earth
Tel: (888) 51-EARTH
Email: goodstuff@abundantearth.com
www.abundantearth.com
For a variety of natural cleaning equipment and supplies, among other things.

Auro Natural Paints and Finishes
See DECORATING & FURNISHING
For natural household cleaners.

Bioshield
See DECORATING AND FURNISHING
For soft chemistry dishwasher detergent, toilet bowl, kitchen, floor, and glass cleaners.

Citrus Magic
Tel: (800) 451–7096
Email: bpi@beaumontproducts.com
www.citrusmagic.com/natureclean.html
For a variety of natural, citrus-based cleaning products.

Gaiam, Inc.
360 Interlocken Blvd., Suite 300
Broomfield, CO 80021–3440
Tel: (877) 989–6321
Email: customerservice@gaiam.com
www.gaiam.com
For a variety of soft chemistry cleaning products.

Real Goods
See HOME BASICS
For a variety of natural, nontoxic cleaning supplies, ranging from vacuum cleaners to liquid cleaning products.

smallplanet
1200 Aerowood Drive
Unit 30, Mississauga
ON L4W 2S7
Canada
Tel: (905) 568 8442
www.smallplanetinc.com/ps/benefect.htm
Produces Nature Clean brand of natural household cleaning products.

WASHING & LAUNDRY

Caeran Incorporated
R.R.#1 Rockwood
ON N0B 2K0, Canada
Tel: (519) 856 0564
www.caeran.com
Biodegradable laundry, cleaning, and personal products.

Green Wave
See SAVING ENERGY
For natural laundry products.

Life Natural
Tel: (888) 271-LIFE
Email: information@lifenatural.com
www.lifenatural.com/launball.htm
For laundry balls.

NaturalHerbalTherapy.com
www.naturalherbaltherapy.com
For information on how to make your own natural laundry detergent, among other things.

Real Goods
See CLEANING THE HOME
For soft chemistry detergents.

RECYCLING WASTE

Air & Waste Management Association
420 Fort Duquesne Blvd.
One Gateway Center
Pittsburgh, PA 15222
Tel: (412) 232–3444
Email: info@awma.org
www.awma.org
For information on air and waste management.

Council on Environmental Quality
The White House
1600 Pennsylvania Avenue NW
Washington, DC 20500
Tel: (202) 456–1414
www.whitehouse.gov/ceq
For information on the government recycling programs.

Enviro Solutions
P.O. Box 2482
Lexington
SC 29071–2482
Email: envirosol@prodigy.net
www.envirosolutionsllc.com
For information on recycling ink-jet printers and printer cartridges.

Global Recycling Network
P.O. Box 24017
Guelph, ON N1E 6V8
Tel: (519) 658–9580 (US and Canada)
www.grn.com
For local, national, and international directories of recycling organizations.

The Literary Empowerment Fund
Tel: (717) 791–6210
Email: rorendi@literacyempowerment.org
www.colorcodedbooks.org/lef/recycling.html
For information on the Reading Recycling Project, which distributes new and used books free of charge to literacy programs.

RetroSystems Inc
7521 Flint Road SE, Calgary
AB T2H 1G2, Canada
Tel: (405) 255 3353
www.retrosystems.com
Specializes in recycling scrap computer and networking equipment.

VirtualRecycling.com
www.virtualrecycling.com
For recycling awareness, initiatives, and information, plus useful contacts.

World Wise
Email: info@worldwise.com
www.worldwise.com
For information on recycling a variety of items, ranging from paper to disposable cameras, batteries, CDs, and cellular phones.

HEALTHY FOOD

Anke Kruse Organics Inc
14191 Crewson's Line
Acton, ON L72 2L7
Canada
Tel: (519) 853 3899
www.ankekruseorganics.ca
For organic food products, including some imported from Europe.

Big Brand Water Filters
Tel: (888) 426–9488
Email: info@bigbrandwaterfilters.com
www.bigbrandwaterfilters.com
For natural water filters, including carbon filtration and reverse osmosis systems.

Biocontrol Network
Tel: (615) 370–4301
Email: info@biconet.com
www.biconet.com
For various agricultural products, including garden soil test kits.

Diamond Organics
PO Box 2159, Freedom, CA 95019
Tel: (888) ORGANIC
Email: info@diamondorganics.com
www.diamondorganics.com
For organic foods and drinks.

Fair Trade Federation, Inc.
See DECORATING & FURNISHING
For information on Fair Trade foods.

Farmer's Market Online
www.farmersmarketonline.com
For organic foods and drinks.

Frontier Natural Products Co-op
Tel: (800) 669–3275
Email: customercare@frontiercoop.com
www.frontierherb.com
For organic herbs, spices, and coffee.

HealthyFoodStore.co.uk
www.healthyfoodstore.co.uk/enumbers.html
For information on European Union permitted additives.

Natural Foods Directory
GreenLeaf MEDIA
2501 University Avenue
Madison, WI 53705
Tel: (608) 233–1737
Email: greenleaf@jvlnet.com
www.naturalfoodsdirectory.com
For a directory of national organic food suppliers and restaurants.

Ontarbio Organic Farmers Co-op Inc
R.R.#1, Durham, ON N0G 1R0, Canada
Tel: (519) 369 5316
www.organicmeadow.com
Organic farmers' co-operative.

Organic Consumers Association
6101 Cliff Estate Road
Little Marais, MN 55614

Tel: (218) 226–4164
www.purefood.org
For information on food safety, organic agriculture, Fair Trade, and sustainability.

Organic Farming Research Foundation
P.O. Box 440, Santa Cruz, CA 95061
Tel: (831) 426–6606
Email: research@ofrf.org
www.ofrf.org
For information on organic farming.

Organic Wine Company
1592 Union Street, #350
San Francisco, CA 94123
Tel: (888) ECO-WINE
Email: organic@ecowine.com
www.ecowine.com
For internationally produced organic wines.

Pacific Western Brewing Company
641 North Nechako Road,
Prince George, BC V2K 4M4
Tel: (250) 562–2424
Email: mail@pwbrewing.com
www.pwbrewing.com
For a variety of organic beers.

Zoglo's
42 Prince Edward Boulevard
Thornhill, ON L3T 7G1, Canada
Tel: 1-877 469 6456
www.zoglos.com
Meatless foods using certified non-genetically modified soy.

PERSONAL CARE

Abundant Earth
See CLEANING THE HOME
For a wide selection of natural personal care products, including deodorants, facial creams, shampoos, shaving creams, dental care products, and feminine hygiene products.

AlternativeBeauty.com
www.alternative-beauty.com
For information on natural cosmetics.

Aveda
4000 Pheasant Ridge Drive
Blaine, MN 55449
Tel: (866) 823–1425
www.aveda.com
For natural hair care, skin care, make-up,
perfume, and products containing oryzanol.

Biocontrol Network
See HEALTHY FOOD
For natural personal care products, such
as organic insect repellents.

The Cascadia Soap Company
Hillcrest P.O., PO Box 29
1453 Johnston Road
White Rock,
BC V4B 5J5, Canada
Tel: (604) 538 8060
www.cascadiasoaps.com
Handcrafted soap and skincare preparations
using natural products.

Frontier Natural Products Co-Op
See HEALTHY FOOD
For a variety of natural aromatherapy and
personal care products.

Hankettes
1734 Pell Road, Roberts Creek
BC V0N 2W1, Canada
Tel: (800) 917–1377 (US and Canada)
Email: info@hankettes.com
www.hankettes.com
For 100% reusable organic cotton products,
including handkerchiefs, towels, and more.

Health Goods
See HOME BASICS
For a variety of natural personal care
products, including shaving products for men.

Liberty Vegetable Oil Company
15306 South Carmenita Road
Sante Fe Springs, CA 90670
Tel: (562) 921–8837
Email: liberty@libertyvegetableoil.com
www.libertyvegetableoil.com
For organic oils for making skin care products.

Mountain Rose Herbs
85472 Dilley Lane, Eugene, OR 97405
Tel: (800) 879–3337
www.mountainroseherbs.com
For a variety of natural clays for face masks.

Natural Choices
See CLEANING THE HOME
For reusable cloth menstrual pads.

Next to Nature Trading
Whippletree Junction, Unit G
Trans Canada Highway, Duncan,
BC V9L 6E1, Canada
Tel: (800) 641–4677
Email: sales@nextonature
www.nextonature.com
For a variety of organic products, including
recycled organic tissues and hankerchiefs.

SaffronRouge.com
304 Stone Road West
Suite 737, Guelph, ON N1G 4W4
Tel: (800) 378–1946 (US and Canada)
Email: info@saffronrouge.com
www.saffronrouge.com
For natural skin and body care items, makeup,
and nail polish and nail polish remover.

Simmons Natural Bodycare
42295 Highway 36, Bridgeville, CA 95526
Tel: (707) 777–1920
Email: simmonsnaturals@pon.net
www.simmonsnaturals.com
For a variety of natural feminine hygiene and
personal care products, including crystalline
deodorant stones.

Tiny Tush LLC
102 Ninth Avenue, Baraboo, WI 53913
Tel: (608) 356–2500
www.tinytush.com
For organic tampons and reusable cloth menstrual and breast pads.

Tom's of Maine
P.O. Box 710
Kennebunk, ME 04043
Tel: (800) 367–8667
Email: orderdesk@tomsofmaine.com
www.tomsofmaine.com
For natural toothpaste and personal care products.

NATURAL REMEDIES

Abundant Earth
See PERSONAL CARE
For an enormous selection of herbs, vitamins, and vegetarian homeopathic supplements.

American Institute of Homeopathy
801 N. Fairfax Street, Suite 306
Alexandria, VA 22314
Tel: (888) 445–9988
Email: aih@bigplanet.com
www.homeopathyusa.org
For information on homeopathy and homeopathic organizations.

Canada's One-Stop Homeopathy Network
www.canadahomeopathy.com
Provides links to and information about a wide range of Canadian homeopathy practitioners and resources.

Elixir
8612 Melrose Avenue
Los Angeles, CA 90069
Tel: (310) 657–9300
Email: herbalist@elixir.net
www.elixir.net

For natural herbal medicine information and products.

Farmer's Market Online
See HEALTHY FOOD
For medicinal plants.

Floraleads GR
PO Box 5546, Cary, NC 27512
Tel: (919) 303–1420
Email: floraleads@yahoo.com
www.floraleads.com
For herbal dietary supplements, natural skin care, hair care, dental care, bath and body products developed from traditional remedies, herbal medicines, and natural cosmetics.

Hahnemann Laboratories, Inc.
1940 Fourth Street, San Rafael, CA 94901
Tel: (888) 4–ARNICA
www.hahnemannlabs.com
For homeopathic medicines and first-aid, home, and professional remedy kits.

Healthy Warehouse
132 Kimberly Lane
Pleasant View, TN 37146
Tel: (888) 403–1896
Email: info@healthywarehouse.com
www.healthywarehouse.com
For a variety of herbal products, including homeopathic remedies.

Herbal Medicine Internet Resources
www.holisticmed.com/www/herbalism.html
For information on herbal medicine.

HMedicine.com, Inc.
4100 Carmel Road #256
Charlotte, NC 28226–7159
Tel: (866) 9–MEDCOM
Email: customerservice@hmedicine.com
www.hmedicine.com
For an enormous variety of homeopathic medicines.

Isis Books and Gifts
5701 East Colfax, Denver, CO 80220
Tel: (303) 321–0867
Email: custserv@isisbooks.com
www.isisbooks.com/herbs-medicinal-
magical.asp
*For a large selection of natural herbs for
homemade remedies and informative books
on herbs and herbal remedies.*

Yoga Directory
Email: info@yogadirectory.com
*For a large yoga resource site with links to
teachers, therapists, centers, organizations,
training, retreats, and products.*

YogaSite.com
www.yogasite.com
*For information on yoga, retreats, teachers,
organizations, and products.*

BABY CARE

Abundant Earth
See CLEANING THE HOME
*For organic cribs, mattresses, bedding,
pillows, baby slings, diapers, washcloths,
shampoos, soaps, breast pads, and toys.*

Beanbuddies and More
912 Finlayson Arm Road
Victoria, BC V9E 1E4, Canada
www.beanbuddies.ca
Cotton diapers, fleece blankets and more.

Breastfeeding.com
4730 Table Mesa Drive, Suite B100
Boulder, CO 80305
www.breastfeeding.com
For breast-feeding information.

Baby's Abode
Tel: (866) 4BBABODE
Email: customerservice@babysabode.com

www.babysabode.com
For organic diapers, clothing, and skin care.

Breastfeeding Basics
www.breastfeedingbasics.com
*For breast-feeding information, advice, and
related products.*

EcoBusinessLinks Environmental Directory
www.ecobusinesslinks.com
links/babyproducts.htm
*"Environmental Directory" of companies that
manufacture natural baby food, diapers,
and clothing.*

Green Babies
Tel: (800) 603–7508
Email: mail@greenbabies.com
www.greenbabies.com
*For an enormous selection of organic cotton
clothing for babies and children.*

Hankettes
See PERSONAL CARE
*For organic receiving blankets, baby wipes
and cloths, and breast pads.*

La Leche League International
PO Box 4079, Schaumburg, IL 60168–4079
Tel: (847) 519–7730
Email: llli@llli.org
www.lalecheleague.org
*For breast-feeding support, information
and advice.*

National Association of Diaper Services
www.diapernet.com
*For information on baby care, natural diapers,
and a US directory of diaper laundry services.*

Natural Babies.
www.naturalbabies.com
*For natural diapers, diaper covers, diaper
accessories, training pants, bibs, baby slings,
and breast-feeding kits.*

Organic Bébé
233 Harvard Blvd.
Lynn Haven, FL 32444
Tel: (866) 734–2634
Email: mail@organicbebe.com
www.organicbebe.com
For a huge selection of natural baby products, including organic formula, juices, food, breast-feeding accessories, diapers, diaper covers, training pants, clothing, bedding, toys, furniture, skin and hair care.

OrganicFormula.com
www.organicformula.com
For organic baby formula, and information on baby nutrition and breast milk.

Sage Creek Naturals
See DECORATING & FURNISHING
For organic baby beds, bedding, clothing, and toys.

smallplanet
www.smallplanetinc.com
See CLEANING THE HOME
Recycling of disposable diapers.

Squeaky Monroe
1205 Pacific Ave., Suite 202
Santa Cruz, CA 95060
Tel: (888) 775–3555
Email: customerserv@squeakymonroe.com
www.squeakymonroe.com
For natural soaps, shampoos, oils, creams, balms, and oatmeal bath for babies and kids.

Tiny Tush LLC
See PERSONAL CARE
For natural cloth diapers, diaper covers, bibs, and cleaning products.

Under the Canopy
See DECORATING & FURNISHING
For organic receiving blankets, baby clothing, and toys.

World Wide Diapering Resource
www.borntolove.com/d-list.shtml
For information on natural diapers, and a world directory of diaper laundry services.

KEEPING PETS

American Holistic Veterinary Medical Association
2214 Old Emmorton Road, Bel Air, MD 21015
Tel: (410) 569–0795
www.altvetmed.com
For information on nontraditional veterinary techniques, including alternative nutrition, homeopathy, and acupuncture.

AnimalsNaturally.com
Email: info@animalsnaturally.com
www.animalsnaturally.com
For information on natural pet care, including natural nutrition and medicine.

Biocontrol Network
See HEALTHY FOOD
For various pet products, including natural insecticides.

Dr Doolittle's
572 Dundas Street, London
ON N6B 1W8, Canada
Tel: (519) 642 1130, 1 888 243 3743
www.drdoo.com
Healthfood store for pets.

EcoBusinessLinks Environmental Directory
www.ecobusinesslinks.com/
all_natural_pet_food.htm
"Environmental Directory" of companies that manufacture organic pet foods, and information on natural pet care.

Farmer's Market Online
See HEALTHY FOOD
For organic pet foods.

Good Dog Express
Tel: (877) 682–PETS
Email: info@gooddogexpress.com
www.gooddogexpress.com
For a variety of natural products for dogs and cats, including food, shampoos, supplements, toys, and accessories.

Gourmet Paws
Winnipeg, Manitoba
Canada
Tel: (204) 663 PAWS (7297)
www.gourmetpaws.com
Homebaked, natural dog treats.

Healthy New Age Success and Creativity Center
Tel: (256) 597–2998
Email: postmaster@healthywage.com
www.healthynewage.com
For a large variety of natural pet products, including supplements, food, medicines, shampoos, and aromatherapy hydrosols.

NaturalPetFood.com
www.naturalpetfood.com
For information on natural pet foods and manufacturers.

Organipetz Natural Pet Care Products
Tel: (866) 223–PETZ
Email: info@organipetz.com
www.organipetz.com
For natural pet shampoos, conditioners, insect repellents, and deodorizers.

PetSupplements.net
Tel: (903) 577–0982
www.petsupplements.net
For natural pet supplements.

Traffic International
250 24th Street, N.W.
Washington,
DC 20037

Tel: (202) 293–4800
Email: tna@wwfus.org
www.traffic.org
For information on wildlife trade and protected species lists.

Vetnat International
1273, St-Louis Street
C.P. 120
Terrebonne
Québec J6W 3L5
Tel: (800) 361–1502
Email: info@vetnat.com
www.vetnat.com
For homeopathic remedies for animals.

World Wise
See RECYCLING WASTE
For a variety of natural pet products, including food, supplements, flea treatments, and accessories, such as cat litter boxes.

WORKING AT HOME

Blue Ridge Technology
100-A Woodwind Industrial Court,
Cary, NC 27511
Tel: (800) 745 5530
Email: info@blueridgetech.com
For telephones made from recycled parts.

Citrus Magic
See CLEANING THE HOME
For natural, citrus-based cleaning products.

Clean Sweep Supply, Inc
10424 N. Florida Avenue
Tampa, FL 33612
Tel: (877) 677–7015
Email: questions@cleansweepsupply.com
www.cleansweepsupply.com
For a large selection of natural office supplies, including furniture, computer supplies, stationery, and equipment supplies.

Computer Recycle for Education
Training Consultants
15150 De La Pena Circle, P.O. Box 619
Rancho Murieta, CA 95683
Tel: (916) 354–3833
Email: recycled@pacbell.net
www.computerecycleforeduc.com
For information on recycling computers.

Co-Op America
1612 K Street NW, Suite 600
Washington, DC 20006
Tel: (800) 58–GREEN
www.coopamerica.org
For information on using your consumer and investment power for social change.

Corporate Governance
Email: jm@corpgov.net
www.corpgov.net/forums/commentary/
entine2.html
For information on ethical investing and links to various ethical funds.

Credit Union National Association
www.cuna.org
For information on credit unions and a directory of credit unions in the United States.

Eco-Mall
www.ecomall.com/biz/office.htm
For a directory of companies that manufacture environmentally-friendly office supplies.

Enviro Solutions
see RECYCLING WASTE
For information on recyclingink-jet printers and printer cartridges.

EthicScan Canada
Lawrence Plaza Postal Outlet
P.O. Box 54034
Toronto, ON M6A 3B7
Tel: (416) 783 6776

www.ethicscan.ca
Provides information and assistance in finding environmentally responsible suppliers of paper, printers and other office equipment.

Flint Ink
4600 Arrowhead Drive
Ann Arbor, MI 48105
Tel: (734) 622–6000
www.flintink.com
For non-toxic inks for printing.

Hampton Toner and Ink
PO Box 796, Bridgehampton, NY 11932
Tel: (631) 725–4204
Email: info@hamptontonerandink.com
www.hamptontonerandink.com
For remanufactured supplies for printers, copiers, and fax machines, and information on recycling used supplies.

National Credit Union Association
1775 Duke Street, Alexandria, VA 22314
Tel: (703) 518–6300
www.ncua.gov
For information on credit unions.

RecycleNet Corporation
P.O. Box 24017 Guelph
Ontario N1E 6V8, Canada
Tel: (519) 767-2913
http://www.recycle.net
For information on recycling a wide range of products, including computers and cellular phones.

Universal Elements Company Ltd.
Tel: (888) 219-1318
E-mail: ueco@therockies.com
http://www.ueco.ab.ca
For a large selection of natural and recycled office supplies, ranging from paper, pencils, and biodegradable ink pens that use cornstarch powder to mousepads.

RECOMMENDED BOOKS

Berthold-Bond, Annie, **Better Basics for the Home: Simple Solutions for Less Toxic Living** (Three Rivers Press, 1999)

Chevallier, Andrew, **Encyclopedia of Medicinal Plants** (DK Publishing, 2nd edition 2001)

Dadd, Debra Lynn, **Home Safe Home: Protecting Yourself and Your Family from Everyday Toxics and Harmful Household Products in the Home** (J. P. Tarcher, 1997)

Elliot, Renee J., and Treuille, Eric, **The Organic Cookbook: Naturally Good Food** (DK Publishing, 1998)

Grant, Doris, and Joyce, Jean, **Food Combining for Health: Get Fit with Foods That Don't Fight** (Inner Traditions Intl Ltd, 1990)

Iyengar, B.K.S., **Light on Yoga** (Schoken Books, revised edition 1995)

Iyengar, B.K.S., **Yoga: The Path to Holistic Health** (DK Publishing, 2001)

Lockie, Andrew, and Geddes, Nicola, **The Complete Guide to Homeopathy** (DK Publishing, revised edition 2001)

Mendelson, Cheryl, **Home Comforts: The Art and Science of Keeping House** (Scribner, 1999)

Rodale's Illustrated Encyclopedia of Organic Gardening (Dorling Kindersley, 2002)

Scaravelli, Vanda, **Awakening the Spine : The Stress-Free Yoga That Works with the Body to Restore Health, Vitality and Energy** (Harper San Francisco, second edition 1995)

Thich Nhat Hanh, **The Miracle of Mindfulness** (Beacon Press, 1999)

Ungaro, Alycea, **Pilates Body in Motion** (Dorling Kindersley, 2002)

Vann, Lizzie, **Planet Organic: Baby and Toddler Cookbook** (DK Publishing, 2000)

INDEX

ticks, 143, 147
tiles, cleaning, 51
tissues, 119
tocopherol, 114
toilet bowl cleaners, 48
toilet tissues, 119
toiletries see cosmetics
toilets, 15, 55
toluene, 98, 122, 191
toner cartridges, 81, 156
tooth care, 15, 137
toothpaste, 112, 113, 119
towels, 31
Toxic Shock Syndrome, 119
toxocariasis, 150, 151
toxoplasmosis, 150, 151
toys, 80, 141
Traidcraft, 160
trans-fats, 91
travel, energy conservation, 28–9
trichloroethane
  perchloroethylene, 66
triclosan, 125
trihalomethanes, 98
TRIS, 41
trout, fish farming, 95
tumble-dryers, 72
tuolene, 42
turpentine, 34, 66, 191

U

ultraviolet rays, 20
  sunscreens, 113, 117
upholstery, 31
  stain removal, 68
urine, pet hygiene, 151

V

vaccinations, pet care, 148
valerian, natural remedies, 131
varnish, shellac, 13
vases, cleaning, 59
VDUs, 158
vegetables, 90
  buying in season, 101
  chemical residues, 93–4
  "food combining," 91
  food hygiene, 107
  growing your own, 104–5

organic food, 92, 100–1
ventilation, 16, 17, 155
vermiculite, 24, 191
vets, 148
video recorders, 26, 27
vinegar, 47
  cider vinegar, 116, 147
  cleaning appliances, 53
  cleaning bathrooms, 54, 55
  cleaning tiles, 51
  cleaning windows, 50
  stripping wallpaper, 35
vinyl chloride, 98
vinyl paints, 32
viscose rayon, 40, 119
vitamins, 90
  supplements for pets, 145
  vitamin C, 117
  vitamin E, 114, 116, 117
volatile organic compounds
  (VOCs), 32, 42, 98

W

wallpaper, 35, 50
walls:
  cleaning, 50
  insulation, 25
washing, 63–73
  bedding, 39
  drying and pressing, 72–3
  laundry, 64–5, 70–1
  natural fabrics, 36–8
  stain removers, 66–9
  synthetic fabrics, 41
washing machines, 64, 65
  calcium deposits, 71
  cleaning, 53
  energy conservation, 26
  water conservation, 14
washing soda, 47, 66
waste:
  recycling, 75–87
  reducing, 76–7
water:
  cleaning with, 45
  conservation, 14–15, 26
  drinking, 77, 98–9
  stain removal with, 67
  treatment plants, 15
  water heaters, 14

water softeners, 52
watermarks, on furniture, 56
wax:
  emulsifying wax, 114
  food coatings, 93
  removing from candlesticks, 59
  stain removal, 68
wheatgerm oil, 145
white spirit, 34, 66, 191
wild foods, 103
willow, natural remedies, 131
windows:
  cleaning, 50
  draft-proofing, 25
  home offices, 155
  natural light, 20
wine, 102
  stain removal, 68
witch hazel, 125, 131
wood, 12–13
  cutting boards, 52
  fires, 17
  floors, 43, 51
  furniture, 56
  pressed–wood products, 11
  recycling, 81
  wood fiberboard insulation, 24
wool:
  bedding, 38
  carpets, 42, 43
  soft furnishings, 37
work surfaces, 52, 53, 107
working at home, 153–9
worms, pets, 150, 151
wormwood, 147
wrapping paper, reusing, 86

X

Xenex, 147
xylene, 42, 122, 191

Y

yoga, 127, 132–3, 159
yogurt, as skin cleanser, 116

Z

zeolite, 71

GLOSSARY

AEROSOL PROPELLANTS

Contain liquified toxic gases and are present in personal care items and household aerosol products. Typical propellants include liquified petroleum gas (LPG), used in household aerosol products, and dimethyl ether, common in personal care products. The gases may penetrate lungs and skin more easily than those distributed by pump-action sprays, because the dispersion is finer and more easily absorbed by the lungs and skin. CFC liquified aerosol propellant gases are no longer used in aerosols in the West, but they are permitted in inhalation aerosols used in the treatment of asthma (*see also CFCs*). They may cause headaches, nausea, dizziness, eye and throat irritation or injury, skin rashes, heart problems, birth defects, and lung cancer,

ACETONE

A manufactured chemical also found naturally in the environment, acetone is a flammable, colorless liquid with a distinct smell and taste. Used to make nail polish, paint, and household chemicals; it is also found in plastics, fibers, and drugs, and is present in vehicle exhaust fumes, tobacco smoke, and landfill sites. Harmless in small doses, but overexposure by touching or breathing in acetone can cause nose, lung, throat, and eye irritation, and shortening of the female menstrual cycle.

AMMONIA

A natural gas with a sharp odor that is soluble in water, and the only volatile alkali on earth. Household products containing ammonia should be used sparingly and with caution since exposure to ammonia can cause eye irritation and conjunctivitis, respiratory tract problems, and skin burn. About 80 percent of the ammonia made in factories is used to make fertilizers. The remaining 20 percent is used in textiles, plastics, explosives, pulp and paper production, household cleaning products, and refrigerants.

ASBESTOS

A mineral that is resistant to heat, fire, and corrosive chemicals. If its microporous fibers are inhaled, they can cause chronic lung disease (asbestosis) and cancer (mesothelioma). Generally, material in good condition will not release asbestos fibers. There is no danger unless fibers are worn or damaged. Until the 1970s, many types of building products and insulation materials used in homes contained asbestos. It was found in roofing shingles, insulation, plasterboard, floor and ceiling tiles, heating pipes, and ventilation ducts. It was also used to make fire-resistant household products, such as oven mitts and ironing-board covers. Most products made today do not contain asbestos. Those few products that are still made with asbestos are required to be labeled as such.

BENZENE

A colorless liquid with a sweet odor. It is highly flammable and is formed from both natural processes and human activities. Indoor air generally contains higher levels of benzene from products that contain it, such as glues, paints, furniture wax, and detergents. Natural sources of benzene include volcanoes and forest fires. Benzene is also a natural part of crude oil, gasoline, and cigarette smoke. It is carcinogenic and a central nervous system depressant. It may cause light-headedness, a staggering gait, disorientation, fatigue, loss of appetite, skin and lung irritation, anemia, reproductive problems, leukemia, and myeloma.

BORAX

Borax, or sodium tetraborate, is a naturally occurring mineral. It is a colorless, crystalline salt; it also occurs as a white powder. Borax is widely and diversely used, for example, as a mild antiseptic, a cleansing agent, a water softener, and in the manufacture of enamels, shellacs, heat-resistant glass, fertilizers, pharmaceuticals, and other chemicals. It contains the element boron (*see below*).

BORON

A mineral element that is a necessary food supplement for some living creatures, but can be damaging at high levels. Pure boron is a little-used dark powder, but boron compounds are important in many industries, such as glass and detergent manufacture and agriculture. Boron compounds are used in fertilizers to aid in plant growth and yield. Boron is an essential mineral for plants but not animals—in fact, it can be toxic in excess.

CFCS

Chlorofluorocarbons, or CFCs, are used as propellants in aerosol cans, in the blowing of polystyrene packaging, in the refrigerants that remove heat from refrigerators and freezers (which accounts for one-fourth of all CFCs), in car seats and foam mattresses, in dry cleaning, and fire extinguishers. They have been linked to the deterioration of the ozone layer and act as a "greenhouse gas," adding to global warming.

CHLORINE

A heavy yellowish-green gas with a powerful odor, used as a bleaching and disinfectant agent. It was used during World War I as a chemical weapon. Chlorine penetrates the skin and can aggravate sensitive areas in the eyes, nose, throat, and lungs, and has been linked with high blood pressure, diabetes, and heart disease. Chlorine bleaching of paper and other items creates polychlorinated biphenyls (PCBs), which are known to cause sterility and cancer.

COLORS

FD&C colors (used in food, drugs, and cosmetics) are made from coal tar, and tests on animals show them to be carcinogenic. They may cause hyperactivity, eczema, asthma, behavioral disturbances in children, dizziness, headaches, mental confusion, skin rashes, and gastritis.

DIOXINS

A group of chemical compounds, some of which are produced by the chlorine bleaching of wood pulp and other industrial processes, including the incineration of waste. The term dioxin is sometimes used to refer to one of the most toxic dioxins, 2,3,7,8-tetrachlorodibenzo-p-dioxin (TCDD), considered by scientists to be the most potent synthetic poison ever created. Exposure to large amounts of dioxins may result in skin diseases and liver damage. Dioxins may cause mutagenic effects on fetal development, and have been linked to cancer. Dioxins find their way up the food chain, and human exposure may come from milk, butter, meat, poultry, and fish that contain traces of dioxins.

EDTA

Ethylene diamine tetraacetic acid is a widely used water-softener processed from crude oil. It may damage the environment and pose a hazard to drinking water.

ENZYMES

Natural catalysts obtained, in the case of laundry detergents, from bacteria and used to break down protein stains. Their action on human proteins may produce skin problems and respiratory complaints: enzymes are considered a factor in the growing incidence of allergic reactions.

ETHANOL

The type of alcohol that is present in wines and beers when fermented from sugars. Much ethanol—not intended for drinking—is now made synthetically from ethylene, derived from petroleum. This type of ethanol is used as an automotive fuel by itself and can be mixed with gasoline. Ethanol may cause depression of the central nervous system, anesthesia, impaired motor coordination, double vision, and nausea.

FLAVORS

Around 1,500 petrochemical derivatives are used as flavorings in food. They can cause hyperactivity and behavioral disorders.

FLUORIDE

Although this mineral occurs naturally in water, some countries add fluoride to the water supply as a treatment chemical to prevent tooth decay. It is also present in most toothpastes. However, a growing number of scientists now question the value of supplementing fluoride intake, even in small amounts. Some studies indicate that fluoridation does not improve dental health. In addition, low levels of exposure to fluoride may lead to tiredness; weakness; kidney, bladder, and stomach disorders; eczema; and a weak immune system. Its use in the water supply is banned in many European countries.

FORMALDEHYDE

A colorless gas with a pungent odor used as a preservative, bonding agent, and fire retardant. A suspected human carcinogen and mutagenic agent, it has been shown to cause cancer in animals. Formaldehyde may be a contributing factor to sudden infant death syndrome (crib death). Exposure may cause coughs, throat problems, eye irritation, respiratory problems, headaches, rashes, tiredness, nausea, and insomnia. Long-term exposure may lead to allergic sensitization. Formaldehyde may be found in carpets, fabrics, permanent-press clothes, particle board and pressed-wood products, paints, lipstick, toothpaste, shampoo, grocery bags, paper towels, facial tissues, and soft drinks, among other items. Formaldehyde may continue to outgas for up to seven to eight years.

FRAGRANCES
Many synthetic fragrances used to scent personal care and household products may contain as many as 4,000 separate, unlisted ingredients. These fragrances can cause headaches, dizziness, skin discoloration, skin irritation, breathing difficulties, coughing, nausea, and behavioral problems.

HARD CHEMISTRY
In the process of "hard" as opposed to "soft chemistry", raw materials, such as crude oil—an unrenewable resource —are unraveled into their basic structure of atoms and molecules and then rebuilt. This process is energy-intensive and polluting, often releasing dangerous by-products into the environment.

LINDANE
An extremely toxic organo-chlorine insecticide that is easily absorbed by the skin. It is used as a seed and wood treatment, an insecticidal spray for a range of food crops, a veterinary insecticide on livestock and pets, and the active ingredient in head lice shampoos and in lotions to treat scabies. Exposure may cause convulsion and seizures, and cancers in laboratory animals. It is a possible human carcinogen, and it has been linked to breast cancer. Lindane is being phased out for use in farming in the European Union, and it is banned in some countries in other parts of the world.

MELAMINE
A thermoplastic polymer of methylene and dimethylene ether based on petrochemicals whose manufacture is polluting. It is resistant to heat, flame, and solvents. Melamine is used in fire-blocking fabrics, aircraft seating, protective clothing, thermal liners, air filters, and as a veneer on particle board for kitchen fittings. If particles of melamine become airborne— for example, when melamine board is sawn—they may cause irritation to the respiratory tract.

NAPHTHALENE
This volatile liquid is distilled from petrochemicals, and is a constituent of bitumen and asphalt. It is also found in some air fresheners and fragrances. Napthalene is a suspected human carcinogen. It may cause skin irritation, headaches, confusion, nausea and vomiting, and sweating.

NITRATES
Naturally occurring and harmless in themselves, nitrates can be turned to nitrites in the body, where they lower blood pressure and may cause headaches, vertigo, and palpitations. Nitrates are present in most waterways because they wash off agricultural land, where they are used as a fertilizer.

NTA
Nitrilotriacetic acid (NTA) is an environmentally polluting water-softener derived from crude oil. It is widely used as a phosphate replacement in dishwasher detergents and washing powders.

OPTICAL BRIGHTENERS
These styrol derivatives are added to washing agents to convert UV light into visible light and so make laundry lighter and brighter. Their chemical structure makes them allergenic, and they are suspected carcinogens.

ORGANOCHLORINES
A family of chemical compounds produced by combining chlorine with organic substances, usually petrochemicals. While many are produced commercially, some occur as unwanted by-products in industrial processes. Organochlorines include dioxins, heptachlor, PCBs, lindane, DDT, dieldrin, aldrin, hexachlorobenzene, and pentachlorophenol. Organochlorines may be used in plastics, paints, dyes, pesticides, deodorants, bleaching agents, refrigerants, wood preservers, and cleaning

solvents. Organochlorines may be connected to estrogen-related cancers in women, and they have a severe negative impact on the environment.

OZONE

Ozone is a gas consisting of oxygen molecules. A layer of ozone protects the earth from UV rays from the sun. At ground level, however, it is a pollutant and contributes to city smog in hot weather. Ozone is vulnerable to gases containing chlorine, such as CFCs (chlorofluorocarbons), which have destroyed parts of the protective ozone layer.

PARADICHLOROBENZENE

This is a white solid crystal with an oily surface. It has a mothball-like odor. Paradichlorobenzene may be found in toilet-bowl deodorizers, air fresheners, and mothballs. It is listed as a poison. Inhalation may cause headaches, and skin, throat, and eye irritation, and ingestion can cause damage to kidneys and liver.

PERBORATE

Sodium perborate tetrahydrate is a white crystalline powder made of sodium borate and hydrogen peroxide. It is the most widely used bleaching agent in laundry detergent, and may release damaging amounts of boron.

PERCARBONATE

Sodium percarbonate is the most eco-friendly stain remover and bleaching agent except for sunlight. It creates no environmental hazards. It is used in laundry products.

PERCHLOROETHYLENE

This liquid chemical solvent is used to remove stains and soiling from clothing in the dry-cleaning process. Highly toxic, it is flagged as a possible human carcinogen (perchloroethylene causes cancer in rats). It may cause headaches, giddiness, nausea, and eye and skin irritation, and high levels of exposure have been linked with damage to the liver and central nervous system. It is suspected of causing birth defects in people who have long-term exposure to perchloroethylene.

PERMETHRIN

An odorless concentrate used as an insecticide and repellent. It is a synthetic version of naturally occurring pyrethrin found in flowers. Permethrin is long-lasting as an insect repellent on clothing fibers, but it is less effective when applied directly to the skin. Although it is generally considered safer than some types of insecticide, there is still concern as to its safety.

PETROCHEMICALS

These are all derivatives of petrochemicals, including mineral oils, petroleum, kerosene, and any compound ending in -ethyl or -enzene. They come from non-renewable resources, and their manufacture is polluting to the environment. Many petrochemicals have toxic side effects, some of them severe (even small doses of kerosene may cause cancer in mice). Petrochemicals are widely used in many household and cosmetic products.

PH VALUE

Measure of acidity or alkalinity of a solution.

PHENOLS

These derivatives of benzene are known to be toxic and they may be carcinogenic. High exposure may cause nausea, skin rashes, and respiratory problems. Phenols are present in synthetic resins in hard plastics, paints, coatings and varnishes, fungicides, and wood preservatives.

PHOSPHATES

These salts of phosphoric acid are used as water softeners. Phosphates are recognized as being environmentally damaging because they may cause eutrophication (encouraging algae to grow faster in water systems, thereby upsetting the natural ecological balance).

PHTHALATES

Chemicals used as plasticizers. These compounds are found in PVC, for example in medical plastic tubing and PVC toys for babies and children, and in a range of personal care products, such as shampoos, hair conditioners, moisturizers, soaps, perfumes, hair sprays, and nail polish. Plasticizers do not bind to PVC and can leach out. The plasticizer DEHA, for example, is used in some food wraps and containers, and may migrate into foods that have a high fat content. Other phthalates used in food packaging may leach into food if exposed to conditions warmer than room temperature. The most widely used phthalate is diethylhexyl phthalate (DEHP). Animal studies indicate that large amounts of DEHP may disrupt normal hormone function and cause birth defects. The Environmental Protection Agency considers DEHP to be a probable carcinogen. The European Union has banned the use of certain phthalates in toys for infants. In the US, the use of phthalates is also limited in baby pacifiers and teethers.

PLASTICS

Plastics cause problems because they may outgas, especially when heated. Many of these fumes are suspected human carcinogens: those from epoxy resin, acrylonitrile, polyethelene, PVC, and polyester may cause lung and skin disorders. Inhaling PVP (polyvinylpyrrolidone) can cause cancer in animals.

POLYSTYRENE

This is a petroleum by-product (a long chain of styrene molecules joined together) and is used to make egg cartons, coffee cups, and packing materials. Polystyrene is polluting in manufacture and is not biodegradable.

PCBS

Polychlorinated biphenyls are an extremely toxic group of chemicals that were once widely used as a nonflammable oil in electrical equipment, fluorescent light ballasts, hydraulic fluids, waterproof wall coverings, adhesives, textile treatments, wrapping papers, fire retardants, brake linings, plastics, and paints. Although the use of PCBS has been phased out in many countries, they are very persistent and remain in the environment for many years. For example, minute traces of PCBs may be found in numerous foods, especially fatty foods. Exposure may cause a severe skin rash, liver damage, a respiratory disorder, thyroid gland imbalance, muscle and joint pain, and headaches. PCBs are a proven animal carcinogen and suspected of causing cancer in humans.

PVC

Polyvinyl chloride (PVC), also known as vinyl, is a chlorinated plastic and one of the most widely used plastics. It may also be one of the most environmentally damaging. PVC manufacture uses large amounts of chlorine, and this process creates polluting waste. Untreated, PVC is a rigid plastic; to make it soft or flexible, plasticizers known as phthalates are added. These ingredients are not chemically bound to the PVC, and can migrate out via moisture, air, or contact with other materials. Metal salts, such as lead, zinc, and organic tin compounds, may be added as stabilizers in PVC; unfortunately, these may also leach out of the PVC. Vinyl chloride, a mildly sweet-smelling gas used in the manufacture of PVC, may outgas from certain PVC materials, especially when new —for example, the plastic parts in a new car may give off vinyl chloride vapours. (Vinyl chloride is also present in tobacco smoke.) Workers exposed to vinyl chloride have reported symptoms such as dizziness, nausea, stomach pain, breathlessness, and circulatory problems. It has been linked to liver and spleen damage, it is mutagenic in humans, and is possibly carcinogenic. PVC is difficult to recycle, so it is either incinerated, which releases dioxins and other toxic chemicals, and leaves behind toxic ash, or it is disposed of in landfill sites, where chemicals may leach into the soil and groundwater. PVC is used to make window frames, wood moldings, pipes, vinyl flooring, wallpaper, toys, adhesives, shower curtains, clothes, food packaging, plastic wrap, and furniture.

RADON GAS

A naturally occurring, radioactive, colorless, odorless gas that is the second-highest cause of lung cancer after smoking. In areas where radon gas is present, sometimes house construction methods can release the gas, so levels may be tested by the environmental health office.

SODIUM HYDROXIDE

Also known as caustic soda.

SOFT CHEMISTRY

This term is used to describe chemical products that are based on ingredients that come from natural sources and that are renewable. Soft chemistry uses raw materials such as coconut, sugar cane, lemon, and spices. Common minerals, such as sand, chalk, lime, and silicates, are also used, since they are present in large quantities in nature and find their way back into the environment without damaging it. The ultimate aim of soft chemistry is to interfere as little as possible with the raw materials to avoid polluting manufacturing processes.

STYRENE

This is a synthetic chemical that is also known as vinylbenzene, ethenylbenzene, or phenylethelene. A colorless liquid with a sweet smell, it evaporates easily and is used in the manufacture of building materials, carpet backing, resins, rubber, plastic, insulation, fiberglass, pipes, and food containers. Styrene vapours are acutely irritating to the skin, eyes, and upper respiratory tract, and they may also affect the gastrointestinal system. Chronic exposure to styrene vapours may affect the central nervous system, causing depression, fatigue headaches, weakness, and minor kidney problems. It is a suspected human carcinogen.

SULFATES

The filler that makes a concentrated laundry detergent a nonconcentrated detergent, but has no effect on the washing action and is a burden on the environment.

SYNTHETIC

"Hard chemistry" cleaning agents that contain surfactants (surface active agents) based on petrochemicals that separate fats and oils and keep the oil droplets suspended in water. They may cause dermatitis, flu- and asthmalike symptoms, severe eye damage, and respiratory tract injury if

ingested. They may cause environmental pollution.

TOLUENE

A preservative and bonding agent used in cosmetic polishes, such as nail polish, and many household and building materials. A suspected human carcinogen, prolonged exposure can cause liver and kidney damage, dermatitis, birth defects, miscarriage, headaches, nausea, and asthma.

TURPENTINE

This natural yellow to brown oleoresin (a semisolid mixture of a resin and essential oil) seeps out of the bark of sapwood pines, firs, and other conifers. Turpentine production is environmentally friendly, since trees are encouraged to grow to maturity and beyond.

VERMICULITE

A natural micalike mineral based on silicates of aluminum and magnesium. Used in insulation, packaging, filler and lightweight concrete, and as a bedding medium for young plants.

VINYL

Otherwise known as polyvinyl chloride (PVC), vinyl is a thermoplastic that was originally developed in the 1920s as a substitute for rubber, with inherent flame-retardant properties. Vinyl is made by converting basic petrochemicals (petroleum, natural gas, or coal), with the addition of chlorine, chemical additives, and modifiers. It is ubiquitous, environmentally

polluting, and can be a hazard to human health.

MINERAL SPIRITS

A colorless solvent made of a mixture of mineral salts. Among its many uses, it is a paint thinner and general-purpose grease remover. Mineral spirits can sometimes be used instead of turpentine and is much cheaper. Flammable and toxic, it dries out the skin's natural oils and may cause an allergy. It may also be a central nervous system depressant, causing headaches, nausea, giddiness, behavioral disorders, nose and respiratory problems, skin cancers, and miscarriages.

XYLENE

A volatile, colorless liquid used in the preparation of artificial dyes. Exposure may cause nausea, vomiting, coughing, hoarseness, headaches, giddiness, and ringing ears.

ACKNOWLEDGMENTS

AUTHOR'S ACKNOWLEDGMENTS

My thanks to all the people I contacted in the course of researching this book, for being generous with their time, information, and enthusiasm: in particular, Edward Milford, Walter Grondzik, Chris Bennett, and Peter Malaise.

Huge thanks to the editorial and design teams at Dorling Kindersley, and to Russell Sadur for his beautiful photographs.

PUBLISHER'S ACKNOWLEDGMENTS

The publisher would like to thank the following:
Diana Craig for help with editing, Margherita Gianni for help with design, Hilary Bird for the index. For baby clothes and household textiles: **Greenfibres**, Freepost LON 7805, Totnes, Devon TQ9. Tel: 01803 868 001, www.greenfibres.com.
For cotton and linen fabrics: **Malabar**, 31–32 South Bank Business Centre, Ponton Road, London SW8. Tel: 020 7501 4200, www.malabar.co.uk.
For natural floor coverings and linoleum: **Sinclair Till** 793 Wandsworth Road, London SW8. Tel: 020 7720 0031. For loan of household props: **Jasmine** 65 Abbeville Road, London SW4 Tel: 020 8675 9475 and **Josephine Ryan Antiques**, 63 Abbeville Road, London SW4. Tel: 020 8675 3900.

For wallpapers: **Neisha Crosland wallpapers** available through Paint Library 5, Elystan Street, London SW3. Tel: 020 7823 7755, www.paintlibrary.co.uk. For natural paints: **Francesca Lime Wash Ltd**, Battersea Business Centre, 99–109 Lavender Hill, London SW11. Tel: 020 7228 7694, Email: francesca@ francescapaint. co.uk; **Lakeland Paints**, Unit 34, Heysham Business Park, Middleton Road, Heysham, Lancashire LA3. Tel: 01524 852371, www.ecospaints.com; **Auro Organic Paint Supplies**, Unit 2, Pamphillions Farm, Purton End, Debden, Saffron Walden, Essex CB11. Tel: 01799 543 077, www.auroorganic.co.uk.
For natural insulation materials: **Construction Resources**, 16 Great Guildford Street, London SE1. Tel: 020 7450 2211, www.ecoconstruct.com.

PICTURE CREDITS
Commissioned photography:
Photographer: Russell Sadur
Assistant: Nina Duncan

Other photographs: Peter Anderson: pp.21cr, 28cr; Simon Brown: pp.101cra, 104tr, 104br, 105cr, 135tr, 136cra; John Davis: pp.93tr, 110f, 112cra, bl; 113bl, 115cra, bl, 120clb, 122clb, 124crb; Jake Fitzjones: pp.152f; Craig Knowles: p.82tr; Ian O'Leary: pp.36cra, 77tr, 100tr, 103tr, 109cra, 135cra, 138cl; Reuben Paris: p.19br; Pia Tryde: p.103bl; Colin Walton : p.154cra; Tim Winter : pp.50cra, 60cla, 118cr, 127crb, 130cra. All images © Dorling Kindersley Limited. For further information visit: www.dkimages.com

ILLUSTRATION
Richard Lee: (floorplan) p.154

ABOUT THE AUTHOR

Rosamond Richardson lives in a 17th-century cottage in the English countryside, and has run it along environmental lines since she moved there in 1984. The electricity is generated from renewable sources, she recycles as much waste as possible, and uses organic products. Rosamond has written over 20 books on vegetarian cooking, food from the wild, and country life. Her books on natural health and wellbeing issues are based on her experience as a yoga teacher. Her more recent titles for publisher Kyle Cathie include: *The Great Green Cookbook* (2002), *The Natural Home* (2001), *NewWoman: A Survival Guide to Growing Older* (2001), and *Natural Superwoman* (1999).

HOME
HINTS
&TIPS